To Nancy and Bill —
Warm greetings and all
best wishes. We regret
that our paths don't cross
more often. We miss you.
    Cecilia and George
        3/7/97

ON THE
Frontline
IN THE
Cold War

ON THE
Frontline
IN THE
Cold War

_____An Ambassador Reports

George C. McGhee

Westport, Connecticut
London

Library of Congress Cataloging-in-Publication Data

McGhee, George Crews, 1912–
    On the frontline in the Cold War : an ambassador reports / George
C. McGhee.
        p.   cm.
    Includes bibliographical references (p.) and index.
    ISBN 0–275–95649–0 (alk. paper)
    1. World politics—1945–   2. United States—Foreign
relations—1945–1989.   3. Cold War.   4. Germany—Foreign relations—
United States.   5. United States—Foreign relations—Germany.
6. Germany—Foreign relations—1945–   I. Title.
D843.M335   1997
909.82—dc20   96–21321

British Library Cataloguing in Publication Data is available.

Library of Congress Catalog Card Number: 96–21321
ISBN: 0–275–95649–0

First published in 1997

Praeger Publishers, 88 Post Road West, Westport, CT 06881
An imprint of Greenwood Publishing Group, Inc.

Printed in the United States of America

The paper used in this book complies with the
Permanent Paper Standard issued by the National
Information Standards Organization (Z39.48–1984).

10 9 8 7 6 5 4 3 2 1

Copyright Acknowledgments

The author and publisher gratefully acknowledge permission for use of the following material:

From the British Archives Public Record Office, the transcript of a meeting between the author,
Walter Gifford, and Herbert Morrison; a letter from Herbert Morrison to Oliver Franks, and
Franks' reply; and a letter from Oliver Franks to Bowker.

To my dear wife Cecilia,
who with her sound judgement, social graces, and high spirits,
contributed greatly to our many diplomatic tasks
while holding together our farflung family of six fine children.

Contents

Foreword *by Casimir A. Yost* ix

Preface xi

1 The Course of the Cold War: 1947–1990 1

2 Importance of U.S. Prewar Defense Assistance to England, 1941–1943 17

3 U.S. Cold War Kickoff: Greece and Turkey, 1947–1951 25

4 Early Days of the Arab Refugee Problem: 1949 35

5 Envoy to the Middle World: 1949–1951 47

6 The Role of Nuclear Weapons—Navy Duty with LeMay's B-29s, 1944–1945 81

7 The Tripartite Declaration of 1950 93

8 Anglo-Iranian Oil Negotiations in 1951 99

9 Meetings with Mossadeq in 1951 113

10 Ambassador to Turkey: 1951–1953 121

11 The Kennedy Administration Takes Over: 1961–1963 135

12 Covert Intelligence in Cuba, Iran, and Vietnam:
1961–1968   143

13 The Congo Crisis in 1962   151

14 Five Years as Ambassador to Germany: 1963–1968   161

Bibliography   187

Index   197

Photographs follow Chapter 9.

Foreword

Three times in this century, the United States has defeated major enemies and has then been confronted with the challenges of reacting to postwar threats to peace. Following World War I, the American people opted for substantial withdrawal from global responsibility by rejecting U.S. participation in the League of Nations. Dictators and autocrats drew appropriate conclusions from our retreat. Within two decades of the Treaty of Versailles, Europe and Asia descended into chaos; the United States sat on the sidelines until December 1941.

Following World War II the United States chose a very different course. After some hesitation, the United States decided to remain actively engaged beyond its borders. This fine memoir is the tale of that different course as told by an insider. For over a quarter of a century, George McGhee was an important player in containing Soviet power through diplomacy, reinforced by aid, and, ultimately, through the threat of force. Credibility—credible diplomacy and credible force—was critical. Ambassador McGhee helped provide the former and assisted in insuring the latter during a series of critical assignments running from 1947 through 1968.

In 1947, the United States was left to pick up responsibilities Great Britain could no longer fulfill in the Eastern Mediterranean. Greece and Turkey were at risk from communist aggression. George McGhee coordinated aid to these two countries, a central task of the implementation of the Truman Doctrine. The aid worked, and aggression was defeated. Both countries subsequently entered NATO and the eastern flank of NATO was secured.

In 1951, Ambassador McGhee became Assistant Secretary of State for the

Near East, South Asia, and Africa—all regions vital to the interests of the West. Next, he was appointed Ambassador to Turkey. In each of these early assignments, George McGhee's task was the same: to help other countries to help themselves. In the 1960s he became Under Secretary of State for Political Affairs in the Kennedy Administration and then Ambassador to Germany for five critical years, 1963–1968. Quite properly, George McGhee viewed the U.S.-German bilateral relationship and Germany's membership in NATO as central to the West's response to the Soviet threat. He made essential contributions in assuring that Germany's ties to the West remained strong.

Former Secretary of State Dean Acheson said, "The function of a diplomatic envoy, since the thirteenth century, has been a two-fold one—to observe and report to his government all which may concern it and to affect the course of events, so far as he is able to do so, in favor of his own country." This is an apt description of Ambassador McGhee's many contributions to American diplomacy during a difficult and dangerous era, when a mistake could have led to a nuclear catastrophe.

Once again, America is reassessing its world role. Contemporary American leaders are seeking to bring peace to a number of particularly troubled and turbulent parts of the world. Challenges to diplomats and warriors continue despite the end of the Cold War. While the risk of a world war is much diminished, the prevalence of mini-conflicts around the globe is a disturbing feature of the closing years of the twentieth century. All who seek peace today can benefit from careful reflection on the experiences of a "Frontline Cold Warrior."

Casimir A. Yost
Director, Institute for the Study of Diplomacy
Georgetown University

Preface

This work focuses on the Cold War of 1947–1968 between the USSR and the United States and our allies. I start with a review of the preceding Japanese (1931–45) and German (1939–45) wars of aggression, which led to and influenced the beginning of the Cold War. Then I describe my direct participation in various aspects of the "hot" wars and the emerging Cold War over the 27 years from 1941 to 1968.

My own participation in the shooting wars started in 1941 in Washington, London, and North Africa when I was a civilian in U.S. logistic support for British defense on the War Production Board and the U.S.-U.K. Combined Raw Materials Board. Both London and Algeria were under German bombardment while I was there. As a naval officer from 1943–1945, I served with the 21st Bomber Command's B-29s in Saipan and Guam for the last year of the war with Japan, under bombardment and in air-sea rescue flights to Japan on combat missions.

With the end of the shooting war, I entered the State Department in 1945 and spent most of the next 30 years of my life in the frontlines of the Cold War in diplomatic efforts designed primarily to contain the spread of Communist aggression starting in the Middle East, South Asia, and Africa. My first assignment came in 1947 as Coordinator for Aid to Greece and Turkey, the initial effort of the United States, under the Truman Doctrine, to assist those countries to defend themselves against the Communist threat through economic and military assistance. While administering Greek-Turkish Aid, I inspected with General James Van Fleet frontline combat in the Gramos Mountains between the Greek army and Greek Communist guerrilla forces. The United States spent $750 million in two years without a loss of life from the 35,000 advisers sent to help these two beleaguered countries from being drawn behind the Iron Curtain. I also took the lead in seeing they were admitted to NATO in 1952 as its eastern anchor and rearmed to meet the NATO commitments. The door to the entire Middle East, once threatened by a Soviet invasion which reached within 18 miles of Teheran, was closed shut for good.

In 1951 I became the first Assistant Secretary of State for the Near East, South Asia, and Africa, the heart of what I call the Middle World. This area then contained 600 million people in 90 political entities, mostly in colonies of the European powers, which now constitute 66 independent nations. Working directly with the heads of dynasties who had led them to freedom to save them from communism, I visited Ibn Saud, Haile Selassie, the Shah of Iran, the Bey of Tunis, and the kings of Afghanistan, Jordan, and Morocco, combating the spread of neutralism and trying to assist them in building up their inadequate economies and military forces to protect themselves against Communist aggression or subversion. In this volume I have recorded verbatim my diplomatic discussions toward this end. Our success is reflected in the fact that only five small countries came under Soviet influence. Later, as Ambassador to Turkey, I helped the Turks build up the military forces required by NATO and to restore their economic base and self-confidence.

After a break of eight years I returned to the State Department first as the head of Policy Planning and later as Under Secretary for Political Affairs, the number three position, with worldwide responsibilities. President Kennedy put me in charge of blocking the Soviets' most severe threat to Africa, which was precipitated by the secession of the President of the Katanga Province, Moise Tshombe, from the Congo. For a year I coped with this delicate problem, negotiating with Tshombe in his own turf and assisting the United Nations in achieving Kennedy's goal of avoiding hostilities, which would have given the Soviets an excuse for intervening. Had they intervened, this would have been the first direct conflict between the USSR and the United States. I advocated holding our position and waiting for a "break," which finally came one Saturday night when Tshombe's troops mutinied during a night off in Elizabethville, and the United Nations' Indian generals moved and took Solwezi, his capital. It was all over.

My final opportunity to play my part in bringing the Cold War to a conclusion came in Germany, where it all started, and where it would have to be won. As I will explain in this work, Hitler's Germany was the principal cause of the Cold War, and later the strength of NATO's defenses in Germany assured victory, when the Soviet Empire finally fell apart. In 1963 I had asked to be appointed Ambassador in Bonn because I considered Germany the key to Cold War victory. If Germany had traded neutrality for unification, the Cold War would have been lost. I spent five very satisfying years in Bonn from 1963 to 1968, helping to bolster the morale of the

German people and their ties to the West. I admired these people who had lifted themselves out of the ashes of defeat in the Second World War, had renounced Nazism forever, and with NATO forces, including 250,000 U.S. troops, had helped to build up the Western defense of the Fulda Gap entry to Germany so strongly that the Soviets could no longer see any hope of victory.

In 1990, with the collapse of the Communist economy and the loss of morale by the Soviet armed forces after their disastrous defeat in Afghanistan, the Cold War was over. The Soviets withdrew from Eastern Europe, thereby restoring those countries to long-suppressed freedom. Much of the progress in uniting Europe and in launching the Non-Proliferation Treaty to prevent the spread of nuclear weapons was accomplished under U.S. leadership in Western Europe during the period of my stay in Bonn. In those years, Germany became our most valuable ally in Europe.

I am indebted in the writing of this book for the valuable editorial assistance given me by Richard N. Billings, a distinguished writer.

1

The Course of the Cold War: 1947–1990

The Cold War was neither declared nor fought, but it was ultimately won. The term was allegedly derived from testimony financier Bernard Baruch gave before Congress in 1947. It had been antedated, however, by Winston Churchill's phrase "Iron Curtain," which he first used in his famous speech at Fulton, Missouri, in February 1946, made on the invitation of President Truman. The Cold War is most often thought of as years of conflicting interests and purposes. I use the term to describe the years of acknowledged but carefully controlled confrontation between the United States and the USSR, which may have started as early as 1941 with the signing of the Grand Alliance by Roosevelt and Churchill at Placenta Bay. However, before the final conclusion of the wars of aggression which Germany had started in 1939 and Japan in 1931, the growing rivalry between the two superpowers was muted by the Four Power Pact, which brought together as allies the United Kingdom, the United States, the USSR, and China in 1942. Minor problems that arose after that time between the Soviets and the Western Allies were deliberately overlooked, or minimized, in order to avoid disharmony within the alliance and get on with winning the war. I review briefly the merging of the two separate wars of aggression and their influence on the onset of the Cold War.

HITLER'S WAR FOR AN EMPIRE FOR 1,000 YEARS: 1939–1945

After seizing power in Germany in 1933, Adolf Hitler had for years given ample evidence to the other European powers (which they largely ignored) that his aim was conquest intended to redress what Germany considered the unjust Treaty of Versailles. After occupying without opposition the Rhineland on March 7, 1936, Austria on March 12, 1938, and the Sudetenland on September 12, 1938, Hitler invaded Poland on September 1, 1939, starting World War II. After conquering France and most of the rest of Europe and entering into an alliance with Italy and Japan, Hitler, ignoring his treaty with Russia of September 28, 1939, invaded Russia on June 22, 1941. After Japan attacked Pearl Harbor on December 7, 1941, the United States declared war on Japan on December 8, and Germany and Italy declared war against the United States on December 11. And so it was that all of the major allies on both sides of the war were joined in battle. Germany and the United States would be at war for almost six years.

THE JAPANESE WAR FOR A SOUTHEAST ASIA CO-PROSPERITY SPHERE: 1931–1945

Starting in 1931, the military dictators of Japan, acting with the acquiescence of their Emperor, began major wars of aggression to create what they called a Southeast Asia Co-Prosperity Sphere. On May 5, 1931, China—after endless bickering with the outside powers, including Japan, which had profited from China's weakness—made the first move to establish its independence by calling a People's National Convention in Nanking to create a Provisional Constitution for a Chinese government. The Japanese, fearing that this might mean loss of trade with China, took advantage of an alleged explosion in Mukden as an excuse to occupy the three eastern provinces of Manchuria, which they converted to an Independent Manchuria under their control.

Thus Japan began a continuing war of aggression, adding territory in China and, on December 7, 1941, bombing Pearl Harbor. The ensuing war with the United States was followed by the Japanese taking the rest of China, the Philippines, Sumatra, Thailand, Indonesia, Borneo, North New Guinea, and the Pacific Ocean Islands up to the Solomon, Gilbert, Marshall, and Wake Islands.

After the bombing of Pearl Harbor the United States, starting from scratch, began the greatest military buildup in history, amassing the forces necessary to win the war being fought all over the world, in the Atlantic and the Pacific and in Europe and Asia. The Office of Production Management was created for this purpose on January 8, 1941; I joined it in June, and after Pearl Harbor, on January 13, 1942, its name was changed to the War Production Board. The Allied war effort became strong enough for the Allies to invade North Africa on November 8, 1942, and plans were made at the Casablanca Conference of January 12, 1943, for the subsequent Allied invasions in Italy on September 9, 1943, and Normandy on June 6, 1944. Germany finally fell in May 1945.

After the United States' first naval victory against Japan at Midway on June 4, 1942, and a massive military buildup, we rolled back the Japanese on all fronts, taking the key intervening islands and, on October 19, 1944, the Philippines. The Marianas Islands had been captured in September as a base for our B-29 air force which, under General Curtis LeMay, on whose staff I served, proceeded to bomb, burn down, and destroy with two nuclear bombs most of the important cities of the Japanese home islands, contributing to Japan's surrender on August 14, 1945. Japan had been at war for 13 years; the U.S. engagement in the Pacific War had lasted four and one-half years.

BEGINNING OF THE COLD WAR: 1947

Differences arose between the Soviet Union and the United States and the other Western Allies almost from the beginning of their alliance. One disagreement concerned the important issue of distribution of weapons and supplies. While serving on the U.S.-U.K. Combined Raw Materials Board in Washington in 1941–1943, I frequently participated in meetings on allocations of supplies with our new Soviet ally. The Russians representing their country were a detached, humorless, disciplined group and would not discuss their requirements. If not met they were repeated as demands in harsh tough voices. Most American negotiators considered them curious allies.

Three years later in Guam, I served as Naval Liaison Officer to the 21st Bomber Command which was bombing the home islands of Japan. Unable to get sufficient weather information, we couldn't time our flights over Japan to get enough visibility to hit our targets from 32,000 feet. This effort would have been greatly facilitated if the Soviets had acceded to our pleas for radio weather information from Vladivostok. They refused right up to the end of the war, again showing themselves not to be true allies.

After the fall of Germany in May 1945, U.S.-Soviet disagreements became more virulent. Since we had not anticipated this turn of events, it took some time for the Allies to learn how to deal with our new relationship with the Soviets. In their postwar negotiations, the Allies were facing many difficult problems that were widening the cleavage between us and the Soviets—the question of German reparations, the postwar government of Poland, and the growing Communist domination of the Balkans.

The first U.S. response to Soviet pressures was necessitated by the United Kingdom's inability to continue furnishing aid to Turkey and Greece. After World War II, the Greek monarchy faced a Greek guerrilla war that was being supported by Communist Yugoslavia and Bulgaria, acting as proxies for the Soviets. The U.S. response was the Truman Doctrine announced on March 3, 1947, which pledged that the United States would support "free people who are resisting subjugation by armed minorities or outside pressures." I administered the Greek-Turkish aid program in the position of Coordinator, created under the enabling Public Law 75. Some observers have assumed that the Truman Doctrine was inspired by Ambassador George Kennan's containment policy, as expressed in his famous Mr. X article in *Foreign Affairs* in 1947, but Kennan himself disclaimed this in another article published in *Foreign Affairs* in Spring 1989. He said that, as "Mr. X," he had not urged assistance in the defense of weak states, such as Greece and Turkey, but in support of policy positions taken by strong states such as England and France "not to make any unnecessary concessions to these people. Make it clear to them that they are not to be allowed to establish any dominant influence in Western Europe and Japan if there is anything we can do to stop it."

In short order there followed a series of U.S. diplomatic accomplishments, inspired largely by Under Secretary, later Secretary Dean Acheson, to fill the policy vacuum then existing: the Marshall Plan of June 1947, the North Atlantic Treaty Organization of April 1949, and the Coal and Steel Community of May 1952, followed by the Treaty of Rome in March 1957 creating the European Community. In January 1963 Germany and France launched a Treaty of Friendship ending their traditional rivalry. The matrix created by these successful organizations became the basis for the conduct of the Cold War by the Western Allies—a formula for their ultimate success.

Many conjectures have been offered as to who started the Cold War. Averell Harriman, from his vantage point in Moscow, puts all of the blame on Stalin. When Europe was divided after the war, Harriman believed that we made every effort to establish good relations with the Eastern European states without dominating them, whereas Stalin insisted on control. Starting with Poland, Stalin eventually took control over the states he had created.

Charles Bohlen, in *Witness to History* (1973), has a different take on the beginning of the Cold War: the satellization of Eastern Europe and its acceptance by the West in the peace treaties of 1947, and the Soviet expansion beyond the traditional Czarist goals of influence into the Middle East and the Mediterranean area. Bohlen goes back to 1917 for the basic cause, when the Bolshevik wing of the Russian Social Democratic party seized power. The Bolsheviks believed so strongly in the inherent wickedness of capitalism that they denounced all capitalist societies as their enemies and the object of continuous hostility. This stance was first taken against Great Britain in 1917 and later against the United States which was the principal capitalist power left after the war. The Soviets have always judged the United States on the premise that all capitalism is evil, which could be considered an origin for the Cold War.

In 1948 Stalin had based his European policy on getting the Western allies out of Berlin; however, the blockade he created for this purpose was defeated by the U.S.-U.K. airlift. Without atomic bombs Stalin could not risk war. Peace followed for nine years until, when the Soviet Union had the bomb, Khrushchev began to mount a new world offensive using a "ban the bomb" movement and pretending to believe in peaceful coexistence. At the same time he was spreading local subversion, sponsoring wars of national liberation, and using the threat of nuclear war. He demanded the end of the Allied occupation of West Berlin, which would become a demilitarized "free city."

A meeting was arranged between Khrushchev and the new young President, Jack Kennedy, in Vienna, following Kennedy's meeting with de Gaulle in Paris in June 1961. The two leaders got off to a bad start when Khrushchev began aggressively demanding de facto recognition of communism, which he said was destined to win over the world peacefully. Kennedy's rejoinder was that all people must have freedom of choice. Khrushchev took strong exception to Kennedy's warning against "miscalculation" by either power of the interests and policy of the other. The USSR did not want war, but it would defend its interests.

After a long and heated conversation, Khrushchev returned to the question of Berlin. He would sign a treaty with East Germany in September. If the United States insisted on occupation rights, and the East German borders were violated, force would be met by force. Kennedy ended with the comment that it "would be a hard winter." The Cold War had gotten colder and reached its most dangerous phase when Khrushchev secretly began placing Soviet nuclear missiles in Cuba in September 1962.

At the time I was in the Congo where I had been for a month negotiating with Moise Tshombe (see Chapter 13). When I checked in with Secretary Dean Rusk on my return, he advised me that he and George Ball, then Under Secretary, were completely occupied in matters that he could not go into at that time. He said that my meeting with the President scheduled for that afternoon would be left on his schedule but would not take place. He also told me that he wanted me to take over the operation of the rest of the State Department. When I returned to my office, I became Acting Secretary of State.

It has long been my belief that the basic origins of the Cold War lay in the historic relationship between Russia and Germany. Throughout the centuries, the Germans have been a warlike people by virtue of their vulnerable position in Central Europe. They were always on the defensive against potential conquerors from all sides. The Romans did not make a serious effort to conquer Europe east of the Rhine and north of the Main River, I conclude, possibly because the area produces no wine but more probably because the martial abilities of the Germans protected by deep forests would have meant unsustainable losses for the Romans. There is a subsequent history of German military prowess, including Frederick the Great's founding of the Prussian Empire, the German victory over France in 1870, and the impressive German effort in World War I.

The Russian Plain, lying west from Moscow, and the North European

Plain with which it merges do not provide any natural barrier against invasion; Russia's only natural protection is the bitter cold of its winter. After the Mongol invasions of the twelfth and thirteenth centuries, the Germanic Teutonic Knights (who colonized East Prussia), the Poles, and the Swedes all invaded Russia repeatedly until the eighteenth century. Napoleon took Moscow briefly in 1812, and the Germans seized the Ukraine in 1918. Lulled into a false security by the German-Russian Pact of August 23, 1939, the Russians felt the full impact of the Wehrmacht force of 3 million which invaded Russia on June 22, 1941. By the end of October, the Germans had conquered most of the Ukraine and had laid siege without taking Moscow.

On August 9 the German forces, diverted by their shortage of petroleum, lay siege to Stalingrad as part of a plan to open up access to the oil fields of Baku. At the same time, Rommel attempted to conquer North Africa and the Middle East to complete a pincer movement for the same purpose. But Stalingrad ended in disaster for the Germans: by February 2, 1943, 22 German divisions had been reduced to 80,000 men. Concurrently, Rommel was stopped and his army captured in Alamein.

Although the Germans lost the war, they inflicted extraordinary military destruction, killing some 20 million Russians alone and an equal number outside of Russia. The Soviets would not soon forget the ability of the dauntless Wehrmacht officers and their disciplined troops to overrun the vast spaces of Russia and solve the logistical problems in attacking the much larger Russian forces. The Soviets developed such apprehension of the German military capability that even after the German defeat in World War II they feared they might still be able to build a new army and march again across the Russian plane to attack Moscow. Indeed, this did not happen, but the Soviets were determined to create a buffer zone under their control in Eastern Europe and to develop enough military force to stop any conceivable German attack. In doing this they overbuilt. This is why I believe that the origins of the Cold War lay in past German invasions, triggered by the terrible invasion of 1941.

On September 6, 1946, Secretary of State Jimmy Byrnes, in a major speech in Stuttgart, announced that the United States was reversing its policy on Germany and would make every effort to assist Germany's economic recovery. This was, I believe, the signal to Stalin to reverse his policy toward the United States. With the winning of the war against Germany the Soviets had less incentive to continue as our ally. If the principal Soviet objective was to keep Germany from becoming a military power, then in assuring German recovery under the Marshall Plan, we had become their principal enemy—hence the Cold War. Tying Germany to the Western Alliance and to NATO, to which the German Chancellor Konrad Adenauer made an indispensable contribution, was decisive in assuring a Western victory in the Cold War.

Alan Bullock in *Hitler and Stalin* (Knopf, 1992) describes the effect of Churchill's fall from power and Roosevelt's demise on the Allies in September 1945. Their successors, Truman, Atlee, and Bevan, had not had wartime experience and were restricted by the return in their countries of more democratic governments. Stalin had already prophesied difficulties in the wartime alliance once Hitler, whose threat had kept the Allies together, had vanished from the scene. According to Bullock, the Cold War did not start in earnest until 1947–1948, and relations deteriorated slowly and unevenly. In early 1947, Ernest Bevin and George Marshall had spent weeks in Moscow in an unsuccessful attempt to reach agreement on the German question. Cooperation was rapidly being succeeded by confrontation.

At this time, Stalin decided to begin emphasizing the sacrifices the Soviets needed to make to achieve victory against the powerful capitalists and imperialists, and so stressed the importance of continuing to expand heavy industry and collectives. In reaction, Churchill remarked: "They fear our friendship more than our enmity." When the Moscow Council of Foreign Ministers met on March 10, 1947, it did little more than highlight the disagreement on German reparations and the dangerous economic situation in Europe which badly needed U.S. economic aid. Marshall for the first time made it clear that "The United States recognizes that its responsibilities in Europe will continue." The meeting broke up without setting a fixed date for another one. By the end of the meeting, the cooperative "Spirit of Yalta," when real progress seemed possible, was a distant memory.

In a followup meeting, Vyacheslav Molotov accused the British and French of using the United States Marshall Plan offer to force other countries to sacrifice their independence. The Soviet Union, therefore, rejected the plan, both for this reason and for ignoring the Soviet and other claims to German reparations, and warned the British and French of the serious consequences if they persisted in their plan. The Soviet rejection of the U.S. invitation to participate in the Marshall Plan provided the first cleavage between the United States and the Soviets, and soon the Cold War was on.

Bullock states that although both sides prepared for confrontation, neither contemplated going to war. Fear of war was already so widespread that both sides took advantage of the opportunity to strengthen themselves. Only the threat of war in Korea in June 1950 and the Berlin blockade in 1948 led either side to believe that conflict could arise between the superpowers. Even so, the Korean War, including the Chinese intervention, could not have taken place without Soviet approval, despite Stalin's knowledge that the United States had nuclear superiority. While excluding the possibility of war, both powers continued to engage in political, economic, psychological, and subversive actions.

Stalin's first objective in expanding his empire was to legalize his control over the Eastern European states, which he had created. By the end of 1946 this objective had been accomplished, and all of them had become recognized Communist states. Stalin's second goal was to gain influence in the so-called Northern Tier of the Middle East—Greece, Turkey, Iran, and the Persian Gulf. The penetration of Soviet forces came within eighteen miles on Teheran. With strong American support, however, the U.N. Security Council forced Russia to end its occupation of Northern Iran. Turkey, with British and American support, refused Molotov's demand to allow the Soviets to participate in the defense of the Straits, and to cede territory in Eastern Turkey around Kars and Erzurum. In 1946, Stalin's Balkan Communist states, Yugoslavia, Albania, and Bulgaria, supplied arms to guerrilla forces fighting to overthrow the Greek monarchy. In February 1947, the British, so weakened by the war that they could no longer support Greece and Turkey militarily, withdrew their assistance. Fearing that Greece, and possibly Turkey as well, would be drawn behind the Iron Curtain, the United States then agreed to give both nations military and economic support under the Truman Doctrine. This action marked a sharp turn in U.S. foreign policy that later would lead to U.S. involvement in the Korean and Vietnam wars.

In 1947–1948, the Soviets also made a strong effort to control the governments of France and Italy through democratic methods, chiefly through the 900,000 Communists in France and the 2 million in Italy. In Italy the Communist rise to power was stopped at the polls by Alcide de Gasperi in May 1947, whereas in France in December 1947 the Communists lost the working classes after an independent trade union was formed. By 1948, the French Communist vote had been reduced from 40 percent to 31 percent. The Communists had better fortune in the Eastern European states where by 1948 they had increased their control from two states, Yugoslavia and Albania, to seven, adding Poland, Czechoslovakia, Hungary, Rumania, and Bulgaria.

During 1947 and 1948 Stalin also lost the only territory he had once dominated; this was the first loss either way in the Cold War. After a test of wills between Stalin and Marshall Tito, the Cominform was asked to expel Yugoslavia for its nationalist deviation. During this same period, the United States and Britain committed themselves to the reconstruction of the German economy, thereby inducing the Germans to associate themselves inexorably with the West, despite strong Soviet opposition. Stalin had wisely chosen to apply the greatest pressure against the West in Berlin; as a result, Berlin was split into four zones, controlled respectively by the Soviets, the United States, the United Kingdom, and France. The Russians' crude blockade of supplies coming into Berlin in 1948, which at one time was down to 36 days' food needs, was broken by the daring U.S.-U.K. airlift, flying in 8,000 tons a day—a great defeat for Stalin. At the same time, the North Atlantic Treaty Organization was created, providing a strong enough link between the West and the West German state that the Allies could now count on Germany to reject the Soviets' proposal that Germany accept neutrality in return for reunification.

During Stalin's final years, the Soviets scored victories in the Far East rather than in Europe. At the end of the war with Japan, the Soviets switched ties from the Nationalist Chiang Kai-Shek to the Chinese Communists under Mao Zedong. Kim Il-Sung, the North Korean Communist leader, upon Stalin's approval, attempted a takeover of South Korea after first inciting a Communist revolution there in June 1950. He took the capital, Seoul, before being stopped. The long and bloody Korean War that ensued ended in a stalemate for the U.S.-led U.N. forces in June 1953 but at the cost of some 53,000 U.S. lives.

U.S. participation in the war against North Vietnam also exacted a big price in lives—about 58,000—but it was conducted on quite a different basis. The Kennedy government became embroiled in Vietnam influenced by the domino theory; the experts were certain that a Communist victory in uniting North and South Vietnam would lead to the loss of Indochina and other Southeast Asian nations. I believe, however, as I did at the time, that we unwittingly interposed ourselves into a civil war that the Western powers had been responsible for creating. The Vietnamese people, having been a colony of France for many years, primarily wanted to expel *all* foreign powers out of Vietnam and to unite their separate states. The United States paid a very high price for its miscalculation—the loss of thousands of young lives, the alienation of a whole generation of young Americans, and the creation of both a U.S. and world recession. It also greatly diminished respect for the United States as a world power and to this day has made us leery about engaging in such wars, as spelled out by the Nixon Doctrine. Thus, the Soviets, with little cost to themselves, had through their proxies in North Korea and North Vietnam extracted an enormous cost from us.

At various times during the Cold War, leaders on both sides waged a slackening or pause in hostilities. Gradually, for different reasons, this effort came to be described by the vague French word détente, which Webster's translates as "a slackening or relaxing, as of strained relations between nations." Those who proposed détente were often accused of being Communists, whereas those who unalterably opposed negotiations to end the Cold War were given the derogatory title "Cold Warriors." At different times I myself was accused of being both, but I ended up being in favor of détente before it had become popular.

The best argument in favor of détente was, in my view, that to avoid a war, one should be willing to go to almost any lengths, short of capitulating, and should be willing to engage in discussions with the adversary, both directly or secretly through intermediaries, with an open mind and a willingness to negotiate and make reasonable compromises. In other words, to avert war one should be willing to negotiate "with the devil himself." The opposing negotiator's internal political problems and his necessity to save face should be taken into account if possible. At the same time, our nego-tiator had to know when to stand firm, even though the result might be failure or even war.

Either course could lead to victory or defeat. Churchill, for example, stood up to Hitler at a time when almost everyone else was giving in to his demands. President Jimmy Carter, although he was defeated at the polls in the end, received some credit for his futile effort to free the captive U.S. Embassy staff in Teheran. At least he did something. In contrast, Bush lost the presidency because he didn't even make a try to turn the nation around economically.

The concept of détente may have emerged from the meeting between Eisenhower and Soviet Premier Nikolai Bulganin at Geneva in July 1955. This meeting resulted in the "Spirit of Geneva"—a relaxation from tensions that should have resulted in détente. Others believe that the turning point leading to détente did not come until the signing of the Test Ban Treaty in 1963. Later, in 1968, President Richard Nixon came into power seeking "to build détente" but received no real response from the Kremlin.

Henry Kissinger, Nixon's chief architect of U.S. foreign policy, blames short-term periods of Soviet intransigence on the internal victories of Soviet hard-liners, not on the dynamics of the Communist system which he attrib-utes to the mature force of Soviet politics. Earlier, George Ball did not believe that we could influence the Soviets simply by changing U.S. policies. After Stalin's death in 1953, however, the Soviets did, after eight years of negotiations, help end the Korean war. Similarly, after the Cuban Missile Crisis in October 1962, Premier Khrushchev did change his policies dras-tically in signing the Partial Test Ban Treaty in 1963 and in setting up the "hot line." After the shock of the Soviet takeover of Czechoslovakia in 1968, the Soviets agreed to the SALT Treaty, resulting in strategic arms limitations.

At the Moscow Summit Conference of May 1972, the United States and the Soviets signed a Basic Principles of Relations professing a common de-termination to conduct their mutual relations "on the basis of a peaceful existence." The Soviets claimed a victory for this agreement while making it clear that they considered war and diplomacy to be synonymous—to ad-vance their interests at the expense of their adversary. Khrushchev in his de-Stalinist period granted internal liberation while opening up ties with the West. His successors, Leonid Brezhnev and Aleksei Kosygin, followed a less clear, more bureaucratic policy until the Spring of 1965, when they reha-bilitated Stalin, increased military expenditures, and repressed many intel-lectuals, reversing the trend toward détente.

In the February 1954 meeting of the Foreign Ministers in Berlin, the Soviet Union had proposed a conference on the security of Europe, but the Western powers did not agree to the conference because of their preoccu-pation with bringing Germany into NATO. When the Soviets made the same proposal in 1968, the United States and Europe were both in a mood of détente and the proposal was accepted that June. Willy Brandt, as Chancellor, had led the Social Democratic Party (SPD) into power in Germany and was, for the first time, able to effect his long-espoused Eastern policy, or Ostpolitik (see chapter 14). At this time, Nixon and Kissinger, who were also pursuing a policy of détente, sought to negotiate with the Soviets under Brezhnev. However, the brutal Soviet invasion of Czechoslovakia made any negotiations toward ameliorating the Cold War impossible.

In late 1969, NATO agreed to hold a conference on European security, and so further progress became possible, with Germany taking the lead by signing a treaty with the USSR establishing the inviolability of the frontiers of the European states. In December 1970, Germany also signed a treaty with Poland renouncing all territories east of the Oder Neisse. In December 1971, the Federal Republic of Germany (West Germany) and the German Democratic Republic (East Germany) signed a treaty agreeing to hold their common border inviolate. Thus, postwar Germany was contained. In September 1971, after hard negotiations, the United States, the United Kingdom, France, and the USSR signed a Quadripartite Treaty on Berlin, agreeing to improve the movement of goods, services, and people between West Germany and the Allied section of Berlin. Having tried in vain to persuade the Soviets to negotiate such an agreement to overcome the severe transit problems that existed during my ambassadorship in 1963–1968, I had great respect for the success of then Ambassador Kenneth Rush, who fortunately had the support of Nixon, his former student at Duke University.

The single most important step toward ending the Cold War took place in Helsinki, where delegates from all the nations of Europe, the United States, Canada, and the Soviet Union met to take preliminary steps for a conference on European security. This conference was to include political, economic, cultural, and cultural-human considerations, and would also create a basis for continuing cooperation through the Conference on Security and Cooperation in Europe (CSCE). After other preparatory phases, the Final Act for the CSCE was concluded on August 1, 1975. The 35 nations involved had agreed to the inviolability of prewar boundaries in Eastern Europe. The Soviet Union had also agreed to the people's greater freedom of movement and right to information within the member nations.

Unfortunately, the accomplishments in founding the CSCE and negotiating the arms limitations under the Ford regime were counterbalanced by the Soviet Union's failure to fulfill its human rights commitments within its satellite states. The Watch Groups created to evaluate CSCE performances found such a deplorable violation of rights in the satellites that a sharp reaction set in against any détente in U.S.-Soviet relations. This attitude was accentuated by the Carter administration's severe economic sanctions against the Soviet Union and its Eastern European Communist states, Willy Brandt's continuation of his Ostpolitik policy, and the breach in U.S.-

German cooperation, which climaxed over the issue of U.S. insistence on Theater Nuclear Weapons stationed in Europe.

Under Carter the United States suffered severe loss in prestige and economic status, accentuated by our embarrassing inability to free our embassy personnel held hostage by the Iranian government. After his election as President, Ronald Reagan sought to reestablish the U.S. world leadership role while resisting continuing Soviet pressures. He took the Cold War back to its darker days by referring to the Soviet Union as the "Evil Empire." He also sought to eliminate the concept of détente which many Americans and most Europeans still held. Reagan also added an extra trillion dollars to the defense budget and forced acceptance of the Strategic Defense Initiative (SDI), called "Star Wars," which most leading U.S. experts in this field opposed and which I do not believe any Soviet experts were taken in by. After the expenditure of $35 billion, no useful weapon was produced. Reagan also sought unsuccessfully to block the building of the Yama gas pipeline from the Soviet Union to Central Europe. During this period Europeans in general refused to follow U.S. leadership in the Cold War and increasingly distanced themselves from U.S. policy. As a result, Reagan, either responding to European pressures or convinced that the time was ripe for an abrupt change in U.S. policy, arranged a meeting with the Soviet leader Mikhail Gorbachev in Reykjavik, Iceland, in October of 1986.

The world's hopes of easing the Cold War rose when it was rumored that Gorbachev was prepared to make deep concessions in Soviet conventional and nuclear forces. These hopes were quashed when Reagan refused to reciprocate by canceling SDI; then general dismay reigned when Reagan, without consulting his allies or U.S. experts, proposed eliminating *all* Intercontinental Ballistic Missiles (ICBMs) and Submarine Launched Ballistic Missiles (SLBMs) in the world. This adverse reaction to his proposal was overcome a year later when Reagan agreed to dismantle the entire class of the INF Theater weapons so feared by Europeans. Although the Berlin Wall did not come down until November 1989, the relationship between the Soviet Union and the United States had increasingly become a normal bilateral one, and less and less a continuation of the Cold War. American presidents, starting with Nixon, have had direct and private proxy channels of communications with their opposite Soviet leaders since Kissinger's effort to personally control U.S. foreign policy. Interestingly, Kissinger and Zbigniew Brzezinski, who in seriatem had a strong influence on U.S.-Soviet relations for 14 consecutive years, were both of European origin.

My first personal involvement in the Cold War occurred when I administered Greek-Turkish aid and took the lead in admitting both countries to NATO, to defend these countries from increasing Soviet threats. In Greece I learned about the brutal atrocities committed by Greek Communist guerrillas against their own people in the mountainous area along their northern borders. I was pleased to be characterized by Soviet Middle East Radio as a "Cold Warrior." Later I helped the Turks build up their defenses under NATO while serving as Ambassador to Turkey. Indeed, I was one of the first Cold Warriors. After my retirement, even though I returned to private life, I continued to support U.S. policy in the Cold War through public speeches and my membership in various organizations, including the conservative Committee for the Present Danger. As the desire for détente spread in Europe and the United States in 1956–1957, I gradually separated myself from the diehard Cold Warriors, who now decried any effort to enter into a dialogue with the Soviets. To many, any contact or negotiation with the Soviets constituted treason. Rather, they should be spoken of only as villains, thieves, and murderers. I resigned from the Committee for the Present Danger in a letter pointing out the difference in my views from those they were expressing in my behalf.

I believe that any rapprochement with the Soviets during the era of Stalin, and probably that of Khrushchev, would have been impossible. With succeeding Soviet leaders, however, I believe that we should at least have persisted in the efforts initiated under Nixon and Kissinger to establish contacts and mutual confidence that might lead to a relaxation of tensions.

The American people had evinced a deep distrust of communism from the very beginning—from the Communist revolution of February 1917 under Lenin and Trotsky through Stalin's long reign of terror. Americans were shocked by the Communists' brutal execution of the Czar and his family, and later by Stalin's starving of millions of Ukrainians in the 1930s. Being devoted to democracy, the free-enterprise system, and Christianity, Americans have been turned off by the followers of Marx, particularly the Bolsheviks, who supported the equivalent of a religious war against all capitalists and so-called imperialists. Adding to this has been the influence of many Americans of Russian origin whose antecedents suffered from Communist oppression.

It is my belief that the final Soviet surrender in 1990 resulted from the cumulative effect of 43 years of a consistent U.S. policy of unyielding confrontation with the Soviets while maintaining military and nuclear parity. The Soviet demise as a world power resulted, I believe, in the failure of their flawed Communist economic system and the gradual deterioration of the Soviets' military force and morale, hastened by their great miscalculation in invading Afghanistan.

The Cold War lasted so long and had such a strong influence on U.S. national life, attitudes, and government policy that we still have not absorbed the depth of its impact. At the world level, it dominated almost all aspects of our international relations. It drew us even closer to those countries that had been our allies (excluding the Soviet Union, of course), and it helped transform our principal enemies, Germany and Japan, into our most important and most valuable allies. At the same time, we reevaluated all of the non-Communist nations in terms of how they could assist or would handicap us in winning the Cold War. It was on this basis that we distributed our military and economic largesse as the only nation that had survived the war with increased industrial potential. Ignoring the fact that many of these nations were headed by dictators with poor civil rights records at best, we gave them aid principally for building themselves up militarily. We gave large-scale economic assistance to countries we had never noticed before, assigning priority to those that were strategically located, like Iran, or vulnerable to communism, like Mobuto in the Congo. We gave aid to weak, poor countries in Southeast Asia and Central Africa not out of altruism, but to save them from communism.

Under Eisenhower, Nixon, Ford, and Reagan, the scale and daring of our covert intelligence activities increased to the point that we reverted to wartime concepts. We made strong efforts to overthrow Communist governments such as Castro in Cuba and the regime in Nicaragua. Many of our covert moves, such as the Bay of Pigs and the overthrow of Mossadeq in Iran, were ill conceived and cost us dearly.

The Cold War lasted a long time. Although it did not directly cost us many American lives, we suffered the tragic loss of 111,000 lives in the proxy wars with North Korea and North Vietnam, and in addition, enormous expenses for military equipment and operations in those wars, as well as the unused nuclear, high-tech, and other capital investments created just to perpetuate a standoff between the two most powerful nations in the world. In doing so, both nations greatly degraded their standard of living and economic progress. President Reagan's last military expenditures resulted in an enormous increase in our national debt which we still bear, making us the major borrower in the world and preventing us from meeting the social, educational, and infrastructural needs of our country.

On the other hand, the Cold War had a strong influence on unifying American public opinion, particularly our willingness to support our government's foreign and defense policies. Leading citizens were willing to assume important government positions, no matter which party was in power, and were protected from the virulent attacks often made on our officials today. The dissolution of the Soviet Union left us without any unifying political force. Americans now seem free to pursue their particular political goals without consideration of the national interest. Many Americans have not been able to adjust to the change, feeling out of habit that we must continue Cold War levels of military preparedness, despite the lack of an identifiable enemy.

In a recent book, *In Confidence* (1995), Anatol Dobrynin, respected Soviet Ambassador to Washington from 1962 to 1986, gives a perceptive summary of his views on the Cold War. He characterized the Kennedy and Khrushchev era as one of "enormous vitality, drama, and even danger." The Johnson tenure was dominated by Vietnam for the United States and by

Czechoslovakia for the Soviets. Under Nixon and Ford the era was dominated by détente and summits. By Reagan's inauguration, the pendulum
had swung sharply from relaxation of tensions and normalization of Soviet-
U.S. relations to the extreme right.

Dobrynin also saw the decade of détente, 1981–1991, as a decade of "lost
opportunities," with "blame enough" for everyone. After Nixon and Carter,
the one question unanswered was: "What was the historic nature of U.S.-
Soviet relations? Was it détente or confrontation?" What were the principal
reasons for our change in relations? More than ever, Dobrynin added, "We
should understand it now in the 90s." Although détente failed, it did show
that confrontation between our systems was not necessary, and it did reduce
the nuclear threat. Important agreements were reached, but unfortunately
negotiations to this end were not given enough time.

When asked who was responsible for the failure of détente, Americans of
that day blamed Soviet "expansionist foreign and domestic policies,"
whereas the Soviets blamed the United States' "aggressive policy." The failure of early arms negotiations proved that "military détente was impossible
without political détente." Soviet leaders were proud to be assisting the
struggles of Soviet peoples toward deliberation and to be directing them on
the familiar road toward socialism. Since the late 1960s under Brezhnev,
Soviet policy was based on achieving "détente with the West, defense of the
East European status quo, containment of China, and support of the liberation movement in the Third World." The key Soviet objective vis-à-vis
Carter was to get back on the détente track after it had been lost.

Soviet foreign policy during this period was "to relax tensions and reduce
military stockpiles." This was unreasonably interfered with by Communist
"ideology," particularly by confrontations arising out of involvement in regional conflicts "to support our duty to other peoples" and the inevitable
transition toward socialism in the Third World. The Soviet leadership also
had great power aspirations, which resulted in inevitable but unnecessary
conflict with the U.S., first in Cuba and then Africa. This happened when
the United States was "trying to establish trust" between our two countries.

Soviet leaders also underestimated U.S. concerns over their regional intrusions, just as the United States underestimated Soviet resentment of U.S.
efforts to keep them out of the Middle East. By the time Carter's term of
office ended, the United States was fighting proxy wars in Afghanistan, Somalia, and Angola, as well as in El Salvador and Nicaragua. All in all, Dobrynin thought that "détente was to a certain extent buried in the Soviet
rivalry in the Third World."

The principal reason why détente failed was the existence of "contrary
concepts of détente"—Stalin's successors saw it "as a form of class struggle," whereas American leaders saw it as a way of managing the Soviets as
an emerging world power, pursuing a global confrontation through the containment of communism. Both countries also pursued military policy in

planning for a "worst possible scenario, a nuclear first strike with maximum devastation of the enemy." Unfortunately, billions were spent to balance such a strike.

Dobrynin felt that the absence of a solid political consensus in America also helped doom détente. The church, business, and foreign policy councils were not organized as a whole. The Committee for the Present Danger as well as Jewish and neo-conservative groups rallied behind Reagan against détente. In the Soviet Union, the growing influence of military and industrial factions worked against détente, as in America those fighting against "the Evil Empire" demanded national unity and high combat readiness, which involved enormous expenditures.

Dobrynin was, of course, a staunch Communist and, as others in his position, would naturally seek to justify his stand on the issues under consideration. However, it is good for nations, as well as for individuals, to "see ourselves as others see us."

2

Importance of U.S. Prewar Defense Assistance to England, 1941–1943

The U.S. military assistance sent to England before the United States entered World War II cannot be appreciated fully without also weighing its effect on the Cold War that followed. With the German invasion of Poland on September 1, 1939, England declared war against Germany and World War II ensued. At this time, the American people generally opposed U.S. participation in the war and did not want to assist England, our closest ally. The general view was that the Europeans had gotten themselves into the war by mishandling their affairs and that America should not have to bail them out.

Gradually, as the initial passive phases of the war developed without revealing the true nature of Hitler's threat, there was increasing apprehension in America that we would become involved. Fortunately for England and for the world, Winston Churchill, although then out of the cabinet, had the courage to speak out against Hitler. After he became Prime Minister, Churchill sought U.S. military support from President Franklin Roosevelt. The two leaders developed a close personal relationship, and Roosevelt gradually initiated U.S. military support for the British through Lend Lease and other means that were not always clearly revealed to the American public. Other forms of assistance, such as the furnishing of destroyers to the British, were done with doubtful legality.

The wisdom of our early support became increasingly clear in light of subsequent events. Since England was not prepared for defense against Hitler's increasing military might and had no reliable armed European allies, Hitler probably could have occupied England by landing forces after saturation air attacks, which would have had disastrous consequences for the world. With England under German control, the United States would have lacked a base for invasion of the continent and could not have played the role it did in winning World War II. Hitler would likely have attained his goal of conquest, making all of Western Europe his vassal.

It is difficult to predict future events. Hitler may have tried to conquer Russia, since the Soviet Union itself was bent on world conquest. On the other hand, Russia might have seemed to Hitler too much to take on. Germany and the USSR might have been able to coexist as contiguous empires covering the entire Eurasian land mass, with the United States dominant only in the Western Hemisphere. Hitler's defeat of England would, in any case, have left the United States in a secondary position rather than the preeminent world role it holds today.

In early 1941 I had been hearing more and more about the increased intensity of Hitler's air war against England, a country for which I had a deep affection. Almost all of my ancestors had migrated from England and I had spent three very rewarding years at Oxford University. Hitherto, I had not taken Hitler's threat to England and Europe seriously. One day while sitting at my desk in reverie, I suddenly realized that England might fall to the forces of a relentless dictator. I got up and left to discuss with my wife these fast-moving events and what we might do to help England. She was quite willing to make any sacrifices involved.

In June we moved to Washington so that I could join the U.S. defense effort. Professor William Yandell Elliot of Harvard, a man of academic distinction and a Rhodes Scholar to whom I had a letter of introduction, offered me a position as a geologist in the Import Shipping Branch of the Raw Materials Division of the Office of Production Management (OPM). The OPM at the time was in the process of being reorganized as the War Production Board (WPB), headed by Edward R. Stettinius. As the Senior Liaison Officer, I served as office manager and performed other duties as assigned by Professor Elliot. I also became Chairman of the Interdepartmental Shipping Priority Committee, the objective of which was to build stockpiles of critical and strategic minerals and other available materials required in the war effort.

This work put me in touch with other government agencies, primarily the Department of State, Maritime Commission, Reconstruction Finance Corporation (RFC), Board of Economic Warfare, and the branches of the armed forces. I also dealt with an array of business leaders who had volunteered to serve their country in wartime, including Thomas K. Finletter at the State Department, William L. Clayton, who headed the RFC, and William McChesney Martin, a former president of the New York Stock Exchange who had enlisted as a private in army logistics.

Elliot, a strong individual with widespread contacts throughout the defense establishment, was head of an all-government committee controlling strategic materials. I not only gained insight into defense policymaking but also got to know the top policymakers. I accompanied Elliot to informal out-of-office evening meetings of a top government group that discussed high policy defense matters.

In March 1942, Roosevelt and Churchill created three British-American Combined Boards: The Combined Raw Materials Board (CRMB), Shipping Board, and Production and Resources Boards. Bill Batt, former head of the Swedish firm SKF, and Sir Clive Balieu, an Australian industrialist, were the U.S. and U.K. co-chairmen of the CRMB and I was named U.S. Deputy Executive Secretary. I accepted, though I felt guilty about leaving Elliot; however, he was given a promotion at the WPB. The CRMB had a joint staff with matching U.S. and U.K. representatives for each position. The Board's decisions were binding on the two governments.

The Board's mandate covered the stimulation of supply and allocation of all strategic raw materials available to the Allied nations. Decisions were made on the basis of technical reports by the joint staff that determined the world supply and requirements for all nations under Allied control including Russia, Canada, and Latin America. I sat in on all Board meetings preparing the agenda, decisions, and records. At the end of the war, I was presented with copies of all Board documents, including those saved for me while I was in the Navy. In October 1942, as the U.S. war effort intensified, I became increasingly determined, however, to get into the armed forces. In the meantime, I was permitted to spend two months in London on CRMB business, arriving by Pan American clipper on December 24.

London was, after an extended lull, again under Nazi bombing. There was something strangely exciting about walking at night in the darkened streets with the sound of nearby hits and the resulting noise of falling structures and fires. Averell Harriman, who headed what everyone called the Harriman Mission, a part of the Embassy, gave me an excellent office and an efficient secretary at 1 Grosvenor Square. Harriman was very helpful, as was his assistant Phil Reed, a former Chairman of General Electric. I saw much of "Doc" Matthews, acting Ambassador in the absence of John Winant, and other members of the Embassy staff, many of whom were old friends.

While in England I was free to make my own arrangements. I looked into all of the CRMB problems with the British, sending a weekly written report to headquarters in Washington; I was also kept advised of activities there. I met personally with most British officials below cabinet rank in my field, including Oliver Franks, who had been my moral tutor at Queen's College, Oxford, and later became the British Ambassador to Washington as Lord Franks. I lunched with him at the American Club my first day in London and since he was the Second Secretary in charge of the Raw Materials Division, we found many common interests to discuss during my stay.

I attended regular meetings of the Harriman staff, and at one point Harriman asked to see me and deftly broached the question of letting him see my telegrams before I sent them to Washington. He had had considerable experience with raw materials in Russia, he said, and although it was my decision, he would be happy to help me if I would send them through him. He handled this request so smoothly that I couldn't say no. Later Harriman tried to get me to stay and work in the Mission, and I was also offered a job and an Army commission by the Office of Strategic Services. I declined both since I had already put in for a Navy Commission and had taken the physical examination in London so I would be ready to report for duty when I returned to Washington.

I also visited three of the British raw materials control centers outside London, the Iron and Steel Control at Leamington Spa, the Non Ferrous Metals Control at Rugby, and the Hemp Control at Chester. In London, I went to many meetings at the Ministry of Supply, the War Cabinet Offices, and the Commonwealth Supply Council, which allocated raw materials among countries of the British Empire. I also visited the London Preemption Committee, which decided what materials went to neutral countries to keep them from joining the Axis, and the Post-War Requirements Bureau under Sir Frederick Leith-Ross, where representatives of governments in exile met and calculated their needs after the war. I attended two sessions of Parliament and discussed CRMB problems with the staff of the Embassy.

I had interesting meetings with C. R. Wheeler, Deputy Steel Controller, about British and American requirements of scarce ferro-alloys, and arranged for him a useful visit to Washington. I also had helpful talks with Anthony J. D. Biddle, U.S. Ambassador to governments in exile, about the Belgian Congo Tripartite Agreement under which the CRMB allocated scarce metals mined in the Congo, and a visit with M. Plevan, Free French Foreign Minister, regarding materials still under French control around the world. I had meetings with officials of the other Combined Boards in London, and worked with David Eccles of the Combined Production and Resources Board and members of the Combined Export Marketing Committee.

On March 2 I met with Harriman about a trip home via North Africa. Since the area had just been freed from Vichy France, the CRMB was anxious to take advantage of the raw material supplies available there for the Allied war effort while the English public revelled in North African oranges and wine. Harriman had attended the Casablanca Conference presided over by Roosevelt and Churchill and was able to give me valuable information from the French, particularly on iron ore, which was much in demand for English steel plants. The British were currently forced to use 20 percent iron ore from Oxfordshire. With the approval of General Eisenhower, I was assigned top priority for a visit to Africa; I was given this good news with pomp at a fashionable London restaurant. Having been given the required immunization shots, I prepared for my departure.

Following is my report to Harriman describing my work in his Mission.

1 Grosvenor Square
LONDON W.1.
27th February 1943

Dear Mr. Harriman,

The following summarizes my activities during the period I have been attached to your Mission.

Cooperation with the Harriman Mission and Ministry of Supply in organization of the United Kingdom Metallurgical Mission to the United States to promote better cooperation between the two countries in conservation and use of the Ferro-Alloys.

Examination of British implementation of the Combined Raw Materials Board recommendation regarding decreased use of molybdenum in substitution for tungsten in high speed steel.

Cooperation with the Harriman Mission and Services of Supply in correlating their joint raw materials studies with the United States and the United Kingdom collaboration in the raw material field in Washington.

Cooperation with the Harriman Mission and representative of the Bureau of Industrial Conservation in the formulation of the Anglo American Conservation Committee, and establishing working relationship between it and the corresponding group in the United States.

Cooperation with the Embassy in setting up under the aegis of the Coal Tar Controller a committee for the allocation of British production of metaporacresol on a combined basis, with the United States as claimant for supplies.

Cooperation in obtaining agreement by the Ministry of Supply of proposed 1943 allocation of sisal by the Combined Raw Materials Board and the earmarking of sisal for immediate shipment to the United States from British East Africa.

Recommendation as to the action to be taken by the Combined Raw Materials Board in connection with proposed Spanish supply-purchase program for the first six months of 1943.

Cooperation with the Economic Warfare Division of the Embassy and the Ministry of Economic Warfare in formulating proposal to obtain surplus production of cotton goods from Spain for North Africa by furnishing additional amounts of cotton to Spain.

Justification to the Combined Raw Materials Board for allocation of 2,360 tons of zinc dust to the United Kingdom for the first quarter 1943.

Explanation to the Combined Raw Materials Board of second quarter 1943 United Kingdom requirement for cupro-nickel for bullet jackets and recommendation that shipment of clad steel to effect substitution be expedited.

Obtaining information on raw material production and supply in North Africa. Data obtained from Mr. Harriman, Major Chambers, and Mr. Blias, all of which is in the Mission files. In addition information on iron ore available in North Africa, and effect on United Kingdom requirements.

Investigation into 1943 United Kingdom requirements for nickel, especially from the point of view of stabilizing operation of the Clydach Refinery and maintaining United Kingdom stocks at an adequate level.

Investigation of possibility for increased utilization of direct process zinc oxide in the United Kingdom to substitute zinc oxide made from slab zinc.

Examination of United Kingdom control of mica, end uses normally allowed and efforts made by United Kingdom to stimulate production in areas allocated to them.

Cooperation with the Embassy and Foreign Office in working out tripartite supply-purchase agreements with respect to the Belgian Congo and Fighting French territories.

Discussions with the Ministry of Supply in economies in use of jute in Eastern Hemisphere countries, with special reference to availability and development of local substitute fibres for Indian jute.

In closing I would like to express appreciation for the splendid cooperation shown by yourself and other members of the Mission during my visit. It is my hope that there will in the future be more effective cooperation between the Combined Raw Materials Board and your Mission.

Sincerely yours,
George C. McGhee

Mr. W. A. Harriman
American Embassy
LONDON

Following my arrival in Algiers on March 10, I met with members of the North African Economic Board (NAEB) and attended a meeting of the board presided over by its president. I spent the rest of the day studying the files of the Procurement Development Division in an effort to determine the availability of iron ore and other raw materials badly needed for the war effort. I arrived in Bone after dark during a spectacular German rocket raid, followed by three more air raids. During the next five days I visited the phosphate docks, where there was an air raid in which we could see the German planes, and met with the Ministry of War Transport representative at Philippeville, where I was shown the Quenza Iron Ore dumps and their stocks of iron ore and pyrites. While I was in Philippeville, there was an air raid during which artificial smoke was created to obscure the town.

Later I visited the El Halia mine, about 15 miles east along the coast, and Djidjelli, where we inspected the docks, boats, cork, and iron ore. On March 15 I visited the docks and saw sunken ships and iron ore dumps. Iron ore was shipped from here via Timerzit, Bou Amrane, and Gueldaman. Next, I was driven to Algiers and spent the afternoon looking through files of the Export Division.

On March 16 I met with U.S. Minister Murphy and participated in a general discussion about North Africa and NAEB. I inspected iron ore stocks at the ports of Algiers, Zaccar, and Timerzit, where iron ore was shipped. I lunched with Murphy at his villa. Also present were Mr. Lang, a *Time* correspondent who was writing an article about Murphy, and the sub-Prefect of Algiers, who had just returned from fighting at the front. I spent the afternoon at the NAEB office. On March 17 I attended an Executive

Committee meeting of the NAEB and had lunch with the Economic Adviser to the British Minister, Harold Macmillan.

I passed through Les Falaises, an open roadstead, with considerable iron ore stocks. I arrived in Bougie about dark, when an air raid took place. I left Algiers about 9:00 in a C-53. Also on the plane were Ensign Reed, Naval Attache to Biddle's Embassy in London. We arrived in Marrakech about 5:00, and I went to Hotel LaMamounia, where I had a room with a balcony overlooking gardens, the Arab quarter, and the snow-capped Atlas mountains. Reed and I visited the Arab town, particularly the 14th century Medersa. I departed on March 20 and, after stopping in Dakar and Belem, I arrived in Miami about 3:00 on March 25.

3

U.S. Cold War Kickoff: Greece and Turkey, 1947–1951

On September 3, 1945, the day after the peace treaty with Japan was signed in Tokyo Harbor, I departed Guam by air after a year's service there in the United States Navy and arrived in Dallas. After a happy reunion with my family, we laid plans for the future. Our situation was quite different now, because the oil field I had discovered just before going overseas would satisfy all of our financial needs as far ahead as I could foresee. I was now free to enter government, a long-held ambition.

Returning to Washington, I applied in the normal way for a job in the State Department as an assistant to William L. Clayton, the Assistant Secretary for Economic Affairs. Clayton had founded Anderson Clayton and Company in 1904 and had built it from Houston into the largest cotton trading firm in the world. I had known and admired him through visits to Houston before the war and during my work with the War Production Board and was anxious to work for him. Since I was too old for a Foreign Service appointment, I was forced to begin at the lowest Civil Service level, sharing an office with Fisher Howe, a lifelong friend, as he rose to high diplomatic posts, and doing low-level chores.

Nevertheless, I seized an early opportunity to take minutes of the many meetings in Clayton's office. Sitting quietly in the back of the room, I developed a technique for taking notes without being observed. I would use this technique successfully throughout my later diplomatic career. With a tiny square of paper concealed in the palm of my left hand, I scribbled notes with a small pencil, designating subjects, key numbers, and key phrases for direct quotations, without looking down. As soon as the meeting ended, I used my scribbled notes in dictating a verbatim transcript. The three memoirs I later wrote and this volume were based on notes taken in this way.

Working with Clayton was a great education, as I was able to absorb the lessons of his vast experience in international trade. When I got to the point where I could predict what his reply would be to any question, I became concerned that I might not be able to think for myself. By coincidence I was later to occupy the same position Clayton had had, with a change in title from economic to political affairs. After two years, I was in a position for an important assignment of my own—Coordinator for Aid to Greece and Turkey under the Truman Doctrine. It was the first U.S. effort under a policy to contain Soviet expansion, as designed by George F. Kennan.

On February 24, 1947, a dangerous power vacuum threatened to replace colonial rule in the Middle East. Amid the wreckage of World War II, the newly emerging, mostly Arab nations struggled to attain self-government and achieve economic stability. They were seriously divided by religious and cultural differences, unprepared to unite in a regional defense—in a region strategically placed, rich in oil reserves, and vulnerable. From behind the shadow of fascism, another threatening force was emerging. Communist movements, which had begun to grow on the open wounds of Europe, probed incessantly for weaknesses in Greece, Turkey, and Iran, seeking to control the Turkish Straits and to open the way for expansion into the Middle East.

The British, who had valiantly borne the burden of preserving the Middle East from Hitler and the Soviet threat that succeeded it, were forced to reassess their commitment to providing Greece and Turkey with economic and military assistance. Their own wartime losses had placed an unbearable strain on their ability to defend their interests in the Middle East and to finance postwar reconstruction at home. The uncertain fate of the Middle East had approached a crisis point. Communist-led guerrillas had gained control over most of Greece outside major cities, and the Greek royalist government was threatened. Turkey, which lay athwart the land route for any Soviet invasion of the Middle East, had been weakened economically by its risky policy of neutrality and its isolation during the war. Turkish weaponry was too limited and obsolete, and Turkish communications facilities were insufficient to defend the country against the increasing Soviet threat. For the moment, the security of the entire Middle East region depended on the survivability of Greece and Turkey.

The fateful transfer was officially initiated at 9:00 A.M. on Monday, February 24, 1947, when British Ambassador Lord Inverchapel handed Secretary of State George Marshall two aides-mémoire—one on Greece and the other on Turkey. In essence, the British stressed the importance of protecting Greece and Turkey against the rising Soviet threat, predicting the fall of Greece within two weeks in the absence of rapid economic and military aid. The United States was asked to assume the major responsibility for providing the assistance to both countries that the British economy could no longer support. Unofficially, the same memos had been presented three days earlier to Loy Henderson, Director of the Office of Near Eastern, South Asian, and African Affairs, in order to give the State Department an opportunity to consider the matter over the weekend. When Henderson convened his task force upon receipt of the British note, the working assumption was that the United States would grant the British request for assistance.

President Truman consulted Monday with Secretary of State Marshall and read the report prepared over the weekend by the State/War/Navy Coordinating Committee. Its working assumption had also been that the administration should decide, in principle, to assume the responsibility involved. Britain's assessment of Greece's financial requirements, as reported to the President by Under Secretary of State Dean Acheson, quoted a figure of roughly $250 million in 1947 and more the following year. Turkey's needs were more difficult to establish and were estimated to be smaller. The special U.S. committee formed to study assistance requirements to Greece and Turkey agreed with the British suggestion that American and British chiefs of staff should jointly make this assessment. Based on the committee's report and following discussions with Secretary of War Robert Patterson and Secretary of the Navy James Forrestal, Marshall wrote to the President on February 26 that he was convinced of four things: the British were sincere about their financial constraints; the situation, particularly in Greece, was desperate; the collapse of the Greek government would put U.S. interests in peril; and the United States should, therefore, immediately extend all aid possible to Greece and, on a smaller scale, to Turkey.

Truman launched into intensive consultations with government and congressional leaders. Sensitive to the reactions of Congress, particularly the Senate leadership of the opposition majority party, he carefully encouraged the support of Foreign Relations Committee Chairman Arthur Vandenberg, whose backing would prove essential to overwhelming congressional support. President Truman decided to request $400 million—$250 million for Greece and $150 million for Turkey—and to commence preparations on a presentation to a joint session of Congress that would explain the sense of his position on the requested aid and smooth the way for the requisite legislation. Marshall delegated Acheson to organize the effort, which culminated in President Truman's speech to Congress on March 12, 1947, and introduced to history the Truman Doctrine.

U.S. foreign policy had reached a turning point. The Truman Doctrine made that departure by declaring that wherever aggression—direct or indirect—threatened the peace, U.S. security was involved. Truman's message to Congress and the nation rang with the conviction of American ideals and drew deeply on the American tradition of democracy. It could not fail to inspire:

I believe . . . that it must be the policy of the United States to support free peoples who are resisting attempted subjugation by armed minorities or by outside pressures.

I believe that we must assist free peoples to work out their own destinies in their own way.

I believe that our help should be primarily through economic and financial aid which is essential to economic stability and orderly political processes.

The seeds of totalitarian regimes . . . are nurtured by misery and want. They spread and grow in the evil soil of poverty and strife. They reach their full growth when the hope of a people for a better life has died.

We must keep that hope alive.

The free peoples of the world look to us for support in maintaining their freedoms.

If we falter in our leadership, we may endanger the peace of the world—and we shall surely endanger the welfare of our own nation.

When he had finished, every member of Congress, with one exception, rose and applauded. Free nations of the world joined in the acclaim, while the Communist world lashed out savagely.

It was necessary, of course, to determine how the new aid package would be administered. At the request of the President, the State Department took the lead among the executive agencies in coordinating the implementation of the policy underlying the Greek-Turkish aid programs, in drafting the necessary legislation, and in preparing its presentation to Congress. The duties of the Washington "back-stop organization," according to a State Department analysis, "seem to be primarily those of planning, organizing, and reporting." For this purpose the Department created the Interim Greek-Turkish Assistance Committee on April 7, 1947. I was asked to serve as chairman. Letters were sent to the Departments of Treasury, War, Navy, Commerce, Agriculture, and Labor, as well as to the Bureau of the Budget, inviting their participation.

The Department of State was formally delegated responsibility for the administration of the act by executive order dated May 22, 1947. The testimony of the executive agencies before the Congress and the reports of the House Foreign Affairs and Senate Foreign Relations committees envisaged small but competent advisory missions in both Greece and Turkey. Each would have a chief of mission, who would exercise a large part of the responsibility for executing the program. It was also made clear that the State Department, in executing the program, would make full use of the best-qualified government agencies. In 1946 the new bureaucracy for foreign operations was only beginning to emerge from the remnants of what was left from the war. The Greek-Turkish aid program was the first of the post-war aid programs, succeeding the United Nations Relief and Works Agency (UNRWA) of 1945. It was later to be absorbed by the much larger Marshall Plan and Mutual Security Agency.

During the effort to get approval of Public Law 75 (Greek-Turkish Aid), little thought had been given as to how it would be administered. When its administration was finally given over to the State Department, there was no precedent to go by. However, a plethora of former participants in the war effort were eager and ready to take part in the new crusade launched by the Truman Doctrine to save Greece and Turkey and other countries threatened by the Soviets. They called me and wrote me by the hundreds. I knew many of them from the war days and was able to recruit excellent candidates for the Greek and Turkish missions.

Although the State Department had never administered anything resembling an aid program, it was naively expected to do so through its normal administrative structure, which had been largely involved in leisurely policy making and only in administering itself. It was decided that a small central administrative staff was required, which was placed inconspicuously in the Department basement.

I and my single purchasing officer, with the assistance of the Army Corps of Engineers, opened negotiations with a consortium of American engineering firms that the Corps had selected to rebuild the docks of Piraeus, the harbor for Athens, which had been destroyed by the retiring Nazis. Contracts on the usual Corps cost, plus fixed fee basis aggregating several tens of millions of dollars, were ready for signature. When I presented the contracts to Under Secretary Robert Lovett for approval, he hit the ceiling. "You mean you want me to sign contracts for these amounts in the name of the State Department? The Department has never done anything like this before. We'll be crucified by criticism. No way."

Feeling that I had committed myself and the Department, I spent a sleepless night. Early the next morning I called the chief of the Corps of Engineers, who had been helping me, and explained my problem. Would he take over the projects and administer them if we would provide the funds? He agreed, and I was off the hook. This increased the cost of the projects and imposed a delay while the Corps formed an Athens District, but the docks were built without scandal.

This being the first of the postwar aid programs, Congress, after putting up token resistance to appropriating the funds, took little interest in how they would be spent. I kept the appropriate committees informed but found no tendency on their part to interfere with the program's administration. They had not yet discovered, much to the increasing distress of government administration to this day, how interesting and politically profitable it was to second-guess the government's decisions. I well recall the day, after the Greek guerrillas had blown up several of the bridges we had just built, that, without getting anyone's approval outside of the Department, I quietly sent the Treasury Department a check transferring $50 million from the Greek economic program to the Defense Department to apply against defeating the guerrillas. No one ever complained or questioned. I concluded that the best way to survive in the Washington bureaucracy was to "lie low," providing you had the authority.

Pursuant to this policy, the Army, Navy, and Air Force assumed responsibility for executing the military aspects of both programs. The numerous other responsibilities were divided along the following lines: *Department of Agriculture,* the agricultural rehabilitation program envisaged as part of Greek recovery; *Department of Commerce,* the development of trade and procurement policies; *U.S. Public Health Service,* execution of the Greek public health program; *Bureau of the Budget,* the development of plans for reorganizing the Greek government calculated to increase its effectiveness; *Department of the Treasury* (although primarily interested in the development of financial and monetary policy), through the Federal Bureau of Supply, the procurement of all nonmilitary supplies not purchased through private channels; *Department of Labor,* all matters affecting Greek labor; *Federal Security Agency,* Greek social insurance; and *Public Roads Administration,* road building under the Turkish program.

As special assistant to William Clayton, I had been advising him on the Greek-Turkish aid issue and had become deeply involved, particularly in the governmentwide effort to prepare for the presentation to the Appropriations Committee that would follow passage of the enabling legislation. Shortly afterward, I became chairman of the interim State Department committee and was later named Coordinator for Aid to Greece and Turkey, a statutory position created when the enabling legislation, Public Law 75, was enacted on May 22.

The rationale for creating such a position resulted from Secretary Marshall's personal experience during his China Mission days. He had been in charge in the field but had requested a trusted Washington aide to serve as his channel of communications with the President, government agencies, and Congress. In the current situation, the heads of the two missions were in the two countries involved. In Turkey, for the two-year duration of the program, was Ambassador Edwin Wilson, and in Greece, initially, was former Nebraska Governor Dwight Griswold, who was chosen by President Truman for the post. A letter of instruction was sent to Wilson in July, giving him complete authority over the military mission insofar as he wished to exercise it.

As Coordinator, I was their representative in Washington and was to fight many battles on their behalf. This was in large part because the lines of authority between Griswold and Ambassador Lincoln MacVeagh tended to overlap, until we realized that the two jobs had to be combined, and Ambassador Henry Grady was chosen for the task. Since Grady reported as Ambassador to Greece through the regional assistant secretary, I had fewer occasions to intervene on his behalf as chief of mission. During the initial phases of planning and coordinating the broad policy of Greek-Turkish aid and shepherding it through the congressional process, there had been little time to focus on the details of the programs, to identify which government agencies would be involved with each aspect of the programs, and to decide how to select and train suitable personnel.

All of these problems fell into my lap at once, even before I had been able to select my own staff. On my first day as Coordinator, I received 137 telephone calls, of which I could return only a few. As quickly as I could, I filled the slots in my own staff of about 20, bringing in Walter Wilds, an experienced administrator, who became my deputy, and William Rountree, a very capable and experienced Foreign Service officer.

During the two-year duration of Public Law 75, I visited Greece and Turkey every several months to meet with the heads of mission, staff, and high officials of the host governments. In Athens, I always visited King Paul and Queen Frederika, as well as the Prime Minister. I once accompanied General James Van Fleet to view, at a respectful distance, a battle between Greek army and guerrilla forces for the Grammos Mountains. The Greek army won, but our elation was destined to be short. The defeated guerrillas, having a sanctuary available in nearby Yugoslavia, wheeled along the border and reentered Greece again unexpectedly, inflicting a crushing defeat that represented a major setback to our aid program. Unfortunately, I had included the claim of victory in my quarterly report to Congress. When it became public coincidentally with the ensuing loss, Walter Lippmann wrote a scathing column accusing us of attempting to mislead the public.

During my visits to Turkey, I became acquainted with Turkish officials who would rise to high positions during the seven years I was to be associated closely with Turkey. These visits also gave me a "feel" for the Turks, operating under what was almost a wartime situation, which was to be very helpful to me later. My friendships with Kasim Gulek, who would become head of the Republican Peoples party during my ambassadorship, and with Nuri Birgi, who would rise to the highest Turkish diplomatic post, date from this period.

Although the United States continued to view piecemeal aid to Greece, Turkey, and Iran as a necessary response to the Soviet threat in the Middle East, it gave priority to the defense of the countries of the North Atlantic region. Progress toward a North Atlantic alliance, however, became a major issue for Turkey, which would continue to press for its inclusion until it finally succeeded in 1952. The dialogue began in force in early May of 1948, when the Turks expressed concern that the United States might extend guarantees against aggression to the Western European countries in NATO without including Turkey. Such steps, they feared, would give the Soviets the impression that the United States would leave Turkey undefended. The State Department, however, explained that it had made no final decision as to which countries would receive security guarantees (NATO was not established until August 24, 1949) and that Turkey, in the meantime, was profiting from military assistance under Public Law 75.

On June 8, 1949, President Truman appointed me to the position of

Assistant Secretary of State for the Near East, South Asia, and Africa, a post
that covered an area with 600 million people in 90 political entities, most
of which had been colonies before World War II. At that time the area
comprised only seven independent countries; today there are almost 70. The
areas included Greece and Turkey, and since my former position as Coordinator of Aid to Greece and Turkey was not to be filled, I continued to
be responsible for the program.

As demonstrated by the State Department's statement, U.S. defense policy in the Middle East continued to focus on Greece and Turkey. A broader
defense policy on behalf of the entire region was not yet part of our Cold
War strategy. This strategy was necessarily influenced by the need to balance
perceived threat against limited resources. Moreover, a Middle East defense
policy was greatly complicated by the desire to enhance relations with both
Israel and the Arab nations, who historically were antagonists. For the time
being, U.S. military assistance would be limited to such measures as the
Mutual Defense Assistance Act of 1949, which permitted the extension of
cash-reimbursable military assistance to any nation whose ability to defend
itself, or to participate in the area of which it was a part, was important to
the United States.

By March 1950 total military assistance to Turkey under Public Law 75
had reached $236 million. Progress was seen both in equipping and training
Turkish armed forces, which had been reduced from 500,000 at the outset
of U.S. aid to 300,000. Turkish military requirements for fiscal year 1951
were estimated at $45 million, down from $81 million in 1950, but economic aid was increasing. Turkish receipts from the EEC (European Economic Community) and ERP (European Recovery Program or Marshall
Plan) for FY 1950 were $114 million, with FY 1951 aid estimated at $76
million. These funds were for economic development—to raise the low
Turkish living standard and to help compensate for the heavy burden of the
defense budget. The Department considered that the objectives of U.S. aid
to Turkey were being achieved and that aid should be continued.

A month after the Democratic party's landslide victory in Turkish elections on May 14, 1950, the Korean War broke out. For the first time Communists and Western forces engaged in battle. At the urging of the United
States, the United Nations sent out a general appeal to members to contribute troops. At this time, Turkey had received no pledges from the Western powers regarding its own defenses, but it clearly showed its own
commitment to the West. The government of Prime Minister Adnan Menderes, without consultation with the opposition party, decided in a cabinet
meeting in Yalova to send a brigade of 4,500 men to Korea.

Turkey was the first nation after the United States to respond to the U.N.
appeal. Menderes stated at the time that it was only by way of a decision
similar to ours, to be arrived at by the Freedom-loving nations, that acts of
aggression can be prevented and world peace can be safeguarded. Scattered

opposition was soon overtaken by pride in the fighting qualities of the Turkish troops, which achieved worldwide recognition. In December an overwhelming majority of the Turkish Parliament approved the government's decision.

A regional meeting of U.S. Ambassadors was held in Istanbul in February 1950. A principal topic of discussion was, of course, Greek-Turkish admission to NATO. I was thoroughly convinced that this step was vitally needed to bring the considerable Greek and Turkish forces, particularly the Turkish army, into the NATO defensive line. Only in this way could the Soviets be prevented from making a military "end run" around NATO. Turkey would be NATO's eastern anchor. No longer would the other weak Middle Eastern states be such easy targets for Communist subversion or military attack. Their morale, as well as that of Greece and Turkey, would be given a great boost.

Both countries ardently desired to become full-fledged allies with us in NATO and to gain a guarantee of collective defense and access to more arms. Acheson and British Foreign Secretary Ernest Bevin had been giving both countries oral assurances, but their full admission had been delayed in September 1950. The invitation to become associated with NATO planning had only temporarily appeased them. At the end of the U.S. regional ambassadors meeting, the conference's most important recommendation was that we enter into reciprocal security arrangements with Greece and Turkey, preferably through their direct adherence to NATO.

During the Istanbul meeting, after a consensus had been reached among the participants, Admiral Mick Carney and I sent a top-secret telegram to the State Department in which we urged that the Departments of State and Defense give renewed attention to Greek-Turkish entry into NATO. We cited not only the well-known arguments but also intelligence that we had received during the meeting to the effect that the Turks, although they strongly wanted to join NATO, were becoming discouraged and were considering alternative courses of action if their entry was further delayed. We argued that we could make a better deal with the Turks when they were eager to join than when their interest might be declining, and we pointed out that the Turkish army was larger than that of any current NATO member. I felt confident that the conference had made a valuable, perhaps decisive, contribution to the successful conclusion of my long struggle to get Turkey and Greece into NATO.

Although the Norwegians questioned this solution to the Greek-Turkish problem, the United Kingdom gradually changed its position in favor of admission. On July 18, the new British Foreign Secretary, Herbert Morrison, publicly announced support and so advised the Greek and Turkish governments. The question was placed on the agenda for the meeting of the North Atlantic Council to be held in Ottawa later in July. George Perkins, Assistant Secretary for European Affairs, was put in charge of the overall conference, and I was named one of the senior advisers on the delegation to handle the Greek-Turkish question.

Bringing Greece and Turkey into NATO proved to be more of a problem than we had anticipated, however, even with U.S., British, and French agreement in advance. We had prepared arguments to meet the expected opposition of the Nordic members, who, having joined NATO to assure protection of the North Atlantic area where they lived, did not want to be drawn into a war in the perilous Middle East. There was much discussion, and finally, Denmark was the last to withdraw opposition.

At this very juncture, with the other nine members waiting in the conference chamber to vote in favor, the United Kingdom and France decided to try to wring national advantage from the decision to which they were already committed. France sought to use its approval as leverage to place a French Admiral as chief of a new Mediterranean naval command; the United Kingdom sought to get Turkey, as the price of entry, to agree to place Turkish troops, in time of war, under a British-led Middle East command. The British proposal, coming when it did, was the dying gasp of an old British proposal the United States had at one time espoused. However, it had been sharply rejected by the Arabs and Turkey. We told the British that if Turkey would accept willingly, we would raise no objection, but that we would not join in any attempt to coerce Turkey to accept wartime Britain command. I was in touch with the Turks through their representative in Ottawa, and, predictably, they held firm against the British proposal.

There remained many hours of wrangling among the three powers on these two issues. This contention became increasingly embarrassing in front of the other NATO members, several of whom had been persuaded against their better judgment to support Greek-Turkish entry. Herbert Morrison, in a clumsy way, attempted to carry out his bluff, lecturing me and other American delegates as though we were junior staff members of his Foreign Office. Although the United States attempted to be patient, we stood firm and in the end reason prevailed. Secretary Acheson and the British and French foreign ministers went back into the council meeting, and the invitation to Greece and Turkey was passed unanimously. I breathed a sigh of relief. The long battle was over.

A protocol admitting Greece and Turkey to NATO was signed by the Council of Deputies in mid-October. Denmark was the last country to sign final acceptance. By a vote of 73 to 2, with 21 members not voting, the Senate approved ratification of the protocol on February 7, 1952. The protocol finally went into effect on February 15, 1952. The area of the treaty was extended to include Greece and Turkey. There could no longer be any Soviet "end run" around NATO. The defense of the Middle East was assured.

4

Early Days of the Arab Refugee Problem: 1949

On November 29, 1947, the United Nations General Assembly approved the partition of Palestine into Arab and Jewish zones. Britain, having held the territory under a League of Nations Mandate since 1920, withdrew its forces on May 14, 1948, whereupon Israel was declared an independent state. Egypt, Transjordan, Syria, Lebanon, Iraq, and Saudi Arabia rejected the partition and invaded Israel on May 15. A truce was arranged under U.N. auspices by Count Folke Bernadotte, head of the Swedish Red Cross, on July 11, but hostilities did not cease until December, following an invasion of Egypt by Israeli forces.

As a consequence, hundreds of thousands of Palestinians, fleeing from the territory that had been mandated to the British, found themselves trapped behind cease-fire lines and were prevented by the state of Israel from returning to their homes. On November 19, 1948, the U.N. General Assembly voted a $32 million fund to provide for the refugees, and on December 11, the assembly passed a resolution (the famous Article II), which mandated that the refugees should be permitted to return to their homes, or else be compensated. The Palestine Conciliation Commission (PCC) was established to help the Jews and Arabs reach an overall agreement on Palestine.

The nations involved fully recognized that the refugee problem had to be resolved if there was to be a lasting peace in the Middle East. On January 28, 1949, the U.S. Embassy in Cairo published an estimate of the number of refugees, based on figures supplied from Middle East capitals: 8,000 in Egypt; 250,000 in Egyptian-occupied Palestine (the Gaza Strip); 302,000 in Arab Palestine (the West Bank of the Jordan River); 89,000 in Transjordan; 90,000 in Lebanon; 100,000 in Syria; and 5,000 in Iraq. The estimates came to a total of 844,000.

In late February 1949, Dean Rusk, the newly appointed Deputy Under Secretary of State, called me into his office and asked if I would like to go to the Middle East and see what could be done about the refugees in the long run. He could offer me the title of Special Assistant to the Secretary with the rank of minister. I accepted.

Mark Ethridge, the U.S. representative on the Palestine Conciliation Commission, was advised that Palestine refugee activities would be concentrated in Washington under me as the Special Assistant to the Secretary of State. It was suggested that I participate in the upcoming PCC conference in Beirut. I would later call on Ralph J. Bunche, the United Nations Acting Mediator on Palestine based in Rhodes, and after other visits in the area, I would return via London, where I would discuss the refugee problem with the British.

Soon after my appointment as Coordinator on Palestine Refugee matters, I directed a memorandum to Secretary of State Dean Acheson, dated March 15, to obtain approval for the proposed terms of reference of my assignment.

1. It be recognized as in the national interest of the United States that an early and effective solution be found to the problem of the Palestine refugees. Such solution should make possible their repatriation or resettlement in such a manner as to minimize present and potential political and economic tensions prejudicial to United States interests in the area affected.

2. The United States be prepared to contribute such technical and financial assistance to the solution of this problem as it considers necessary, while at the same time refusing to accept sole responsibility for solution of the problem and seeking to confine U.S. financial assistance there to within limits consistent with its national interests.

3. A plan be developed as a matter of urgency for the implementation of this policy, including proposals for relief, rehabilitation, and long-range resettlement projects, estimated costs, expected source of funds and operational procedures, including the part to be played by the U.S., the governments in the affected area, other interested governments, and the UN.

United Nations Ambassador Warren R. Austin arranged for me to meet with Israeli Foreign Minister Moshe Sharett, who was in New York. Keen and highly articulate, Sharett said he believed the PCC meeting in Beirut would result in the Arabs uniting in forcing Israel to take back Arab refugees, thus relieving them of the problem and perhaps destroying Israel in the process. As for the long-range solution, Sharett admitted it was possible that some refugees would be repatriated in Israel. This would, however, depend on the state of the peace. It would also require land, money, and technical assistance on a large scale. Since the Arab homes of Palestine had largely been destroyed, Sharett insisted that most refugees must be absorbed in Transjordan, Iraq, and Syria. The money for this relocation must come in part from Israel in the form of compensation and in part from the international agencies. It was unlikely that the Arabs would be willing to accept technical assistance from Israel. (Sharett was later to prove quite intractable on the refugee issue.)

Sharett said that, had the Arabs remained and constituted a majority, the situation in Israel would have been quite different from that which emerged after their departure. They would, in the first instance, have been able to assure themselves certain rights; however, it was too late, he said "to turn the clock back." The settlement of the refugee problem, according to Sharett, must be part of the overall peace settlement. There would be some small-scale repatriation; however, the only real solution was resettlement in Arab countries where there was plenty of land for the refugees. Lasting peace, he said, could only be achieved through separation of the races into separate states.

All Arabs belong to one race, according to Sharett. The differences that had arisen since their delivery from the Turks were slight. They could all be assimilated, and this could be paid for with international funds, plus compensation by Israel for Arab losses, though he admitted these monies would be slow in coming. Israel would gladly furnish technical assistance if it was wanted. Sharett had submitted a plan for this to Ethridge, warning Ethridge that the Beirut meeting would probably serve only to "harden Arab-Israeli differences." In the Near East political bravery is in inverse ratio to the size of the meeting—the larger the meeting, the less likely those present will speak courageously. Palestine, according to Sharett, did not need Arab labor, but other Arab countries did. Syria, for example, had already absorbed some refugees.

I flew from New York to Beirut, arriving on March 20. I entered into discussions with Ethridge and attended the PCC meetings, where I sat quietly in the back and listened to the seemingly futile debate. It soon became apparent that Ethridge and I held similar views on helping the refugees. On March 23, he and I sent a telegram to the State Department seeking approval for our preliminary recommendations. We assumed that the U.N. relief program would not last long. The key to our long-range solution was economic development, for which the PCC would have to appoint a technical commission to develop plans and provide technical and financial assistance. My task was to spell out just how this could be done. The Department had agreed that in the meantime, I would join Bunche at Rhodes for a few days and then proceed to Damascus, Baghdad, and Amman. Lebanon already had too many refugees, and neither Saudi Arabia nor Egypt was a likely prospect for any considerable number. Since the PCC was seized with discussions between Israel and the Arab states over refugees, my visit to Tel Aviv would come later.

The following account is based largely on my field notes taken at the time. Ethridge and I were fully aware that both the Arabs and Israelis held completely negative attitudes toward refugees. The Arabs stood by the U.N. Resolution of 1948 affirming the right of refugees to return to their homes, and they did not wish to relieve Israel of its responsibility by settling refugees in their countries. Moreover, they gladly seized on the refugee issue as a political weapon against Israel.

I arrived in Rhodes during the final days of the difficult negotiations over the Israel-Transjordan cease-fire agreement, which provided for withdrawal of forces and provisional boundaries. This was the last of a series of such agreements that lifted Bunche into world renown and won for him the coveted Nobel Peace Prize. I developed a close relationship with Bunche, whom I held in high esteem. Upon his return to America, he spent a week-end with my wife, Cecilia, and me at our farm in Middleburg, Virginia. He had learned a lot about the Middle East from experience, and in Rhodes he gave me the full benefit of that experience. When I later became Assistant Secretary for the Near East, South Asia, and Africa, it was only because Bunche had turned the job down when President Truman offered it to him. I was not in the least embarrassed to be considered second to Ralph Bunche.

In Rhodes, I had discussions with John Reedman, senior political adviser on the Mediators Staff in Rhodes. Reedman said the Negeb below the 31st parallel was unsuitable for cultivation. The terrain was wild and dry, getting rainfall of only 5 inches a year. Only a few Bedouins lived there. There was no plan for an Egyptian Negeb frontier, which was a geographical and ad-ministrative term. In the Beersheba subdistrict, 100,000 Arabs were milling around. The district going south was Birashug, the coastal strip around Gaza plus the worthless strip along the Egyptian border, where there were to be the Arabs of the partition. In the Gaza subdistrict, including the towns of Gaza, Majdal, and Khanyumis, there were according to Reedman 39,000, 11,000, and 12,000 refugees, respectively. Adding 90,000 in these villages would bring the total to over 150,000. There were, in addition, 50,000 refugees compressed in smaller areas south of Majdal and 50,000 who had come from Jaffa and the surrounding districts. In the Faluga there were 2,800 men well dug in. They could have gotten out but their commander refused to retire because he was afraid they would lose their arms. Only a few hundred Jews were surrounding them.

Of the 3,500 Arabs present in Faluga after the Armistice, 1,800 elected at first to go to Gaza. Later, more came out saying the Jews scared them. Some went first to Hebron under the Transjordan Red Cross Committee but later returned to Gaza "because the relief was better." According to Reedman, Bernadotte wanted to give all of the areas taken by the Jews beyond the partition line (Jerusalem, Lidda, and Ramle) back to the Arabs, and the U.S. approved. There were 16,000 Arabs in Ramle, 18,000 in Lidda, and 67,000 in villages in the Ramle subdistrict, totaling approximately 100,000. There were no Jews.

Reedman estimated that there were 69,000 Arabs left in Israeli territory, 5,000 in Jaffa, 4,000 to 5,000 in Haifa, 1,000 in Acre, and 25,000 to 30,000 in Nazareth and Nazareth district. The rest had scattered into Galilee. He divided the Arab population in this area as follows:

1. Under the Partition Plan there would have been 390,000 settled Arabs as well as 100 Bedouin or nomadic Arabs, some in the Beersheba district.

2. There were 80,000 to 100,000 Arabs in the area taken by Israel beyond the partition line and 100,000 in West Galilee.

3. This totaled 500,000, from which 70,000 could be deducted, leaving 430,000-plus refugees, and in addition an indeterminate number of Bedouins. In addition, many Arabs, perhaps 100,000, had been evacuated from villages near Jewish territory because of fear or isolation. Any additional refugees had to be identified locally.

Reedman reported that the Jews were making minor land grabs in Jerusalem, Lidda, and Ramle, and 1,300 new refugees had emerged in the last few days. Some assurance could be given to Israel, he said, that development in the area could ultimately enable the Jews gradually to buy out the Arabs, who might then take the money and buy new land opened up to them.

In my meetings with Bunche in Rhodes, he had emphasized that there was no basis for linking compensation for land with claims for war damages, which had been levied against the invading states, not the Palestinian Arabs, who were invaded. (A corollary to this was that the Jews had no moral case against the Palestinians on which to oppose repatriation.) Bunche and his associates reported that the homes of the Arabs had been systematically destroyed in areas invaded by Jewish forces, both inside and outside of the Israeli zone. In Jerusalem, Lidda, and Ramle, the Jews had occupied Arab homes, but in Haifa, Jaffa, and elsewhere, they had left many homes unoccupied.

Israel was represented at Rhodes by Moshe Dayan, who later became Chief of Staff of the Israeli armed forces and then Secretary of Defense and foreign minister. Dayan told me about his youth in Palestine and the action he participated in during World War II, as part of a British-Jewish joint operation against the Vichy French, in which he lost his left eye. In conversation, Dayan was a gentle, kindly man. His background was well suited for his future responsibilities. In his memoirs, he recounts the secret behind-the-scenes negotiations he conducted in March 1949 with King Abdullah of Jordan, from which he had just returned when I first met him and which resulted in a successful cease-fire agreement completed on April 3. Our paths were to cross again in years to come.

After returning to Beirut, I held several days of talks with Ethridge and with the U.S. Ambassadors to Middle Eastern nations, who were there for the PCC meeting. Among them, James H. Keeley, U.S. Minister to Syria, opined that the Arabs needed a face-saving mechanism. The Israelis should therefore admit the principle of repatriation even if they didn't intend to do much about it. For our part, he felt that the United States should not question this principle and should not tell the Arabs to be realistic. Instead, we should determine how many Arabs wanted to go back under Jewish rule and then see if the Arab leaders really wanted them to go back. He saw the need to recognize the conflict between the concepts of Arabs being considered a "fifth column" and a "hostage." Israel's first step was to give up the lands it had taken outside the partition area, including East Galilee, and to repatriate the Arabs from there and as many more as could be accommodated.

The Arab states would not take refugees in return for economic "bait" without Israeli concessions, Keeley said. If they were convinced that the United States had taken a strong position for repatriation, and Israel had made a suitable gesture, they would probably take refugees if adequate economic help was granted. The PCC should recommend to the United Nations that economic assistance be provided the Arab countries, both by the World Bank and countries like the United States, the United Kingdom, and France. The Arab countries might ask the United States to conduct a survey that would help them formulate a request to the World Bank. A mission headed by an American with U.S., U.K., and French nationals could make such a survey, with help from the World Bank, the Export-Import Bank, the oil companies, and the U.S. Congress, all dealing with the Arab countries bilaterally.

Dean Hinton, a Foreign Service officer on Ethridge's staff, summarized his views with a number of questions: "What is Israel? Is it the partitioned area, as it existed after the cease-fire? We must first obtain a breakdown of refugees as to where they are from. Some 150,000 to 350,000 of them came from Galilee. Western Galilee, which is out of the partitioned area, holds 100,000 and could hold more. The Israelis occupied western Galilee after the truce, on July 24, 1948."

Hinton continued by posing more questions: "What was our policy toward Israel? Would we apply sanctions or grant a loan? What was the United Nations' position on Israel's actions? Would there be a public statement regarding the Israeli actions?

What are the opportunities for employment of the refugees on the Saudi Arabian tapline and refineries, which will require 55,000–70,000 workers at the maximum? The first to be offered jobs are the 10,000–15,000 jobless in Syria. Beyond this refugees are available and will probably he hired, since they will work for less and it will be difficult to get people to leave their land. The League of Nations effort to resettle Assyrians in Syria failed. Better transportation could help settle refuges in the Gezirah area of Syria; however, there is more Communism there already than in Palestine. The Syrians could not organize the settlement of Gezirah—we would have to. We should not, however, undertake such projects without careful planning and initial Arab requests. Arab reaction to a failure would be great.

In discussions in Beirut, Lowell Pinkerton, our Minister to Lebanon, noted that Lebanon had requested $15 million from the World Bank through the Food and Agriculture Organization (FAO), which was too large a sum. Judging by the denial of the recent Lebanese loan for development of its airport, he felt that Lebanon should not request a direct loan from the United States or any other country. Lebanon did, he believed, have some industrial development possibilities.

Pinkerton did not believe Lebanon could assimilate its present refugee population, much less take any more. Many Lebanese refugees were in more difficult straits than those from Palestine, who constituted about 50 percent of the urban and agricultural population. Rich refugees were spending their money fast. Lebanon was not in a good position, Pinkerton said, to exercise leadership among the Arab states because of its Christian majority. Part of the resentment of Israel would be taken out on Lebanese Christians. Lebanon never participated in the fighting against Israel because its 3,500-man army was so small; as a result, there was little residual feeling against Israel. The Lebanese also had little antagonism toward the United States and so would probably be willing to request U.S. assistance in getting loans. If the United Kingdom participated with the United States in providing technical assistance, France, because of its historic role in Lebanon, would be jealous, said Pinkerton. France itself might have something to offer.

While in Beirut I also spoke with Brigadier General William E. Riley, the United Nations Chief of Staff for supervision of the truce in Palestine and senior U.S. military observer in Palestine. He emphasized that the Arabs would never consent to remain herded together as they now were, nor would they think to press for compensation for their lost lands. There were no such entities as tribal groups, Riley asserted, and there was no more room for refugees in Nablus. Finally, no practical way existed to control the Arabs through registration, and the high number of displaced Arabs was due in part to duplicate registration.

During my stay in Beirut, since I would not be visiting Israel, I had long talks with James G. McDonald, the Special Representative of the United States in Israel. McDonald asked me to tell Ethridge he considered it important that a general peace conference be held, concentrating on Transjordan, which he felt was the key to an ultimate solution. With a peace treaty, McDonald believed, the refugee problem could be dealt with more easily. Egypt "posed no threat," said McDonald, and "when Transjordan made peace, the United Kingdom had too."

Events had proved, McDonald said, that Egypt and the other Arab states did not constitute a barrier to a Soviet threat in the Middle East. The Jews and King Abdullah understood each other. As for the refugees, he said, the Israelis might ultimately take 150,000, but not in Jaffa where the Jews had taken over all living space. (I had observed in Jaffa that Jews owned about half the shops.) It was difficult for Israel to put refugees in Lidda and Ramle because of their strategic importance. Israel wanted to hold its wedge into Jerusalem, moving in new kibbutzim or agricultural settlements, which were strong points where they could dig in.

McDonald thought that since Israel viewed West Galilee as having less strategic value, it might offer better prospects for refugee settlement than did North Gaza. Where there were originally 60,000 Arabs in Haifa, there were now 3,000, of whom 2,000 were employed in the oil refinery there. Half of the oil came by tanker, and the other half by pipeline, which Baghdad had shut off. According to McDonald, the Negev was a "sacred cow" to Israel, although they were not developing it. The Bedouins roamed the Negev from Galilee to Sinai, employing a destructive economy. Their goats destroyed the grass, and they pulled up the vegetation that held the soil. The United Kingdom, according to McDonald, wanted Transjordan for strategic reasons, for it was the only place where they could retain troops in the area.

On April 3, I made a brief visit to Cairo, where meetings with Egyptian officials were arranged by our able Chargé d'Affaires, Jefferson Patterson. Prime Minister Abdul Hadi Pasha took the usual Arab line: the refugees must be permitted to return to their homes, and any who didn't want to must be paid. They could then go to the country of their choice, which would take them if they had money. Neither Syria nor Iraq would be willing to borrow money to take care of refugees they did not feel responsible for.

Egyptian Foreign Minister Ahmed Kashaba did not believe it was realistic to expect the Arabs to go back, for they could not live under Jewish masters. Israel, he predicted, would go broke, since the country lacked a sound economy. The Arabs in Israel would be slaves, working for low wages: 5 to 10 pounds against the 20 to 30 piasters in Egypt. According to Kashaba, the problem should be attacked piecemeal, with the Arabs going back to predominantly Arab areas that were not presently under Israel such as West Galilee, Lidda, and Ramle. I also met with Azzam Pasha, Secretary-General of the Arab League who reported that the League was not strong enough economically to handle the refugee problem, although it had raised 450,000 to 500,000 pounds for refugee relief. If Israel took what it had gained by force, the Arabs must reply with force, he said. The Arab League was not strong enough economically to handle the refugee problem. It could only go after technicians and available Egyptian private capital.

In Damascus, I stayed at the home of James Keeley, our Minister to Syria, who was valiantly trying to maintain relations with an unstable Syrian government. Keeley was of great help in arranging my meetings with Syrian officials. He advised me that Syria was not willing to discuss refugees, and I found the reaction to any refugee assistance to be entirely negative. "If Abdullah takes refugees, that will be the end of Abdullah," said Keeley. "The PCC's job is to get the refugees back to Palestine—not to resettle them." This was very disappointing to me inasmuch as we had had high hopes that the relatively vacant but fertile Jazirah region of northern Syria would be used to settle refugees. My memories of Syria are still influenced by this unsuccessful visit and by another in March 1951, when in my absence my bedroom in the legation was blown to bits by a bomb.

When I arrived in Baghdad, our minister was away, although our legation provided valuable assistance. In deference to British primacy in Iraq, I called on the British Chargé d'Affaires, Humphrey Trevelyan, who was related to Sir George, the famous historian and who himself was to ascend to the highest ranks of the British service and a peerage. Trevelyan tried to talk me out of approaching the Iraqi government, since he knew Iraq was the most adamant of all the Arab states against accepting refugees. He said the question could not even be discussed in Iraqi circles in view of Iraq's categorical refusal to negotiate with the PCC until Israel agreed in principle to permit the refugees to return. Iraq was rabidly anti-Zionist and was threatening retaliation against Iraqi Jews, so it wanted no part in settling the refugee problem.

I replied that the refugee problem existed and that some workable solution had to be found. The United States and the United Kingdom were the only countries that could do it. I urged that refugee settlement be linked with the large-scale economic development schemes being sought by Iraq and other Arab states. Trevelyan did not believe that refugee settlement should be linked with Iraq's current request for flood-control projects before the International Bank. Development schemes for refugees should be clearly labeled as such. The British reasoned that refugee resettlement would be automatically furthered if the right projects were undertaken.

Trevelyan did not agree with my suggestion that the PCC be assigned responsibility for surveys and negotiations with the Arab governments. He felt that any organization connected with Palestine would be suspect by the Arabs. Although we were not in full agreement, my discussions with Trevelyan were most helpful. He was, of course, correct in his analysis of the Iraqi position. I found that no Iraqi official was willing to consider taking refugees. The net of what the Embassy told me was that Iraq could do nothing in the short run, but it might, within five years or so, take many refugees because of the demand for labor. He said we must push the IBRD to make a loan to Iraq. Our Embassy, meanwhile, urged the launching of a Middle East Survey Mission by May. I left Baghdad by the overnight desert bus that travels on no road, making its own path through the desert.

Our Chargé Wells Stabler arranged for me to meet with King Abdullah and his Finance Minister. The King understood the refugee problem very well and promised to do all he could to help, if certain inducements were forthcoming. I had received the same impression in my earlier talks with Prime Minister Tawfiq Pasha at the PCC meeting in Beirut. Although Pasha followed the common line with other Arab officials in meetings, he expressed to me an awareness of the resettlement problem and a willingness to consider concrete proposals. He did not feel that such a parallel approach worked against the Arab states, and he was a help to the PCC in working out overall solutions to problems.

The problem was that the Palestinians would in fact be hard for Jordan to assimilate, for most of them, under the British Mandate, had received a better education and were more experienced politically than other Arabs. Abdullah undoubtedly understood that the Palestinians constituted a possible danger to his old-fashioned Hashemite regime. Having received so many displaced Arabs, Jordan was already threatened with becoming a poorhouse for refugees. Even so, Abdullah was tempted by the additions to his population the refugees would represent and the economic assistance he might receive for taking them. Ultimately, we became concerned that Jordan would take more refugees than it could support.

While in Amman I also had an interesting meeting with E. C. Bryant, Field Director for the League of Red Cross Societies. He took me to a Red Cross camp, where the refugees appeared to be reasonably well housed and fed, but they were milling about without anything to do or any hope for the future.

I did not enter into discussions with the Israeli government at this stage. The number of refugees they would be willing to repatriate and the compensation they would pay were key problems that were being considered at the highest levels in the capitals. Nor did I have any discussions on refugees with the Lebanese government. With more than 250,000 refugees, Lebanon was strained to capacity, and fully understood the economic and political implications for its future. The Palestine Liberation Organization (PLO) and its terrorist activities had not yet emerged in Lebanon, although the rise of such an organization might have been anticipated. In any event, it was clear that Lebanon needed to be relieved of some of its refugee burden, not given any more.

Later, after I became Assistant Secretary of State for the area, three opportunities arose which, if they had succeeded, might have resolved the refugee problem. First, on one occasion, Israel offered to take a total of 250,000 refugees as part of a general settlement. Since at the end of hostilities there were about 125,000 Arabs in Israel and Israel had already repatriated 25,000, this meant an additional 100,000 refugees in Israel. There were an estimated 400,000 refugees in the territory Israel originally occupied, which left 150,000 refugees. Before this offer, we had urged Isreal to take 200,000 more refugees. The Arabs responded with a counter-offer of acceptance if Israel would take a total of 500,000 (250,000 more than offered). Israel, however, declined to raise the ante. The game of numbers of refugees continued.

Second, Ethridge had received another interesting feeler from David Ben Gurion, the Prime Minister of Israel, as early as April 18. The Israelis would take the 250,000 refugees in the Gaza Strip, occupied in the war by Egypt, in return for the strip itself. This proposal seemed to offer good possibilities for a breakthrough, since the number of refugees involved was greater than the 200,000 we had been urging. We asked the Egyptians to give the Israeli offer careful consideration, but they turned it down. Egypt did not want to be accused of trading land for refugees, and perhaps it also felt it would end up with the refugees and lose the strip in the bargain.

Third, on April 29, Minister Keeley reported that General Husni Zaim, the mercurial military ruler of Syria, would accept 250,000 refugees for settlement in Syria, if enough economic assistance was provided. We were elated and tried to pin him down, but Zaim had great difficulty working out a cease-fire with Israel. He felt he could not make concessions on refugees without a quid pro quo from Israel, which was not forthcoming. Zaim was assassinated on August 14 by some of his officers, whose motive was apparently personal.

As early as May 16, Ethridge reported that the Arabs had admitted privately they would have to take refugees. But the Israelis, even under the extreme pressure of one of the strongest diplomatic notes I have ever seen, sent by Truman to Ben Gurion on May 28, refused to make any definitive statement on refugees or to separate the question from a general peace settlement. Truman wrote to Ben Gurion that if Israel continued to reject the General Assembly Resolution of 1948, "the U.S. government will regretfully be forced to the conclusion that a revision of its attitude toward Israel has become unavoidable." Ben Gurion refused to budge. The Israeli representative in Lausanne offered no meaningful concessions on refugees. Despite heroic efforts by Ethridge and others, the Lausanne Conference finally floundered on this issue.

On May 2, my office prepared a memorandum for Secretary Acheson, who was due to discuss refugee resettlement with the President. Among other recommendations, I suggested consideration of holding up the remainder of the $100 million Export-Import Bank loan to Israel, which was $49 million, to put pressure on Israel to take at least 200,000 refugees. On June 10, following Israel's rejection of our latest proposal on refugees, a memorandum was sent to President Truman recommending that the Ex-Im Bank "be immediately informed that it would be desirable to hold up the allocations of the $49 million as yet unallocated of the $100 million earmarked for loan to Israel."

I was advised that the President had approved this recommendation and that I should so inform the Israeli Ambassador. I invited the Ambassador to lunch with me at my club and put our decision to him in the most tactful and objective way I could. In light of the costly military demands on Israel to defend itself against the Arabs, whose enmity arose mainly from Israel's failure to carry out the U.N. resolution on the refugees, Israel would not be able to make effective use of the Ex-Im Bank loan unless Israel took at least 200,000 refugees. The Ambassador looked me straight in the eye and said, in essence, that I wouldn't get away with this move, that he would stop it. There was other conversation, but I had gotten the point. Within an hour of returning to my office, I received a message from the White House stating that the President wished to dissociate himself from any withholding of the Ex-Im Bank loan.

These were, I believe, the last opportunities we had to find a real solution to the Arab refugee problem. My efforts, as well as those of many subsequent sincere and able intermediaries, have all ended in failure.

The number of Arab refugees and their progeny, originally 900,000, now total between 4 and 5 million, scattered throughout the Middle East and around the world. The present situation represents a human tragedy for the millions of homeless and stateless Palestinians involved. Sadly, decisions made by politicians determined the fate of innocent people, most of them farmers and peasants. Refugees still in U.N. camps live in idleness in tents and shacks on a meager diet, often in sight of their former lands, which are now occupied by Jewish residents. The remaining 2 to 3 million refugees who are now outside Palestine and their descendants live insecure lives in other Arab countries: 200,000 of these were recently forced out of Kuwait after the Iraqi invasion in 1991; others were forced to leave Saudi Arabia in time of depression.

Our great concern in dealing with the Arab refugee problem in 1949 was to prevent the embittered displaced refugees from coming under the control of international communism. In 1956, Egypt accepted the Soviet-built Aswan Dam and cooperated for a period with Moscow in meeting economic and defense needs. Syria was the only Arab state, however, that developed a continuing alliance with the Soviets, which was ended by the Gulf War in 1991. The remaining refugees, I believe, resisted Communist overtures because of the strength of their adherence to Islam and because of U.S. efforts over the years to ameliorate their situation.

5

Envoy to the Middle World: 1949–1951

In mid-1949, I was appointed Assistant Secretary of State for the newly created Bureau for Near Eastern, South Asian, and African Affairs, responsible for a vast area extending from the Strait of Gibraltar to the Bay of Bengal. I became the first American envoy to what I chose to call the Middle World. It included all of Africa except the Union of South Africa; the Middle East, including Greece and Turkey; and South Asia through Burma, including Afghanistan. Once they emerged from colonialism, the area would comprise 90 sovereign states populated by some 600 million people.

My government service during this period was made much more challenging by Secretary Dean Acheson, a man I admired greatly. He stimulated me and gave me freedom to carry out my task. Acheson possessed, in my judgment, one of the most brilliant minds that has been applied to American foreign policy. He became Secretary of State in 1949 at a time when we desperately needed to re-create the Western alliance and develop an overall strategy for overcoming the ravages of war and standing up to the Soviets in the Cold War. Acheson provided the leadership through this period, which resulted in the enormous success of the Marshall Plan, Greek-Turkish aid, and NATO. He instilled confidence in the Department, the Congress, the public, and our allies. We were all fortunate to serve under Harry Truman, a great President.

Before the postwar era, most of the countries of the Middle World had been European colonies, and so had not dealt with the outside world either diplomatically or commercially. Their external relations had, of course, been handled in the European capitals—London, Paris, Lisbon, Rome, and Brussels. Consequently, I was the first ranking U.S. official to visit most of the Middle World countries, many of which gained independence during the years of my tenure as Assistant Secretary of State. There had been a Middle World setting for a few head-of-state meetings during World War II, as when President Roosevelt, returning from the Yalta Conference in February 1945, met with Farouk of Egypt, Haile Selassie of Ethiopia, and Ibn Saud of Saudi Arabia. But it was not until 1949, after I became Assistant Secretary, that Prime Minister Jawaharlal Nehru of India and Mohammed Reza Shah Pahlavi of Iran were official visitors to Washington. I handled the arrangements for their visits, and I made two complete tours, meeting with them and the other leaders of Middle World capitals.

Today colonialism is no longer an issue and is only of historical interest. The world, acknowledging its civilizing contributions, has passed it by without regret. At Oxford in the 1930s, however, I had been influenced by the life of my benefactor, Cecil Rhodes, who was largely instrumental in establishing the British Empire in Africa. My heroes were Rhodes and the imperialist rulers in India, Robert Clive and Warren Hastings. Colonialism seemed to me at that time not to be an instrument of oppression but a way of bearing the white man's burden.

By 1949, however, I had come to disapprove of both racism and colonialism. I did not fault the British, for they had begun to adapt colonial rule to changing world attitudes and appeared quite willing to withdraw once a colony had shown it was prepared for self-government. The Dutch also seemed ready to retire from colonialism at appropriate times. In contrast, the French, Portuguese, Italians, and Belgians seemed determined to preserve their colonial benefits until they were forced out, showing them to be not only impractical but also immoral.

Upon undertaking my new duties as Assistant Secretary, I gave careful thought to the vast area under my jurisdiction, analyzing the problems there and formulating a broad strategy for our government in dealing with them. As Coordinator for Aid to Greece and Turkey, the first of our postwar policies aimed at stopping communism, I had clearly developed the point of view of a "Cold Warrior," as the derogatory Soviet press and Soviet broadcasts in the Middle East constantly reminded me. I was not displeased with this. With my new responsibilities, however, I began to recognize the existence of a great many problems in the Middle World, a region five times the size of the United States, which were not related to the threat of communism.

Upon undertaking my new duties, I devoted most of my energies to devising a strategy for the successful carrying-out of our foreign policy objectives in the Middle World that would enable us to use the limited instruments of policy we had available so they would reinforce each other and thereby be more effective. Naturally, I started out with the perceived Soviet threat to the new Middle World states. The Free World's confrontation with the Soviets has often been described as an ideological conflict between communism and capitalism. However, Marxist economic doctrine had been revealed not only as a threat in itself but also as a front for Soviet imperialism under dictatorial rule.

The Middle World had had ample experience over the centuries with conquerors and would-be conquerors. Thus, the Soviet threat was new to the Middle World only in its technique, not in its objectives. I was hopeful, however, that the non-Communist states of this area would develop a realistic awareness of the threat and would join us in resisting neutralism.

By 1951 in Europe, the forces of communism no longer had the initiative that they had had only two years before. To the west of the area conquered by the Soviet army, the European nations had successfully withstood Communist initiatives. Under the Marshall Plan, they had made progress toward economic recovery and the restoration of public confidence in their future. In Eastern Europe, the Soviets had recently suffered a major reversal in Yugoslavia and were fully occupied in holding the remainder of their bloc.

In China, the expansion of militant communism was a great setback for the West. It would be impossible to gauge the full effects of communism's victory in China until their new leaders had come to grips with the difficult practical problems they faced. At the same time, the rapid Communist takeover in China posed grave problems and competition for the Soviet Union. The Soviets could be expected to attempt to maximize their influence over the Chinese Communists and then to consolidate this vast area within their orbit.

The Middle East was vulnerable to Communist subversion, particularly along its northern borders adjacent to the Soviet Union and the satellite states. However, with U.S. help progress was being made in strengthening these exposed states. Greece was successfully liquidating the remnants of the guerrilla movement based in Yugoslavia and Bulgaria, which had been organized and supported by the Soviets since 1946. By 1949, fewer than 2,000 guerrillas were fighting in Greece, compared with a maximum of 28,000 two years earlier. Turkey, with its traditional national unity and determination to resist Soviet encroachment, had successfully withstood demands for territory and military bases, renunciation by the USSR of the Turko-Soviet Treaty of Friendship, and an intensive propaganda campaign. Having survived 13 wars with Russia in modern history, Turkey was not likely to capitulate now.

Among the other nations threatened by the Soviets, Iran deserved special credit for having, with our support, expelled in late 1946 a Soviet-sponsored puppet government in Azerbaijan, a province of Iran bordering the Soviet Union. For the past five years, Iran had firmly stood its ground against the intimidating troop movements along its frontiers, Soviet-inspired incursions into Iranian territory, repeated demands for a Soviet oil concession as a front for penetration, and the full force of Soviet propaganda.

Despite the progress achieved, I felt we should not underestimate the seriousness of the Soviet threat, just as we should not overestimate the progress we had made in stemming the Communist tide. The conflict was drawing heavily upon our resources and upon the strength of other threatened nations. This was not the time for complacency. At the same time, I was well aware that the Soviet threat was by no means the only problem facing the world, and by acting as though we thought it was, we would be according the Soviets undue credit and would surely fail to meet other challenges. There were many other world problems that I felt we should tackle with equal determination.

Countries only recently freed from colonial rule were struggling for political and economic viability and self-respect within the family of nations. Their feelings of insecurity made it all the more difficult for them to work out compromises over long-standing conflicts with their neighbors. Looking to the future, I felt that these problems would constitute a threat to the Middle World even in the absence of the Soviet menace. Their diversity and complexity precluded any simple formula for their solution. Certainly, the mere extension of material aid, even if it were available in adequate amounts, would not in itself ensure a solution.

In the Middle East, Iraq, Egypt, Saudi Arabia, and Yemen had achieved independence only since the 1920s. Lebanon and Syria had followed during the Second World War, and Jordan in 1946. All these states were still struggling to overcome the effects of a long-lived foreign influence, and were only beginning to seek opportunities for economic development and social reform. The political structure of the Middle East had been drastically changed by the emergence of the new state of Israel in 1948 and by the resulting large-scale Jewish immigration to Israel. Though reassured that Communist ideology had gained so little influence in the Middle East, I felt it necessary to do our utmost to continue to exclude this influence.

In the late 1940s, Africa had only four independent states: Egypt, Liberia, Ethiopia, and the Union of South Africa. However, a resolution of the Political and Security Committee of the U.N. General Assembly called for independence for Libya by 1952 and for Somaliland after 10 years. These states would be confronted with problems similar to those faced in the Middle East. With Libya as an example, other African states could be expected to press for an acceleration of their time schedules for independence. The limitations on technical skills and investment capital in Africa made that continent a prime candidate for our Point Four Program of technical assistance. We had for some time been cooperating with the Liberian government in such a program, which showed what might be done in other African countries. Development in Africa seemed to us the best antidote to communism.

In South Asia, the threat of Chinese communism was creating growing apprehension, but thus far Communist ideology had appeared to have gained little influence. The more pressing problems of this area were largely internal. India, Pakistan, Burma, and Ceylon had achieved independence within the last few years, and all of them except Burma within the framework of the British Commonwealth. They faced the difficult task of creating a new administrative structure. India and Pakistan had the additional problem of integrating their diverse ethnic groups, religious sects, and social classes, as well as the former princely states, and of settling the 10 million refugees resulting from their separation.

South Asia's long domination by foreign powers had left a legacy of suspicion toward the West which would be overcome only slowly. This negative attitude had been aggravated by our initial concentration on Europe, which South Asia had interpreted as indifference to their plight and even as Western solidarity "against the East." Although we recognized that these states desired to be neutral in the struggle between the Soviet Union and the West, we hoped that they would increasingly associate themselves with the Free World on important issues, on the basis of equality and partnership.

I felt that we must continue to help free nations resist Soviet expansion, seeking at all times to minimize the conflict and keep it from becoming military. But such a goal was only a minimum; it alone would not rally the people of the world to a common purpose. If we hoped to attain their voluntary association with us, we needed to meet the challenge of the dynamic forces at play in the world, which had appeal for the new developing nations.

In retrospect, we underestimated the overriding preoccupation of the new states of the Middle World with the conflicts they had inherited from their past: such as those between India and Pakistan, Arabs and Jews, Ethiopia and Somalia, Morocco and Algeria, Iran and Iraq. These seemingly intractable problems, of which the Middle World appears to have a disproportionate share, are deeply rooted in ancient religious and dynastic struggles. So far they have proven impossible to resolve and they continue to be overriding barriers to progress.

JAWAHARLAL NEHRU

In October 1949, in making arrangements for the first visit to the United States by Pandit Jawaharlal Nehru, the Prime Minister of India, I was assisted by Loy W. Henderson, our Ambassador to India, who prepared an evaluation of Nehru and offered advice on how to handle him. Coming from a prominent Indian family and educated in Britain (Harrow School and Cambridge), the high-handed Nehru tended to deprecate most things American as being inferior to the British, and he had little respect for U.S. government officials. He seemed determined to bypass the U.S. government and appeal directly to the American people; in so doing, he succeeded in making himself so unpopular in our country that it would later prove difficult to muster congressional support for much needed wheat shipments to India. During his visit Nehru and Truman didn't hit it off. At their first informal meeting the Prime Minister was offended because in his presence the President engaged in a lengthy conversation with Vice President Alben Barkley on the qualities of bourbon whiskey.

I myself found Nehru all but impossible to deal with. In contrast, his sister, Madame Pandit, the Indian Ambassador to Washington, was a friendly and appealing person. She often came to my office to chat, and we developed a good relationship. I was disappointed when Nehru chose his daughter Indira, rather than Madame Pandit, as his successor. Madame Pandit confided to me that her Washington favorites were Walter Lippmann and Felix Frankfurter, and that she encouraged her brother to spend most of his spare time with them. Hubert Humphrey, a newly elected Democratic Senator from Minnesota in 1949, invited me to meet with him on the Hill. "I want to specialize in India," he said. "You arrange for me to get invited to the Embassy, maybe a trip to India, and I can help you up here when matters arise affecting India." I held out my hand, saying, "Senator, you just made a deal."

MOHAMMED SHAH PAHLAVI

The son of Reza Shah Pahlavi, Mohammed Shah Pahlavi acceded to the Iranian throne on September 23, 1941, and although the United States had enjoyed good relations with him from the beginning, he had never paid an official visit to the United States. Educated in Switzerland and an avid sportsman, particularly in skiing and flying, he appeared to be thoroughly Westernized. Though not prepossessing in appearance, his intensity and air of self-importance definitely gave him a kingly aura. At age 30, he already had nine years of experience as a ruler; with his reformist and modernist views, and his liberal and open mind, he promised to be an enlightened monarch. He seemed sincerely interested in educating his people and in breaking up large estates to distribute land to the peasants.

Starting in January 1942, the Shah had sought large-scale military aid and expanded trade with the United States. The Millspaugh Mission, whose purpose was to explore how we could aid Iran, had ended in failure in June 1944. But we had cooperated in furnishing military aid in the form of surplus equipment in 1947. Our military and police missions in Iran had done good work. However, Iran's Seven-Year Plan of internal development, which had been headed by Max Thornburg, formerly of the State Department, had been too grandiose. After an assassination attempt in February 1949, the Shah attempted to ban the Communist Tudeh party and curb the power of the Majlis, a parliament without the powers of a democracy. His difficulties and frustrations, however, only increased, and his expectations of the United States soon reached unrealistic proportions.

At the invitation of the President, the Shah of Iran arrived in Washington on November 16, 1949, on President Truman's plane, the *Independence*, and on November 18 he met with the President at the White House. He stressed the importance of his country in any defense strategy against Soviet advances into the Middle East, and on this basis he made a strong appeal for military aid. Truman assured him that his request for aid would receive respectful attention, noting at the same time that Congress had reduced the administration's military assistance program. The Shah also outlined his economic program, a Seven-Year Plan that would drain his country's oil proceeds. He hoped a way could be found, either through the barter of strategic materials or a form of lend-lease, to obtain products such as wheat.

Later that day, I attended the Shah's meeting with Secretary of State Acheson, at which the Shah repeated his request for early military and economic assistance in substantial amounts. It was vital that Iran's defenses be built up immediately—an army of 150,000 was required, plus 30,000 frontier guards—anticipating a Soviet onslaught. The Secretary agreed that an increase in Iranian military strength was desirable, but he stressed the need to give priority to economic and social development. All nations in the Free World faced the same problem, said Acheson. If we all tried to build our military forces to the level of the Soviet Union, we would wreck our economies and collapse before being subjected to military attack.

The Secretary cited the example of China. At the end of World War II, Chiang Kai-shek had a large and well-equipped army enormously superior to the Chinese Communist forces. We had urged him to concentrate on improving the economic lot of his people, but he had opted instead for military strength, with the result that the people lost confidence in the Nationalist government. The vast quantities of American military equipment sent to China had been used to arm the Communist army after the Nationalist forces surrendered.

What went wrong? In retrospect, we know that the Shah's aspirations for himself and his country were far too ambitious. He attempted to justify his insatiable appetite for military equipment by citing Iran's strategic situation as guardian of major oil reserves and the approaches to the Persian Gulf. But more than that, for him military might was a source of prestige designed to strengthen his regime; assure the loyalty of his army; and make Iran not just a Middle Eastern power, but, as he was to claim later, an Indian Ocean and African power. To those unrealistic ends he sought the very latest in aircraft, tanks, and naval vessels.

The scope of the Shah's plans increased more rapidly than Iran's income. This was true even after 1973, when it rose to $20 billion a year. With the blank check given the Shah by the Nixon administration, in my view a great mistake, he purchased billions of dollars worth of military equipment, most of it too sophisticated to be maintained and operated by the Iranians. The Shah's economic and military programs not only exceeded Iran's infrastructure and available trained manpower but also helped the conservative Iranian religious hierarchy rally discontent against him. The Iranian people, who had never been consulted about the Shah's plans, were not enthusiastic followers, and the Shah never tried to develop a political base or any participation in government by the middle class he had created. More and more, the Shah withdrew into himself, accepted little advice, and resorted increasingly to dictatorial and repressive measures based on his SAVAK intelligence apparatus.

We would not be successful in Iran, even after sending Henry Grady there as Ambassador, as I had recommended because of his experience with aid programs to Greece. The Shah took this appointment to mean that more money would be available than was actually given to Iran, and so U.S.-Iranian relations steadily deteriorated. On November 4, 1950, the Soviet-Iranian Trade Agreement was announced, and cooperation with the United States came to a halt. When Iranian Prime Minister Ali Razmara was assassinated in March 1951, we entered the Mossadeq era; during this time, I negotiated with Prime Minister Mohammed Mossadeq, in an attempt to prevent Iran's nationalization of oil. (For more detail on Mossadeq, see Chapter 9.) The Shah was at his lowest level of confidence.

Years later, as a private businessman in 1974, I spent an hour with him in Teheran, and at once noted the change in his demeanor. Now the recipient of massive U.S. military aid, he was at the peak of his self-confidence and full of ambition to transform Iran into a regional power. Only five years later, his reign would end in utter collapse.

After World War II, the United Kingdom realized India was ready for self-rule. The population of India was about 350 million, and Mohandas Gandhi, the revered apostle of nonviolence, had led the Indian Nationalist Congress since 1919. Independence was granted by British Prime Minister Clement R. Attlee in 1946, subject to working out the details. The Dominion of India was created on August 15, 1947, as was the Dominion of Pakistan, following partition and the exchange of Hindus and Muslims between the two new countries. This bloody process produced some 10 million refugees. A constitution was adopted in January 1950, and India became a republic of the British Commonwealth. Pandit Nehru, a follower of Gandhi (who was assassinated in 1948) and Congress party leader, became Prime Minister, and his party won a sweeping victory in the country's first general election in 1952.

Pakistan, meanwhile, was undergoing a similar evolution. Following the creation of the Muslim League in 1930, its president, Mohammed Ali Jinnah, led a movement for an independent Muslim state. When the dominion was founded on August 15, 1947, Jinnah became its Governor-General. Immediately, tension arose over Indian control of predominantly Muslim

Kashmir, and after armed clashes in 1948, the United Nations was asked to settle the dispute.

Pakistan faced the daunting problem of caring for millions of Muslim refugees, and neither country had the resources to alleviate the suffering of its people. Tensions between the two were exacerbated by the Cold War. Nehru was not willing to compromise his neutrality, although he would still accept American wheat, whereas Pakistan, hoping it would gain our military and economic assistance, lined up on our side.

LIAQUAT ALI KHAN

The purpose of my trip to Pakistan in December 1949 was to extend a personal invitation to Prime Minister Liaquat Ali Khan to visit the United States, but Liaquat was in Peshawar, far to the north of Karachi, the capital, where I arrived. As a result, I spent a day meeting with Pakistani officials, in particular the Minister of Finance, Ghulam Mohammed, who had become my friend on frequent trips to Washington. That night, Ghulam gave a dinner for me and my wife, Cecilia, in his big old-fashioned house, and we found ourselves caught up in the enthusiasm of the other guests, British-trained Pakistani officials for the most part. Disillusionment had not yet set in over the problems of being a poor divided country locked in bitter rivalry with a more powerful neighbor.

We arose at six o'clock on December 10 for the flight to Peshawar, the capital of Northwest Frontier Province, where we were driven to Government House for our meeting with the Prime Minister and his wife. Liaquat, as second only to Jinnah in his party during the pre-independence era, had become the unchallenged leader of his country since the great Jinnah's death in 1948. This big, strong, confident man had considerable international stature, and we sought to enlist his services as a strong anti-Communist ally in the subcontinent, for his country had strategic territory on both the northwest and northeast borders of India.

Arriving at Government House, Cecilia and I were immediately received by the Prime Minister and his wife. They were a friendly and attractive couple, he brimming with smiles and she bursting with energy and exuberance, which had earned her the nickname "Tiger in Silks." Before Pakistan radio and a television recording, I presented the President's letter. The Prime Minister read it, asked me to thank the President, and accepted the invitation. I liked his forthrightness; truly he seemed to be a man you could do business with.

After a delightful lunch, we were taken through the Khyber Pass to the Afghanistan border, 20 miles west of Peshawar. In my youth, I had conjured an image of the Khyber Pass—rugged, mysterious, the route of conquerors such as Alexander the Great—and I was not disappointed. We were in an area called Pushtunistan, whose Muslim, Pushtu-speaking natives are known for their warlike independence. (The issue of whether to make Pushtunistan a separate state had disrupted relations between Pakistan and Afghanistan, which explains why I did not visit Kabul at that time.)

In May 1949, the Prime Minister and his Begum came to Washington for an official visit, and it was a great pleasure to see them again. Cecilia and I accompanied the pair by train to New York and were worried by Liaquat's drinking two strong Orange Blossoms before his arrival speech in New York. But we need not have worried. I appeared with Liaquat on Eleanor Roosevelt's radio program. Not being a world figure on the order of Nehru, Liaquat did not command as much attention in the press as Nehru. However, his talks with President Truman were more substantial, and his assurances that Pakistani forces would be available to meet any Communist threat to South Asia were indeed welcome.

Liaquat Ali Khan was assassinated in October 1951 by an Afghan fanatic who espoused the cause of an autonomous Pushtunistan. It was a terrible loss for Pakistan.

JAWAHARLAL NEHRU: MY FIRST VISIT

We arrived in New Delhi on December 11 and were met by Ambassador Loy Henderson and his wife, Elise, old friends from Washington. We were immediately caught up in a round of receptions—at Government House, where we were greeted by the Governor-General, and at the Embassy, which was attended by Prime Minister Nehru, his daughter Indira, and Sardar Patel, the Deputy Prime Minister. The success of my visit would depend on the outcome of my meeting with Nehru, so I was glad to catch a glimpse of him in a social setting.

At nine the next morning, I met with Patel, who launched into a lengthy spiel on India's position with regard to Kashmir and other issues vis-à-vis Pakistan. I emphasized how important it was to us for India and Pakistan to remedy their differences. Patel agreed, though he insisted that the fault lay with Pakistan. We also discussed economics, and I told Patel that American investors did not have a favorable view of the Indian investment climate. Could he not do something to improve it?

Nehru received me at noon in his office in the Council House. He was evidently having a busy day and seemed hurried. When he asked me to speak first, I outlined U.S. India policy. We were not attempting to enlist India into a power bloc, I explained, although we did hope to depend on India's cooperation in discouraging aggression and other violations of the United Nations Charter. I also stressed that we were not trying to dictate India's economic policy, although I tried to describe the kind of environment that might attract American private capital. I cited our policy toward Greece as an example of how the United States assisted countries without taking advantage of them.

When I had finished, Nehru said: "Mr. McGhee, I am sure you would like me to be very frank with you. I will." With that, he proceeded to ramble in his inimitable form of double talk. Nehru spoke easily and sonorously, but the words that came out had little meaning to me. They sounded fine if you didn't have to report or analyze them, but if you had a mental pencil poised to record his thoughts, nothing worth jotting down came through. In the end I had nothing to report. I would not say that he was being deliberately duplicitous or evasive or insincere; his mind simply did not move from cause to effect, or progress from *a* to *b* to *c* as most Westerners' would. Perhaps the Indian mind, particularly after centuries of coping with conquerors, had adopted a more cautious and circuitous line of reasoning than prevails in the West. In any event, it was an unsatisfactory experience, and although I respected him as a national leader, I doubted that we would ever forge a firm relationship with India while Nehru was the Prime Minister.

Loy Henderson, who sat in on the meeting, wrote in his report that, though friendly, Nehru "was, as usual, rather reserved and evaded in his rather lengthy replies any discussion of the rather concrete matters touched on by Mr. McGhee." I would never know the reason for Nehru's behavior. Was he preoccupied by grave problems, or did the reason simply have to do with the age-old mismatch of the Eastern and Western minds?

Without question, Nehru was devoted to his country and the Indian people, but he approached the masses aloofly as one would expect of a member of the ruling class. During his first U.S. visit, for example, I was with him outside of official U.S. circles on a number of occasions and saw him treat members of his staff so rudely, even brutally, over some real or imaginary dereliction of duties, that I was embarrassed for both him and them.

U NU

After a visit to Calcutta we flew east to Rangoon, Burma, and on the morning of December 23, I met with U Nu, who had been Prime Minister of the Texas-sized country since it had gained independence from Britain on January 4, 1948. U Nu was a sincere adherent of his Buddhist religion and had recently announced that he was temporarily forsaking his wife, much as a Christian might give up chocolate for Lent. He had also moved out of his official residence during his period of deprivation, although he was able to return home for our meeting.

I first asked U Nu (everyone in Burma called him by that name, although his real name was Thakin Nu) whether he thought his country faced a serious crisis in the insurgency of the Karen tribal minority in the north. He voiced the belief that the worst of the crisis had passed. He was disappointed that the peace he had attempted to mediate had failed, but he would have nothing to do with the rebels until they laid down their arms. We discussed whether China might take advantage of the unrest and move against Burma, a point I always raised in my talks with Middle World leaders to emphasize the Communist threat.

We also discussed economic aid, and I expressed the hope that Burma would be interested in technical assistance under the Point Four Program proposed by President Truman. I stressed the importance of internal stability, since American companies weighed this factor heavily in making decisions about investments abroad. The Prime Minister was surprised that businesses would be guided to such a degree by the prospect of a return on their investment. He thought, naively, that containing the spread of communism was a greater motivator for them than profits. I replied that, while the U.S. government supported undertakings for political reasons such as defense against communism, private companies did not. I don't believe, however, that I succeeded in establishing much contact with U Nu. Smiling all the time, he was shy and noncommittal. All the same, I attempted to persuade him that we wanted to be friends with Burma, and that we had no desire to draw him into any bloc or tell him how to run Burma's economy, which, since independence, had been highly socialistic. Later, after I had left government, U Nu accepted my invitation in 1961 to represent the Buddhist religion in the Conference on Religion and Freedom organized by the Dallas Council on World Affairs during my presidency.

JAN CHRISTIAAN SMUTS AND DANIEL F. MALAN

In early March 1950, having presided over the East-West African Conference of U.S. Diplomatic and Consular Officers in Mozambique, I made an official visit to the Union of South Africa. The country was not in my jurisdiction, but I had been asked to hold talks with Prime Minister Daniel F. Malan, who had come to power on the basis of separate development of the races, or apartheid. It was virgin territory with all the attendant risks, since no one at the policy-making level of the State Department had ever visited the Union of South Africa and there had been no U.S. Ambassador in Cape Town since North Winship resigned the previous November.

En route from Mozambique by auto, I was given a tour of Kruger National Park, a wildlife sanctuary in the Transvaal, and I literally held my breath as lions walked up to our car and herds of elephants meandered in the distance. We saw giraffes, jackals, leopards, monkeys, baboons, antelopes, and many more—it was an extraordinary visit. And when we reached Johannesburg, where I was the Mayor's guest of honor, I was reminded of Chicago by the skyscrapers and industrial plants that stood as symbols of business dynamism. When I went to Soweto, however, and glimpsed a few of the half million underclass blacks in their dingy wooden shacks, I was apprehensive about South Africa's future.

In the 1948 election, Malan's National party won only 45 percent of the vote, but by forming a coalition with the small Afrikaner party, it was able to defeat the United party of renowned soldier-statesman Jan Christiaan Smuts. Since becoming Prime Minister, Malan had faced repeated incidents of racial unrest, climaxed by rioting in Johannesburg three weeks before I arrived.

I quickly learned that native rights was the single most important issue in the country. All political parties were essentially in agreement on the principle of an inferior class of blacks, although they argued over details and definitions. The whites basically despised the blacks, although most knew them only as servants, and they feared for their own survival. They resisted criticism—that from within was based on hopeless idealism, they felt, and that from abroad was resented as outside interference. Advice from the United States, they believed, was rooted in ignorance, for in our country blacks had not turned to communism and posed no serious threat to white supremacy. In general, however, South Africans had a high regard for Americans, which was reciprocated, though we could not agree on race relationships.

Upon my arrival, it was suggested that I might like to meet with General Jan Christiaan Smuts. Aware that the 80-year-old Afrikaner was the most famous of all South Africans, I gladly accepted. Because he was the opposition leader, it was left to our Chargé d'Affaires to make the arrangements. Smuts, world-renowned South African general and political leader, was born in 1870 near Riebeeck West in Cape Colony. Although also eminent as soldier, philosopher, and botanist, the Oubaas (old master), as he was called, was regarded in his own country primarily as a politician. He was admitted to the Cape Town bar in 1895 and became a political ally of Cecil Rhodes. After the ill-fated raid to seize tribal territory led by Dr. L. S. Jameson, however, Smuts moved to Johannesburg and transferred his loyalties to the Transvaal. During the Boer War he led the Afrikaners in the Cape.

Smuts co-founded Het Volk (The People) party and emerged as the leading Afrikaner exponent of reconciliation between Boer and Briton in South Africa. World War I projected him onto the world stage as a military commander in East Africa and as a member of the Imperial War Cabinet in London. Smuts represented South Africa at the Versailles Conference and contributed significantly to the creation of the British Commonwealth and the League of Nations. He became Prime Minister for the first time in 1919, brought South Africa into World War II during a second tenure in office, and returned to London to serve in Churchill's war cabinet. At the time of my visit, his party had just been defeated at the polls by Malan's Nationalists, largely on the apartheid issue. He was opposition leader at the time of his death in May 1950, only two months after I saw him.

We met after dinner on my first evening in Cape Town, and I found it easy to like this friendly and open man. Avoiding internal Union political issues, he opined that the world situation was more serious now than at any other time in his career. In the contest between the West and communism, we were facing one of the real crises of history, he declared. He felt that the only hope for the world lay in the West, where the burden of world responsibility had rested for hundreds of years. Close cooperation among the Western powers was essential to survival, Smuts insisted. When I asked for his assessment of the United Nations, he replied that it had been rendered ineffective by the Soviet Union.

Smuts predicted that as a result of Indian neutrality and the loss of China to communism, the Western democracies would have to look to Africa for natural resources for their struggle with the Soviets. Africa had untold mineral wealth—ferro-alloys, coal, and uranium. He said the United States could have an important part in developing Africa, through both private investment and the new U.S. development aid Point Four Program. With regard to seeking Soviet economic cooperation, he seemed to be looking 40 years down the road: only when there was some fundamental change, such as the breakup of the USSR's unwieldy political structure, would a new Union of South Africa approach to the USSR be possible.

In Smuts' opinion, the forces at work in the Far East were beyond the control of the Western powers. He was pessimistic about the Marshall Mission to China and considered it probable that Southeast Asia would fall to communism. Even so, Communist domination of Asia would ultimately fail for economic reasons, and a period of chaos would ensue. Of special concern was India, whose leaders, Smuts felt, were out of touch with the people. I felt very fortunate to have met Smuts and was impressed with the clarity and sagacity of his analysis. I was greatly saddened by his death.

My first meeting with Prime Minister Malan was over luncheon at Groote Schuur, the home Rhodes had left to South Africa for its Prime Minister's official residence. I enjoyed the surroundings, but my impression of Malan was less than favorable. A large, impassive man of 76, he seemed to epitomize the dogmatic Boer attitude held by their ancestors in Friesland in the Netherlands. Although he was educated in theology and had served as a minister in the Dutch Reformed Church, he was deemed more politician than thinker, a man practiced in manipulation. In our conversations, he tried to appear concerned about the human aspects of political issues, but to me at least, he was not convincing. He seemed to regard apartheid as a desirable end in itself, rather than reluctantly, for lack of an alternative.

Because my main interests related to security, I tried to draw Malan out on the Communist menace and on the position the Union of South Africa would take in the event of East-West hostilities. The natives were susceptible to propaganda, he said, but his government would do all it could to prevent the growth of communism. Europeans in his country were outnumbered four to one, which made segregation an absolute necessity. The government was attempting to separate whites and nonwhites into separate residential areas, so that the natives would be able to live in accordance with tribal customs. When he advocated white supremacy, Malan assured me, it was his policy to treat natives with justice.

I fully realized Malan had used my questions about communism to make a case for apartheid, but I was left with misgivings. I doubted his flexibility in dealing with the problem of racial equality and the moral issues involved. In response to my question about Union reaction to possible hostilities between the United States and the Soviets, Malan said his government would assist by supplying ships, but whether he would send troops abroad would depend on internal order and other circumstances.

In discussions with Sir Evelyn Baring, the British High Commissioner to South Africa, I found that we were in agreement. The Smuts government had made an earnest effort to find a solution to the "non-European problem," said Sir Evelyn. They had appointed a commission that produced a report in 1948 rejecting total separation of the races. They had, however, been defeated by the Nationalists with their policy of apartheid. While not pretending to offer a solution, Sir Evelyn did not believe the present government was going about it in the right way.

HAILE SELASSIE

My next stop was Addis Ababa, the capital of Ethiopia, where I was immediately taken on a tour of the sights by Ambassador George R. Merrill. He had packed a supper of martinis and hors d'oeuvres, and we drove to a plateau high above the city to watch a magnificent sunset. We could see the Imperial Palace, the Coptic Christian churches, and other symbols of the world's oldest empire. I was there to meet with Emperor Haile Selassie.

Following nearly two decades of internal power struggles after the death of the ruler Menelik II in 1913, Haile Selassie (until then known as Ras, or nobleman, Tafari) was crowned as the sole Emperor of Ethiopia in 1930. His full title was Haile Selassie I, Conquering Lion of the Tribe of Judah, Elect of God, and King of Kings of Ethiopia. Five years later Mussolini attacked the country and seized Addis Ababa the next year. Haile Selassie and his family were forced to spend a few years in England, but when British and Ethiopian troops drove out the Italians in 1941, he returned to the throne, initiating a series of reforms, including the abolition of slavery. At the time of my visit, the country was relatively stable, except for Eritrea. Reports had been circulated, however, particularly from French sources, that Addis Ababa was being built up as the headquarters for communist propaganda and other subversive activity in Africa.

The invitation to dinner that evening read, "By Command of His Imperial Majesty Haile Selassie I." As I entered the palace, I walked through a hallway lined with cages of lions, their eyes flashing from the light of torches in the palace yard. The Emperor was a small man but striking in appearance. He had a long, aquiline nose, a black beard, and close-cropped black hair. Standing beside him was the Empress, who was taller than he and equally impressive, with black hair and a full face. She wore a light white fur jacket over a black satin dress, and a Coptic cross hung from her neck. After champagne, we sat down to dinner, where I was placed between the Empress and the eldest son, the Duke of Harrar (who would one day be banished after his alleged involvement in a plot to overthrow his father). The conversation was in English. After dinner, I was invited to sit with the Emperor for a get-acquainted chat. I said I would be interested in listening to his hopes for his country, and he said he had something he particularly wanted to take up with me.

The following morning, I handed Haile Selassie a letter of greeting from President Truman, and our official talks began. The topic he wished to discuss was Eritrea, originally an Ethiopian possession but an Italian colony from 1890 until British troops drove the Italians out of Africa in 1941. In November 1949, the United Nations General Assembly had approved a resolution placing former Italian Somaliland under a trusteeship administered by Italy. The United Nations had also established a commission to examine the future of Eritrea. Ethiopia opposed Italian reentry into East Africa but appeared willing to acquiesce if it could gain control of Eritrea. Ethiopia had the backing of the United States, but at the time of my visit no final decision had been reached at the United Nations.

Haile Selassie outlined to me the findings of the U.N. commission since it had started to study the problem in 1947. Supporters of federation with Ethiopia were in a clear majority in Eritrea, he said. Opponents of the so-called Democratic Front now realized that the Italian government had duped them. Muslims had withdrawn from the Front and formed the Muslim League. Christian Liberal Progressives had also left the Front. The reasons for these defections, said Haile Selassie, were bribery and acts of violence by the Italians. The Emperor mentioned three factors that had contributed to unrest in Eritrea: trade union activities, Italian efforts in behalf of independence, and the Italian presence in Somaliland. If the United Nations did not soon recognize the realities in Eritrea, there would be a general uprising. I realized, of course, that this assessment did not come from a disinterested party.

Haile Selassie also raised the question of loans to his country. Since the war, the United States had become the largest importer of goods, I said, but Ethiopia needed to expand its means of production and transportation facilities. We were in a position to offer aid in the form of technical expertise and capital, provided American companies were welcome. (I was aware that Sinclair was drilling for oil in Ethiopia.) Haile Selassie said he hoped for an economic boom, with assistance from the Export-Import Bank and the Point Four Program. (In December 1950, the U.N. General Assembly adopted a federation plan, granting self-government for Eritrea under the Ethiopian crown. Foreign Minister Ate Aklilou Habte-Wold, whom I had met in Addis Ababa, came to Washington to thank our government for its help in settling the dispute. I gave an official luncheon for him.)

IBN SAUD

I arrived in Saudi Arabia on the afternoon of March 18, planning to spend a week traversing the country from the Red Sea to the Persian Gulf, stopping in the main city, Jidda, the capital Riyadh, and Dhahran, site of both the U.S. Air Force Command and the Arab-American Oil Company (ARAMCO). The country—with its desert, the Bedouins, the centers of Islam at Mecca and Medina, and recently the discovery of vast oil reserves—had always intrigued me. It was my first visit, and it promised to be a fascinating one.

Saudi Arabia's oil reserves were recognized as potentially the greatest of any country in the world. The first major field was discovered in 1938, but during World War II, development was limited to exploration. (Oil was not in short supply during the war, but the steel needed for drilling equipment was scarce.) In 1942 Secretary of the Interior Harold L. Ickes sent a technical mission to evaluate the Saudi Arabian oil potential, headed by distinguished geologist Everette L. DeGolyer, my father-in-law. DeGolyer reported proven reserves of 4 billion barrels, and possibly much more. Against present Saudi reserves with more yet to be discovered, the figure seems small, but in 1945 it was enormous.

As a geologist, I was well aware of the U.S. interest in Saudi oil and would later help resolve problems that arose, particularly with regard to the payment of royalties. The decision by ARAMCO to offer a 50–50 profit-sharing plan to the Saudi government, which would result in 22 years of uninterrupted production, was reached by the parent companies of ARAMCO in my office at the State Department in November 1950.

The House of Saud, including the family of the young Abd al-Aziz, was exiled from Saudi Arabia in the early nineteenth century and took refuge with their Bedouin followers, living later in Qatar and Bahrain. Abd al-Aziz, known as Ibn Saud, returned to join his family's struggle to regain their power and, in 1902, captured Riyadh from a rival amir. (At dinner he told me about his great victory in great detail.) By the eve of World War I, Ibn Saud could claim the allegiance of most of the Arab tribes in northern Arabia. During the war, the British courted both the Sauds and the Hashemites, who had ruled Mecca since the eleventh century, to enlist their support against the Turks. The Hashemite leader, Sharif Hussein, proclaimed Arab independence in 1916, drove the Turks from the Hejaz, and significantly aided British military operations in Palestine.

In launching the Arab revolt against the Ottoman Empire, Hussein had also presumptuously declared himself "King of the Arabs," but the tribes in the region even rejected his title to the Hejaz. When Hussein attempted to assume the mantle of Caliph, formerly worn by the Ottoman sultans, Ibn Saud retaliated in force in 1924. In 1926, he seized Mecca and was proclaimed King of the Hejaz and Sultan of the Nejd and Dependencies, thus uniting into a single state that formed the major part of the Arabian peninsula. In doing so, he won both the allegiance of the Arab tribes and British recognition. In 1932, he announced the creation of the United Kingdom of Saudi Arabia, making his capital at Riyadh in the Nejd the Saudi heartland.

Washington responded to Saudi fears of the Hashemites in 1949 by dispatching a military mission headed by General Richard J. O'Keefe to study security requirements. O'Keefe's report was submitted to the Joint Chiefs of Staff in January 1950, but while a copy was en route to the State Department, it had been decided not to send one to the Saudis because "it would only give us headaches." One objective of my visit was to allay Saudi suspicions of our sincerity and to reach agreement on how we might meet their military needs.

I met with Prince Faisal on the second day of my visit. (Faisal, the second son of Ibn Saud and Foreign Minister, would ascend to the throne in place of his brother, Saud, in 1964, and rule until his assassination in 1975.) I told Faisal that the United States felt the only important security threat facing the world lay in the Soviet Union's aggressive designs. Even though it was against our traditions, in order to preserve the independence of nations threatened by the Soviets, we had given large-scale military assistance, first to Greece and Turkey and now to Western Europe under the North Atlantic Treaty. I said that fortunately Saudi Arabia was not menaced by the Soviets and had no internal Communist problem.

We also understood that Saudi Arabia was apprehensive about Jordan and Iraq. I had discussed this question with the British Foreign Office and with all of our Middle East Ambassadors at the Istanbul Conference the previous November, after which we concluded that Saudi Arabia was not threatened by its neighbors, which I thought should be reassuring. There appeared to be little reason to expect a joint action by Jordan and Iraq against Saudi Arabia, and the British had assured us that they would restrain any such aggression if it did occur.

Faisal replied that everyone with sincere feelings toward Saudi Arabia had been pleased to see the U.S.-Saudi friendship strengthened. He was eager to witness the further cementing of this friendship. Even though differences in points of view might arise, he hoped they would not have an adverse effect on our relationship. He was acquainted with the report submitted by General O'Keefe's survey mission, which he considered a bare minimum. "We need more," said Faisal, "but not less than that."

Turning to the Arab refugee problem, Faisal observed that if the refugees took residence in other countries, there would be no one to return to Palestine. In the U.N. resolutions on the partition of Palestine, he said, the

Arab nations had been forced to accept U.N. terms. But Israel had flouted U.N. Resolution 75 by not permitting the refugees to return. We deeply regretted Israel's action, I said, and our notes to Israel urging compliance were known to his government. We had come to the inevitable Arab-Israeli problem, one the Saudis, the "most Arab of the Arabs," felt most keenly. Fortunately, they did not allow it to hinder U.S.-Saudi relations.

Accompanied by Ambassador J. Rives Childs, I flew to the U.S. air base in Dhahran, where we were met by General O'Keefe, three ARAMCO representatives, and a lone Saudi official. We lunched at the ARAMCO Executive House, and it was good to be back among oil men, many of whom were old friends. We toured Dhahran, inspected an oil refinery and an export terminal there, and flew by Air Force plane to Riyadh. During the trip, Childs confronted me with a delicate problem: he asked me if I would mind wearing Arab dress while in Riyadh. My initial reaction was negative, but Childs argued convincingly that doing so would make it easier for the King to have me, a nonbeliever, as his guest in a holy city. When he added that Ibn Saud also wished to present me with fine winter and summer robes and a headdress he had already ordered for me, I agreed.

I was granted five audiences with the King. Usually, the precise time of a meeting was not revealed until the moment arrived, and meeting times were changed abruptly—all of which, I gathered, was for the purpose of security. I got the impression they were playing a cat and mouse game: lesser officials would sound me out on what I intended to ask, and would then return with additional questions from the King. But Childs assured me this was typical treatment of an emissary in an oriental court.

When I was received by the King, he extended warm greetings and recalled his meeting with President Roosevelt in 1945. I was not prepared for his overpowering appearance—he was a big man with a large face and nose, a jet-black mustache and beard, and he kept his eyes half closed, as if to shade them from the sun. He smiled easily and had a friendly manner.

In the afternoon, I presented a letter from President Truman, which an aide translated for the King. I then repeated what I had told Prince Faisal about our proposed response to Saudi security needs. If the integrity of Saudi Arabia were threatened, I declared, we would act immediately. But in light of unpredictable complexities, it was not possible to state precisely what that action might be. His Majesty expounded at length on his concerns with respect to his neighbors to the north. The two Hashemite rulers had been imposed on their respective countries, he said, and had never been accepted wholeheartedly by the people. Their military power was entirely derived from British support, whereas Saudi Arabia had no such outside support.

He himself had been well aware—based on information obtained by the Turks from the Germans prior to World War I—that Saudi Arabia was potentially one of the richest oil countries in the world. Even though the British had been given first refusal, they had always resented that the oil concession had been awarded to the United States, an action that had become the basis for subsequent Saudi difficulties with the British. The King made it clear that he was telling me all this to impress on me the importance of U.S. support for Saudi security. That evening, the King entertained me at a state dinner, which included 50 of his sons. Except for the dishes given to the King, we were served Western style. I had been looking forward to Arabic food, and since I was sitting to the King's right, I asked if I might share his meal. He readily assented.

I met with the King again on March 23 and went down a checklist of items we had discussed: a treaty of friendship, commerce and navigation, technicians under Point Four, Ex-Im Bank loans, the Dhahran airfield agreement, and military aid pursuant to the O'Keefe report. I assured the King that he would be advised before congressional action on the report was sought. He agreed with my proposals and also said that when it was time to work out the final details of military assistance, someone from Washington—perhaps I would be the one—would come and review the plan with him. In my last talk with Ibn Saud, I expressed pleasure with the outcome of our meetings and with his firm statements of friendship for my country. He reciprocated his satisfaction, reiterating his rejection of communism because of its aggressiveness and its animus against religion, which was the basic element of Arab life.

MOHAMMED V

On a stop in Rabat, Morocco, in late September 1950, I met with Sultan Mohammed V and the chief official of the French protectorate government, General Alphonse Juin. I felt the French were in a tenuous position, ruling Morocco as a virtual colony when the colonial era was fast drawing to a close. Little did I know that I would have a hand in ending French rule. Morocco had supported the Allied cause, and at the end of the war a freedom movement was spearheaded by the Istiglal (Independence) party. In early 1947, violence broke out in Casablanca and French police opened fire on nationalists, killing several hundred. When the Sultan spoke out for self-government, the French responded by naming the hard-line General Juin the new Resident-General. An impasse developed with Juin refusing to accede to any demands for reform, and Mohammed V declining to sign decrees presented to him by Juin.

This was the country of the legendary Abd el Krim, who in the early 1920s conducted one of the most remarkable anticolonial campaigns in modern history. Leading a force of Berber tribesmen, Krim, an educated man who had held colonial posts before joining the rebels, founded a Riff Republic in 1923. It took the combined forces of 400,000 French and Spanish troops finally to force him into exile and put down the rebellion in 1926. His story served as an inspiration to the generation of Moroccan nationalists who finally liberated Morocco in 1956. Years later, while attending an Arab League meeting in Cairo in 1948, this story came to life for me when I sat next to Krim at a dinner in my honor. A short, stout man with a ruddy complexion and little trace of age, he recollected for me the five years he ruled the Riff as sovereign (and outlaw). He had escaped on a merchant ship headed for the Suez Canal, from which he jumped off and swam ashore to begin an asylum in Cairo.

When I arrived in Rabat on September 29, 1950, I was accompanied by Edwin Plitt, the Consul General in Tangier, and in the villa of John Madonne, Consul General in Casablanca, we discussed our objectives in Morocco. We considered Morocco important because of its historic ties to us and its strategic location on the Atlantic and the Strait of Gibraltar, and because of its phosphate, manganese, and other mineral resources. Recognizing that tension between the French and Moroccans might lead to serious unrest, U.S. policy was to encourage the French to proceed with social, political, and economic reforms, while helping Moroccans move gradually toward self-government. Fortunately, the Communists had not yet succeeded in establishing any real influence.

With these guidelines I paid a call on Juin the day after my arrival. He had invited me as well as three Embassy and consular officials to lunch at his residence. Born in Algeria, son of a French gendarme and a Corsican mother, Juin was a career officer and a graduate of St. Cyr, where he was a classmate of Charles de Gaulle and stood at the head of his class. As commander-in-chief of Vichy French forces in North Africa, he had deserted the pro-German Marshall Petain, joined the Allies, and proven himself a brilliant commander. A tough, hard soldier, he was later suspected of planning a coup in France which would have made him dictator of Morocco. He had been sent to Morocco to restore order after the Moroccan uprising against French control called the "Casablanca Affair."

Juin was terse and to the point, exuding confidence. When I asked him about progress in developing the Moroccan economy and furthering education, he displayed no knowledge or interest and rather abruptly ordered an aide to bring statistics on new schoolrooms. I assured him that we had no desire to encroach on French responsibilities, but it had been agreed that France's duty was to lead the Moroccan people to eventual independence. It was not a pleasant meeting, for Juin was not accustomed to visitors who questioned French policy.

In preparing for my meeting with the Sultan, I had reviewed Moroccan history, learning that Islam had been brought to the Berbers of the Maghreb, as North Africa is called, by Ugba Ibn Nafi in 683, only 51 years after the death of the Prophet Mohammed. Berbers and Arabs have lived together under six dynasties, the last being the Alawites, who assumed power in 1666. Mohammed V, or Sidi Mohammed Ben Youssef (meaning the son of Sultan Youssef), was the fifteenth of the Alawites Dynasty. Although he was the youngest son of the pro-French Sultan Mulai Youssef Ben Hassan, he had been chosen to succeed to the throne at the tender age of 16 by the ulama, the religious scholars, on the death of his father in 1927.

Juin, who was in effect Foreign Minister to the Sultan, normally did not permit him to receive foreign visitors. My audience was a concession, made more difficult by the French suspicion of U.S. motives in Morocco which had been aroused by President Franklin D. Roosevelt's private meeting with the Sultan during the Casablanca Conference of January 1943. The Sultan had already made clear his pro-Americanism after the American landings in Casablanca in November 1942. Urged to take flight, he replied, "The Americans are my friends. I will meet them here." At Casablanca Roosevelt, who had presented the Sultan a high-powered automobile, had made clear America's keen interest in the future of Morocco, and had given the Sultan the impression that we would support Moroccan independence. Roosevelt followed this with two letters along the same lines before his untimely death in April 1945.

I was quite taken by Mohammed V, who would be remembered as the father of modern Morocco. Dressed in a long white robe and white hood, he had a handsome, gentle face, and the careful way he chose his words conveyed an intense sincerity. There was an aura of dignity about him, but not a trace of condescension in his manner. Indeed, I was struck by a trace of humility. Although I had no specific instructions from my government, I knew that I was to make clear our continuing interest in Morocco and let the Sultan know he could depend on our support. But since I wanted to avoid a conflict with the French, whose representative was present, there was little of a specific nature that I or the Sultan could say. I attempted to get my message across by showing empathy and acting in a friendly way. For his part, the Sultan sought to make me aware of the importance he attached to American interest in his country and what it could mean for the future.

We discussed the Communist threat, not only to Morocco but to the world in general. I said that we considered Islam a significant barrier to the spread of communism. The Sultan agreed, pointing out that the tenets of Islam were fundamentally at odds with Communist philosophy. I complimented the Sultan on the economic progress that Morocco had made since my last visit to his country 15 years before and observed that we stood ready to assist him in any way we could. Mindful of the French official, the Sultan replied only that we had been informed of Morocco's needs.

Little did I know that my visit to Rabat would have an effect on the future of Morocco. Eleven days after our meeting, the Sultan traveled to Paris at the invitation of French President Vincent Auriol. The *New York Times* reported on October 12 that he was seeking more power for himself and his cabinet, despite the objections of General Juin. The *Times* also re-

ported that divergences characterized French relations with the Sultan and
with diplomatic representatives of the United States as well. These had resulted from the "frequent contention that the best way to block the expansion of Communism in North Africa is to encourage Arab nationalism, a
view that the French attribute to George C. McGhee, Assistant Secretary of
State, who visited Morocco late in September, and Edwin A. Plitt, U.S.
Minister in Tangier."

A few months later, Juin accompanied the French Premier on an official
visit to Washington. Just before departing, he had demanded that the Sultan
either denounce the Istiqlal party or abdicate, giving him until his return
from Washington to decide. This ultimatum shocked the entire Arab world,
and I obtained approval from Secretary Acheson and President Truman to
meet with Juin and inform him of our position of support for Mohammed
V.

Other State Department and French officials were present when Juin met
with me in Washington on March 31, 1951. I told him that the United
States opposed any French move to remove the Sultan from power. I added
that Juin's demands that the Sultan denounce the Istiqlal party had put the
Sultan in an untenable position. Moreover, in view of the Sultan's popular-
ity, his removal would result in a severe setback for French relations with
Morocco and French efforts to prepare Morocco for independence. Although reluctant to do so because of our close ties with France, we would,
if Juin persisted, be forced to denounce the threatened action publicly and
declare our support for the Sultan. To make our position very clear, we
advised our Embassy in Paris, for their discussions with the French Foreign
Office, as follows:

France does not have unqualified U.S. support in their confrontation with the Sultan,
and we will say this publicly if our position is misrepresented. We are concerned over
the effect on the stability of Morocco of the French threat to remove the Sultan. If
the French take such action, the U.S. will publicly oppose it. If the question is raised
in the U.N., we will not support France. We are not advocating immediate independence for Morocco, only an evolution of the present situation.

Juin was still in Washington when he received a report of our Embassy's
followup demarche with comment by the Quai d'Orsay. He was furious,
but by the time he returned to Rabat, he was reportedly somewhat chas-
tened. There was no more talk of forcing the Sultan to abdicate, at least for
the time being. In 1953, Juin was replaced by General Augustin Guillaume,
who made a renewed effort to depose Mohammed V. When he again refused
to abdicate, Guillaume ordered his security chief to escort the Sultan at
gunpoint to exile, first in Corsica and then in Madagascar.

After angry Moroccans had rallied to the nationalist cause, Mohammed
V returned in triumph in 1955, and independence was declared on March

2, 1956. When I met the first Moroccan Ambassador to the United States, I told him about my intercession with Juin. He smiled wryly and said that by preventing the Sultan's exile, "you merely delayed our independence by two years."

JAWAHARLAL NEHRU: MY SECOND VISIT

Cecilia accompanied me on yet another trip to India in March 1951. On the evening of our arrival, I consulted with Ambassador Loy Henderson. The background of my meeting with Prime Minister Nehru was dominated by the Korean War, in which the United States had suffered severe casualties, and an Indian request for food grains that was pending before Congress. Henderson had explored Nehru's attitude toward the Soviet Union and Communist China's entry into the Korean War. When Henderson expressed U.S. regret at Stalin's recent attack on the United Nations and the Soviets' continued efforts to overthrow non-Communist governments, Nehru replied in his usual equivocal way. He cautioned against accepting available evidence of aggressive intent by the Soviets, urging instead an analysis of the situation in its entirety, to avoid a world war. India's efforts, Nehru had said to Henderson, were directed toward this end, as evidenced by India's position on China. Nehru did not believe China had an aggressive intent in Asia beyond retaking Formosa (present day Taiwan) and Tibet.

When I met with Nehru on March 8, I began by explaining Secretary Acheson's desire to emphasize that whatever differences might exist between India and the United States regarding Communist China, they should not affect our basic understanding or impede progress on matters of common interest. I asked the Prime Minister how he assessed the present intentions of the Soviet Union and Communist China, making it clear that it was their aggressive intent, more than their ideology, that gave us concern. Nehru then embarked on a long and boring historical discussion in which he sought to prove that wars, rather than achieving their objectives, merely led to new wars. He noted the undesirability of war in terms of the social and economic chaos it creates, and he argued that even if the Soviets were defeated, the world would be left as easy prey for communism. Russia was what it was, he said, largely because it had been isolated when a young nation. He maintained that the same mistake was being made with respect to China.

I replied that we were as thoroughly convinced as anyone about the undesirability of war, but we would rather face a war than fall under Soviet domination. Although the world might still face a Communist threat after a destructive war, domination would appear a certainty if we were not prepared to stop the Soviets in their objective of world conquest. I pointed out Americans' great disappointment over India's present policies, which appeared to run counter, even to undermine, our efforts and those of other nations to develop effective collective security against aggression.

It was a great disappointment to us, I continued, that India had voted against the U.N. Security Council resolution condemning China's aggression, and appeared to be actively seeking to influence other states toward neutralism. This constituted a great danger. It distracted from the strength of the Free World, which could only come from unity. It also provided encouragement to the aggressor states by raising doubts as to whether the neutral states would be willing or able to defend themselves. Nehru agreed that the Russians had aggressive designs, but he did not believe that China now had such intentions. It would take China a long time, perhaps a decade or so, to consolidate its newly won independence. Nor did Nehru agree that China's actions in Korea and Indochina were a clear indication of aggression. He also refused to accept our view that China posed a threat to Burma, even though I told him of evidence we had to this effect.

Pressing my basic point, I asked Nehru how any responsible government could fail to take steps to protect its people against a threat that had at least some degree of probability. He did not yield, refusing to respond to a suggestion that there was any such threat to India. I expressed admiration for the strong leadership qualities he had displayed, and I said his greatest possible contribution to world peace—and perhaps the only way to assure there would not be another war—would be for him to lead the wavering states in supporting the principle of collective security against aggression.

Nehru then proposed that the United States and India seek more complete consultation on matters of common interest. He agreed that it was better to discuss issues between ourselves privately rather than publicly or in the press. It was, of course, presumptuous of me to press the acknowledged leader of world neutralism to abandon a fundamental premise of his political philosophy. For him, neutralism was deeply rooted in India's long struggle for independence. (India would soon prove unable to defend itself: on October 20, 1962, a large-scale Chinese invasion was virtually unopposed. On October 29 Nehru asked the United States for military aid.)

Nehru could not have been expected to yield at the time of my visit, illogical as his position seemed to those of us who were convinced that communism posed the greatest threat to all free nations. In my view, he was simply hiding his head in the sand. The idea that a state should not try to defend itself against an aggressor was to me incomprehensible. But then there was really very little Nehru could do. He had no choice, even assuming he did understand the threat, but to rely on us and others to build any defense against Soviet expansion. His stance obviously enabled him to hold sway over his people and in his mystical role as leader of the former colonial developing nations. In the end, he did not really respond to my appeal. Instead, he tactfully ignored it and reverted to the message I had brought from Acheson: We would not permit our conflicting views of communism to affect our basic understanding. In brief, I made no more progress with Nehru now than I had during my first visit.

KING MOHAMMED ZAHIR SHAH

On March 10 we arrived in Kabul, where I hoped to make some headway in resolving the Afghan-Pakistan dispute over Pushtunistan. There were global issues to be concerned about, since Afghanistan shared a long border with the Soviet Union, but our main interest at that time was in resolving the Pushtunistan issue. Afghanistan had maintained an attitude of cautious correctness toward the USSR combined with firm resistance to Soviet penetration. But Afghan activity in the Pathan tribal area on the Pakistan border, which had led to occasional fighting, offered the Soviets an opportunity to intervene. Aware of the danger of setting a precedent that the USSR could take advantage of, we had advised the Afghans not to ask for U.S. military aid.

In November 1950, we had expressed concern over the Pushtunistan issue, which was impeding social and economic progress in the region and inviting Soviet intrigue. We offered to be a go-between, though not a mediator, in the hope of reaching agreement on a set of rules: Both governments would cease attacks on the other and would seek to prevent violence through mediation by private parties. They would try to eliminate inflammatory incidents and statements; exchange ambassadors within two months; and appoint representatives who would meet within three months for exploratory talks without preconditions or publicity. The Afghans had accepted our proposals, but the Pakistanis had not, so my hope was to use the results of my negotiations in Kabul to gain approval in Karachi.

In the absence of the Prime Minister, my meeting with King Mohammed Zahir Shah was the highlight of my visit, but it was also largely perfunctory. A tall, dignified, imposing figure, he received me in his brightly lighted, bejeweled throne room. We discussed the general relations of our respective countries, and I emphasized our willingness to strengthen our ties and to help settle the issues between his country and Pakistan. I said only the Soviets could benefit from the present discord.

The King made what I was finding to be a standard Afghan pitch for Pushtunistan, suggesting that I discuss the details with Foreign Minister Ali Mohammed Khan. He professed a desire to improve relations with Pakistan, but observed that this would depend on the Pakistani attitude toward the Pushtu people. Zahir Shah struck me as a cold man, difficult to approach, though he obviously was trying to be agreeable. He presented me with a photograph of himself in a splendid silver frame and sent my wife a fine Afghan rug.

My main discussions were with Ali Mohammed Khan, who was also the Acting Prime Minister, and he read a statement on the Pushtu issue. Afghanistan had always been interested in the tribal peoples and had sought a peaceful solution to their problems. When the partition of India took place, Afghanistan expected to be consulted about the tribal area but was not. Subsequently, a referendum was held in the Northwest Frontier Province, although the Afghans advised Pakistan that under no circumstances would they accept the outcome. Later, the Afghans agreed to send a special envoy to Karachi on condition that the tribal area would be discussed. It was not. Still later, when the exchange of ambassadors had been agreed on, the Afghans renewed an offer to the Pakistan Ambassador to discuss a negotiation of differences over the Pathan tribes, but no reply was ever received. The Foreign Minister said that Afghanistan had been pleased to accept our proposal of November 6, 1950, for the initiation of bilateral talks with Pakistan.

I replied that while I understood Afghanistan's interest in the Pathan tribes, this problem had to be considered in the light of Soviet Russia's expansionist policy. There was no question about Soviet intentions. The United States wished to help all countries protect themselves from communism, and we had already given evidence of a willingness to help Afghanistan. I assured the Foreign Minister that our objective in the Pushtunistan issue was simply to help solve the matter by bringing the two parties together.

I then made the following points. In our judgment, Pushtunistan was not economically or politically viable. An independent Pushtunistan would have no experienced leaders to handle its relations with neighbors. The internal political situation in Pakistan was such that Liaquat Ali Khan could not maintain his position were he to make considerable concessions on the tribal area. The timing of Afghan sponsorship of Pushtunistan was very important. We were trying now to prepare as rapidly as possible for a united effort in containing Soviet aggression. Keeping the Pushtunistan issue alive could harm Afghanistan by creating conditions that could lead to Soviet intervention. Without foreclosing action in the future, it would be better now for Afghanistan to seek a modus vivendi with Pakistan.

When I asked the Foreign Minister whether he thought any good would come from continuing to explore solutions to the Pushtu problem short of the sovereignty issue, he replied that he could not say but he hoped so. Finally, at my urging, he remarked that he saw no reason why I should not mention to Liaquat that Afghanistan was hopeful that good would come out of the meeting, even if agreement was not immediately reached on sovereignty.

LIAQUAT ALI KAHN: MY SECOND VISIT

Cecilia and I flew from Kabul to Karachi on a U.S. Air Force plane on March 14, arriving at Maripar Airfield, where we were met by Ambassador Avra Warren. We spent the night in a luxurious apartment in the Governor-General's residence, and the next morning I held a press conference. Asked about the touchy Kashmir question, I pledged U.S. support for the resolution before the Security Council, as modified by debate in the Council, looking toward early acceptance. On March 16, however, I was quoted in the *Civil and Military Gazette* as saying a catastrophe would result if the matter remained unsettled. We attended a dinner in our honor given by Prime Minister and Begum Liaquat Ali Khan. It was a happy reunion, and we reminisced about their visit to our country.

The next morning, accompanied by Ambassador Warren, I called on the Prime Minister with great hopes for a breakthrough on Pushtunistan. I was not disappointed. Liaquat stated that he would call off the propaganda campaign against Afghanistan if the Afghans would do likewise. He was also agreeable to naming an ambassador to Kabul and expected that an Afghan ambassador would be sent to Karachi. After their accreditation, he was prepared to receive any representations on differences between the two countries as part of the normal discussion on the ambassadorial level. In the event that problems arose that could not be settled in this manner, he was prepared to work out with the Afghan government the organization of a special joint conference that could take up outstanding tensions.

Encouraged, I immediately said that I understood that the Prime Minister had accepted in substance the points in the American offer of good offices, to which he agreed. It was also agreed that at the beginning of the week, Ambassador Warren would work out mutually satisfactory language with the Secretary-General of the Pakistani Foreign Office and inform Washington officially of the results of our conversation. Although I left Karachi hopeful that our proposals had been accepted, Pakistan would soon lay out new difficulties, leading to hard negotiations ahead.

When I returned to Washington in April, I met with Afghan Prime Minister Sardur Mohammed Kahn, who often came to the United States for medical reasons. He appeared to be in fine fettle, and he came to visit Cecilia and me at our farm in Virginia. A great fisherman, he welcomed an opportunity to fish in my lake; however, he caught only blue gills and none of the larger bass. He was mollified when I assured him that the more lively blue gills were considered the more sporting catch.

As we chatted after dinner, I pressed the Prime Minister to tell me whether the Pushtunistan issue was deeply felt by Afghans, including himself, or whether the regime had seized on it only to gain favor with the people. It was perhaps an improper question to ask a member of the royal family (Sardur Mohammed Khan was the King's uncle), but it received what appeared to be a sincere response. Tears came to Sardur's eyes as he recounted the plight of the Pathan tribesmen under Pakistani rule. Traditionally freedom-loving nomadic people, they had been forced into an impossible dependent situation, separated from their fellow tribesmen in Afghanistan and stripped of their liberty. I was moved by his reply.

Apparently because of Pakistan's inaction and despite Liaquat's personal assurances, the issue of Pushtunistan was not resolved. After a series of disappointments, our good-offices proposal was withdrawn on October 12, nearly a year from the time it was offered. The government of Afghanistan expressed regrets, and Pakistan's attention was diverted by the assassination of Liaquat on October 16. The opportunities presented during my visits to Kabul and Karachi were not to be realized. Such often happens with gratuitous offers made by sincere and disinterested friends to assist rivals of long standing find an answer to problems they cannot solve.

KING ABDULLAH IBN-HUSSEIN

I arrived in Amman, the capital of Jordan, on March 25, having come by desert bus, without roads, from Damascus, Syria. I had the feeling I was in a war zone, even though more than two years had passed since my first visit to Jordan in April 1949, soon after the cessation of hostilities over the formation of a Jewish state. As Special Assistant to the Secretary of State in charge of U.S. efforts to solve the Arab refugee problem, I had met with King Abdullah. Since then, however, no progress had been made in peace treaty negotiations with Israel or in the resettlement of Arab refugees.

A wartime atmosphere prevailed because Jordan was still adjusting to peace. The country was overrun by refugees, and its limited facilities were strained. On my first night, I met for dinner with the Prime Minister and other officials along with the British, French, and Turkish Ministers, and I was deluged with questions. Would the refugees be permitted to go back? Would hostilities be renewed? Would the United States help the Arabs bear the burden of supporting their refugees? I felt very much on the spot.

I was looking forward to my meeting with King Abdullah, set for the next morning, for he was a very interesting leader indeed. In 1949, following the Arab-Israeli War, he had annexed about half of what had been Palestine—the West Bank of the Jordan River and territory set aside for an Arab state. This created problems, such as the assimilation of a million Palestinians in an impoverished state that had gained independence from Britain only in 1946. Other Arabs were jealous of Abdullah, and they might have suspected that he was engaged in secret negotiations with Israel. At any rate, this suspicion was said to have supplied the motive for Abdullah's assassination on July 20, 1951.

The King received me in the throne room of his comfortable but unpretentious palace at 9 A.M. on the morning of March 26. He was a short, wiry man with a handsome face, smooth dark skin, and a mustache and goatee. He wore a light white wool shirt buttoned at the top and covered with an unbuttoned light wool jacket. His eyes shone. He talked quickly and with extravagant gestures. He offered me Turkish coffee, and during my hour with him, we talked about many things. He took a long view of the Palestinian problem and was willing to be patient. After all, the hostilities had resulted in a territorial windfall for him. He had never forgotten his family's loss of the Hejaz to Ibn Saud in 1924, which gave the Saudis control of the Arabian peninsula. Although he knew he could never recover it, he could still dream. "If I had your power I would not be able to restrain myself," he said to me with a roguish smile.

I sensed that Abdullah still feared a Saudi invasion, and I recalled that Ibn Saud had expressed a similar anxiety about him during my visit to Saudi Arabia in March 1950. It was in part to relieve tension between Abdullah and Ibn Saud that I had helped formulate the Tripartite Declaration of May 25, 1950. (Signed by Britain, France, and the United States, the Tripartite Declaration provided for the supply of arms for defensive purposes to Middle Eastern states that had been embargoed by the United Nations after the Arab-Israeli War.)

I expressed appreciation for the way Jordan had taken care of its Arab refugees. The King said he was convinced that large numbers of refugees, if not all, could be settled in Jordan if sufficient assistance was forthcoming and if changes were made in the U.N. administration of relief and settlement. I agreed that changes were required and that with the cooperation of Jordan and other Arab states, large numbers of refugees could be settled. I assured the King that we would continue assistance to countries receiving refugees, and we would make contributions to the relief and integration fund. I noted that Jordan could also seek economic aid under the Point Four Program.

The King then raised the question of the Middle East as a whole. The defenses of Greece, Turkey, and Iran required strengthening, he said, particularly Iran, since it was most exposed geographically to Soviet attack. He also said that indecision and political instability had prevented most Arab states from building effective defenses. I assured the King that the United States recognized the danger the Soviet Union posed to the Middle East, and I explained that we and our West European allies were engaged in large-scale mobilization to protect the area. If the Soviet attack could be delayed for at least 18 months, I said, the West would have overwhelming superiority in war material and manpower. I gave the King the precise number of aircraft, tanks, and guns we were producing, and he was surprised.

He noted, however, that disunity among the Arab states would prevent them from mounting strong defenses even if weapons were available. He stressed that the unity of the Arab world must be encouraged, suggesting that if Syria and Jordan could be united under the Hashemites, he could build up a strong Arab region that would contribute to stability and end the threat of a fifth column. In order to avoid any misunderstanding, I replied that we were not opposed to voluntary union of like-minded people and would not sanction a union imposed by force.

I told the King that we were pleased by his cooperation in resolving problems between Jordan and Israel. Should there be violations of borders in the Middle East, I said, we would meet our commitments made in the

Tripartite Declaration. The King said he had no fear of Israel, although he had found the Jews unwilling to make concessions. After his assassination four months after my visit, I sent a comment to the Secretary of State about the King of Jordan: "Of all the Arab leaders, Abdullah was most cooperative toward Israel."

After a press conference, I had a good meeting with the well-known Englishman Glubb Pasha, commander of the Arab region. He was quite different from what I had expected. He appeared quiet and reserved; although his cherubic face showed where his jaw had been shot away, he still maintained a soft, merry smile. Glubb was a romantic figure much like Lawrence of Arabia had been, and had identified himself completely with the nomadic Bedouins. He was reputed to be withdrawn, self-sufficient, emotional, of strong convictions, and devoted to the cause of Middle Eastern peace. He was not in such a political position that I could discuss major policy with him: my call was social and out of interest in the man. Nevertheless, he told me of his deep affection for the Bedouin soldiers and for Jordan, and hoped the time would come when we could help strengthen the Arab Legion which, since the Arab-Israeli War, had suffered shortages of equipment and loss of morale. I promised to do what I could to help him.

THE MIDDLE WORLD IN PERSPECTIVE

Looking back at what has happened to the Middle World since the early 1950s, in the light of U.S. hopes and policies at that time, I have tried to appraise the results of our efforts. U.S. objectives in 1949 were fairly clear-cut. We wanted to make friends with those new states, allay fears of our motives, and establish a basis for future political, cultural, and business ties with them. Through our diplomacy, we also sought to help the new states get a fair start in the world and begin to solve their difficult, inherited problems.

We wanted, in particular, to help the new Middle World states cope with their internal economic problems, making use of the limited tools we had available at the time to offer them. We wanted to convince the new states of the dangers of Soviet communism and help them develop internal security forces adequate to protect themselves from Communist subversion. We tried to persuade them that neutralism would weaken their defenses against communism, and to encourage them to accept a generally pro-Western and democratic point of view. Greece, Turkey, and Iran, border states already under Soviet attack, were the only countries we thought could develop forces strong enough to deter Communist aggression against the Middle World.

These were our aims. Were they realistic? Were our efforts to carry them out helpful? Was our overriding concern in 1949–1951 about the Communist threat to the Middle World in the aftermath of Korea justified in light of subsequent events? Did it lead us to push those states in the development of their security forces too fast and too far, harming their econo-mies, endangering their leadership, and eventually alienating them from us? Would they have been endangered by closer ties with the Soviets? Certainly India, which was never attracted to alignment with us, gained from the close relationship it developed with the Soviets. At times, certainly during the height of the détente efforts of the 1970s, some observers might have con-cluded that we had exaggerated the Soviet threat to the Middle World, that we had misinterpreted longer-range Soviet goals. Subsequent events in Af-ghanistan have, I believe, reconfirmed our original interpretation of Soviet intentions.

Of the 90 states of the Middle World, Afghanistan, which was occupied by the Soviet army in December 1979, is the only country that temporarily lost its freedom to the USSR. India suffered loss of territory to Communist China in 1962 and had to increase its military forces greatly to prevent further incursions. It was a pity that Nehru had not done this when I warned him to do so in 1951. A few other countries have come under varying degrees of Communist influence or control. Guerrilla activity to achieve independence from Portugal began in Angola in 1961 and in Mozambique in 1956. Both movements were assisted from the beginning by the Soviets and other Communist states. The United States, largely because Portugal was a member of NATO and because we hold our Azores base only at the pleasure of Portugal, did not become involved in Angola until 1974, through our unsuccessful support of the National Front party. The Soviet-backed Popular Movement in Angola and the Front for the Liberation of Mozambique received massive Soviet aid and established Marxist govern-ments after the two colonies achieved independence. In Angola, Soviet in-fluence was strengthened by 25,000 Cuban forces as well as East German and Soviet advisers and the remaining Portuguese Communists.

Among the other newly independent African countries, Guinea turned to the Soviet bloc, with a push from General de Gaulle, when it broke with France in 1958. Since that time, however, it has strengthened its contacts with the West. In Ethiopia, the military regime that had overthrown the monarchy in 1974 switched dramatically from dependence on the United States for arms to total reliance on the Soviets, when the Carter administra-tion halted deliveries in 1977. The Soviets lost their Somali clients and signed a cooperation accord with the strategically more significant Ethiopia, which accepted as many as 20,000 Cuban combat troops and a large number of Soviet military advisers. Ethiopia also absorbed large quantities of Soviet military equipment, to turn back the Somalis in the contested Ogaden area. As a result, Somalia has been negotiating an arms aid and base agreements with the United States. Both Somalia and Ethiopia accepted Soviet military aid because of their war with the other, just as Angola and Mozambique had in their wars for independence against Portugal.

After South Yemen achieved independence in 1967, the South Yemen

National Liberation Front, which had been aided by both the USSR and China, came under Communist influence. The war South Yemen provoked with North Yemen in 1979 was terminated, at least officially, by a unification agreement later in the year negotiated with an assist from the Arab states. North Yemen, which remained torn by civil war, also received significant Soviet military and economic assistance, but more aid from Saudi Arabia and the Western states.

Of the other Middle World states, many have at various times accepted assistance from the USSR and other Communist states, and have come temporarily more or less under Communist influence. Egypt, particularly after American withdrawal of support from the Aswan Dam project in 1956, accepted large-scale economic and military assistance from the Soviet Union (which had actually started in 1955), including some 20,000 Soviet military personnel as advisers to Egyptian forces. This relationship was terminated abruptly in 1972 by President Anwar Sadat. Soviet personnel were expelled, and Soviet influence has not returned. In 1972, Iraq signed an aid pact with the Soviets, who furnished arms on a large scale, as well as several thousand advisers. After the government's execution of 21 Iraqi Communists in 1978 and a shift of trade to the West, however, relations with the Soviets became strained. General Saddam Hussein, who came to power in Iraq in July 1979, turned to the Soviets for arms for his war against Iran, but there was no evidence of any overall shift back to the Soviet bloc.

Of all the Middle World states that have flirted with the Soviets, Syria has been the most consistent. The Ba'ath party came to power in 1957 on a wave of anti-Western sentiment. Syria received large quantities of arms from the Soviets in 1972 (perhaps before) following fighting between Syrian-supported Palestine guerrillas and Jordan, and again in 1973 when Syria joined Egypt in an attack on Israel. Further large-scale shipments of Soviet arms to Syria occurred in 1974 and 1978. Soviet military assistance to Syria, including Soviet-manned anti-aircraft missiles, was stepped up after the Israeli invasion of Lebanon in 1982.

The Middle World countries that came under Soviet influence started distancing themselves following the Soviet seizure of Afghanistan. India, although it still accepted Soviet arms and maintained close relations with the Soviets, nonetheless publicly opposed the Soviet occupation of Afghanistan. The Islamic states took a strong position in demanding Soviet withdrawal from Afghanistan.

Our warnings in 1949–1951 of the Soviet threat to the new Middle World states seemed at the time to have had little effect. In particular, our attempts to persuade Nehru and other South Asian leaders to reverse their trend toward neutralism fell on deaf ears. Both they and the new states of Africa as they emerged in the 1950s and 1960s became strong supporters of the nonaligned movement, which was the response of these nations both to the Soviets and the United States. Gamal Abdel Nasser of Egypt, then leader of the Arab nations, was a co-founder of the nonaligned movement, and Nehru, prime minister of the most influential South Asian country, was a strong nonaligned backer. This group at its peak reached two-thirds of the nations of the world, 94 in all, including almost all of the Middle World. The essence of nonaligned policy is to avoid association with either bloc and to work against political polarization and bloc rivalries.

The United States' early efforts in the Middle World states may at least have influenced them to carry out their nonaligned policy impartially. Many Middle World countries, despite their nonalignment, were willing to accept favors from the Soviet bloc, and some undoubtedly profited thereby. Egypt got its Aswan Dam from the Soviets and Tanzania its railway to Zambia from China. But in the process there emerged little basis for a lasting tie between the Soviets and the emerging nations of the Middle World. Angola, Mozambique, Ethiopia, South Yemen, and Syria would have accepted arms aid from the devil himself to use against their mortal enemies. Arms were not at the time available elsewhere. But neither these nor other Middle World countries developed any lasting affinity for the Russians as a people or communism as an ideology. The ideological base for communism, as devised by Karl Marx while he was in England studying the problem of how to help the workers of the industrialized countries seize power from the bourgeoisie, was not applicable to an agricultural and pastoral society that was struggling to emerge as a modern state. Marxism had no monopoly over socialism.

The United States was not wrong in 1949–1951 to warn the Middle World about the dangers of Soviet communism. Any doubts anyone may have on this point have been removed by recent events. Some of the states involved may have suffered because we pushed them too indiscriminately and too fast. I believe, however, that as a result, they were better able to protect themselves from the Communist dangers they later avoided. Viewed in perspective, the Russian Middle World "take"—4 or 5 relatively unimportant countries out of 66—was pretty thin, for in 1949–1951, we feared the whole Middle World might be lost.

6

The Role of Nuclear Weapons—
Navy Duty with LeMay's B-29s,
1944–1945

Nuclear weapons evolved from the work of outstanding theoretical and research nuclear physicists starting in 1911 by the discovery of the inner structure of the atom by Ernest Rutherford in Cambridge. Ernest Lawrence, in California, developed at this time the cyclotron for bombarding the nucleus of the atom and predicted the creation of atomic energy, which Einstein had predicted theoretically in 1905 and which was verified experimentally in 1932 by John Cockfield and E.T.S. Walton. James Chadwick of Cambridge discovered the neutron particle in 1932, followed by the discovery in 1933 in Paris of artificial radioactivity by Frederic Julio and his mother-in-law Irene Curie, which was later further elaborated by Enrico Fermi in Rome.

A major breakthrough was made in 1938 by Otto Hahn and Fritz Strassmann in Berlin which led to the discovery of nuclear fission. This became known through Niels Bohr, leader in his field as head of the Institute of Theoretical Physics in Copenhagen, who departed shortly afterward for America. Here Bohr, as well as Julio and Curie, exchanged nuclear findings with Enrico Fermi at Columbia. Although the creation of atomic energy was early recognized, there was no interest at that time in atomic weapons and new nuclear discoveries were published, rewarded by Nobel Prizes, and generally available to Americans working in the field including Arthur Holly Compton of Chicago.

At the outbreak of World War II in 1941, the young Werner Heisenberg, of "uncertainty principle" fame and an expert in the basic physics of uranium fission, was brought into the German army to work on uranium problems. At the same time, theoretical and experimental physicists were unhappily separated from each other in Germany. Robert Oppenheimer, himself an experimentalist, was later to bring the two factions together successfully as head of the U.S. Los Alamos project. Fortunately, Heisenberg and his superior Albert Speer did not press Hitler to make a major effort to attain nuclear weapons, knowing how easily he could go to extremes in a field where they had little hope for success. As it turned out, only the United States and the Soviet Union were to develop nuclear weapons that could virtually destroy whole nations.

The decision to develop the first atomic bomb was made in deepest secrecy by President Franklin Roosevelt on October 9, 1941, on the recommendation of Vannevar Bush, his chief of defense research. Since this was two months before Pearl Harbor, which brought war with Japan and open war with Germany, it was not necessarily planned with Japan in mind. Its immediate cause was based on information readily available of the consideration being given to nuclear weapons in Germany. Japan was, however, destined to be the only country to be attacked by nuclear weapons.

Even while we were still fighting Germany and Japan, the USSR became an increasingly uncooperative ally, and after the defeat of Germany in May 1945 and the surrender of Japan on August 14, 1945, it became our only enemy. Although the United States and the USSR never used nuclear weapons to attack each other, the growing confrontation between the two enemies became more dangerous. Their increasing nuclear arsenals threatened not just military defeat but also no achievable victory through the destruction of both countries.

The great cost of the Cold War was drastically increased when both countries began to build ever more effective nuclear forces, including the hydrogen bomb. The cost of ground forces could not be reduced because of the uncertainty that strategic nuclear weapons could ever be used; the cost of destruction would be more than either country could risk. However, the two protagonists, for purposes of deterrence alone, felt compelled to match increases in nuclear strength by the other, adding not only to the cost but also to the danger of accident or miscalculation on either side. In retrospect, as Ambassador Anatol Dobrynin later confirmed, neither side ever seriously considered making the "first strike," although both hinted and threatened that they would.

In the end, we must conclude that the massive, fairly equal nuclear weapons attained by both sides had the beneficial effect of preempting their use. We knew we took no nuclear risk when we dropped bombs on Hiroshima and Nagasaki in 1945. But those who have subsequently developed nuclear weapons have faced the possibility and even the certainty of nuclear retaliation. The new nuclear powers, with limited nuclear backup and opportunities for testing, face the truth of the saying that "a limited nuclear capability is worse than none at all." The success of nuclear weapons and the tremendous numbers available to the two powers in the late 1980s—more than 50,000 warheads—were responsible for preventing a "shooting nuclear war" resulting from the Cold War.

The first dispute over the international control of nuclear weapons arose in the early war years between Roosevelt, who had made the first production decision in June 1941, and the British, who had made invaluable contributions toward nuclear development through their Maud Committee. In July 1942 in their meeting in Quebec, Roosevelt and Winston Churchill agreed that they would not use a nuclear weapon either against each other or against a third party without the other's agreement.

Several leaders in the nuclear field, including Niels Bohr, James B. Conant, Felix Frankfurter, and Field Marshal Jan Smuts of South Africa, questioned whether their major ally, the Soviet Union, should be taken into their confidence. This confidence was never shared until the Potsdam meeting between the three powers in 1945, when Roosevelt was dead. President Truman informed Stalin only casually of work on a new weapon and the plan to use it against Japan. Stalin's surprising failure to raise any questions was interpreted as indicating prior knowledge through Soviet spies, which has now been fully confirmed. A heated debate has been conducted ever since as to whether an earlier sharing of U.S.-U.K. nuclear plans with the Soviets might have deterred or prevented the Cold War.

A considerable body of opinion still holds that the only hope of containing the nuclear problem at the time was through international control, as first emphasized by Smuts. McGeorge Bundy, in *Danger and Survival* (1988), believes that more thought should have been given to convincing the Soviets to join us and our allies in such an endeavor. Since no such effort was ever made, we may never know how events may have been changed. Once the Cold War had set in, making understanding between us and the Soviets very difficult, it was probably too late, and the Cold War had to run its perhaps predestined course.

As I explained earlier, I joined the defense effort in June 1941, before Pearl Harbor, and served with the War Production Board and U.S.-U.K. Combined Raw Materials Board for two years. Although based mostly in Washington, I visited London and North Africa when both were under German bombardment. But anxious to get into the shooting war, in 1943 I joined the Navy as a Lieutenant (j.g.) in Air Combat Intelligence. After training in Quantset Point and in a naval experimental squadron, I applied for and was accepted as the Navy Liaison Officer for the 21st Bomber Command being assembled for duty in the western Pacific.

The 20th Air Force was born in Washington on April 4, 1944, with General Henry "Hap" Arnold as its first commander. Under a special charter, the 20th operated directly under the Joint Chiefs of Staff at a time when the Air Force was still part of the U.S. Army. The 20th's mission was based on a very unusual aircraft—the Boeing B-29, conceived in 1940—and on the latest strategic doctrine—high-level precision bombing of the home islands of Japan. B-29 raids were first conducted from bases in India and China by the 20th Bomber Command in June 1944, on Bangkok, and 20 days later on Kyushu in Japan. Massive bombing of Tokyo was begun on November 24, 1945, by the 21st Bomber Command from the island of Saipan in the Japanese Marianas, which had been captured by U.S. forces in 1944.

The B-29 was an extraordinary plane. Weighing 60 tons, it had four 2,200-horsepower engines and a 20,000-pound bomb capacity; it was manned by a crew of 18 and had a 16-hour mission capability. By the end of the war, the 21st Command was capable of sending 850 of its 1,042 B-29s on missions over Japan every other day. During the course of the war, the 21st flew 28,329 sorties and lost 354 planes, a 1.3 percent loss ratio.

I flew by naval plane to Hickman Field north of San Francisco and from there to Honolulu, arriving on September 15. I spent five very busy weeks in Honolulu. My main duty was to receive briefings on the Naval Commands in the Western Pacific Area, Commander Forward Area, from Admiral John Hoover in Saipan on down. I was also thoroughly briefed on a submarine, and I met with Admiral Lockweed, Commander SUBPAC, to discuss the availability of submarines for air-sea rescue. Lockweed was very cooperative, particularly when rescuing downed airmen, which assured that a sub got credit for a successful mission. This was a time when decorations for combat valor against the Japanese were becoming scarce.

Toward the end of the war, in June 1945, we had exclusive use of 14 submarines that were under the control of the Marianas Area Sub Commander, "Bud" Ward. The submariners seemed to be fairly independent of Admiral Chester Nimitz, the Pacific Fleet Commander, who moved his headquarters from Honolulu to Guam soon after my arrival. I also was briefed by the Chief of Intelligence, Pacific Ocean Area. I happened to be in his office when he took an emergency call advising that a large Japanese flotilla had appeared in the Leyte Gulf off the Philippines. "Where did they come from?" he shouted. "How will they try to get out?" There followed a major U.S. naval victory of the Pacific war. In my letters home, I had begun complaining about being held so long in Honolulu that I would miss the war, when I received orders to Saipan.

Saipan had been selected to be taken by the Marines, for use by the B-29s in the first air attacks against Honshu, the principal island of the Japanese mainland. Saipan, Tinian, and Guam, all of which eventually had B-29 Bomb Wings (Guam also had the 21st Bomber Command headquarters), were selected because they were the closest suitable land within return flight distance from the principal Japanese targets. Preparation of the airstrip in Saipan and construction of temporary headquarters and support facilities began before the island was secure. A number of B-29s and personnel were in place when I arrived on December 15. I was warmly received by the Commander, Brigadier General Heywood Hansell. Later I came to admire him greatly and consider him a good friend.

On November 24, after six trial runs against Japanese-held islands, the 21st made its first, long-delayed raid on Tokyo, called San Antonio No. 1. Of 110 planes of the 73rd Bomb Wing, two were lost, and the mission was considered only a qualified success. We were deeply disappointed, despite a more successful attack on Tokyo two days later. Those of us in 21st Bomber Command headquarters had also realized that there had been a considerable delay in making the initial attack. However, there was no way to know the concerns of the 20th Air Force and its Commander, General "Hap" Arnold. (Arnold had suffered three serious heart attacks and so was more than normally impatient.) To most of Hansell's peers and close friends in the Air Force, including Arnold's select group (Larry Norstad, Harry Kuter, and Rosey O'Donnell), Hansell had done a creditable job in completing construction of an air field on a newly taken island, training inexperienced crews, and completing the organization and command structure of a new bomber command. Much as everyone admired Hansell, some reasoned that he was more of a planner than an operator. Arnold finally made his move: He tapped the best operator produced during the war so far, Major General Curtis LeMay, a 34-year-old expert bombardier technician.

Later, when I got to know LeMay, I understood why he was chosen. He was successful because, in addition to native intelligence and good judgment, he could concentrate 100 percent on the job at hand. He permitted nothing to distract him, whether desire for recognition or acclaim, personal friendships or obligations, need for relaxation or pleasure. At all waking hours he was 100 percent on the job. His usual scowl, which added to his reputation for toughness, was caused by a facial injury. He was a congenial companion for an evening of poker, at which he usually won. If a Wing Commander was in trouble, LeMay would ask him to come to Guam for a conference. After a thorough review of the situation, always smoking his cigar, he would make his decision as to what should be done. If the trouble was not overcome, there was no harsh talk or second meeting—the offending officer simply went home. LeMay was a loyal friend to those who served him well. After the war, he came over to my house in Washington for a few poker games, but I lost touch with him after his unfortunate race for the vice-presidency in 1968, sharing the ticket with Governor George Wallace of Alabama. He was a master in his own profession but no politician.

All of us at Bomber Command headquarters knew something drastic was up when General Lauris Norstad, Chief of Staff for the 20th Air Force (whom I had known in Washington), came out to confer with Hansell. We soon knew who would replace him. All of his staff felt a great sadness that Hansell, whom they so much admired, had lost his chance to lead the most powerful Air Force in the world to a successful conclusion of the war with

Japan. When LeMay arrived in Guam to take over, Hansell received him gracefully with no show of remorse, and so we all admired Hansell even more. But a new era had begun, and we were ready to support LeMay wholeheartedly.

LeMay took a hard-nosed attitude toward Nimitz and refused to attend his morning briefings for all of the island commanders. He designated me as his representative, which was great for me since I got exclusive use of a jeep that was also available when I wanted to go to the beach, where the 21st Bomber Command had its rest camp—complete with free rum drinks. I did not, however, always get a seat at the CINCPAC (Commander in Chief Pacific) meetings, where rank meant everything. Since most of the routine coordination between CINCPAC and the Bomber Command now came through me, I tried to improve relations.

One evening, I arranged for Nimitz and his top staff to have dinner with LeMay, who behaved very well. It was a very productive meeting. I urged CINCPAC to furnish LeMay and General "Augie" Kissner with flag-rank bungalows like those built for Navy officers of similar rank. Eventually, they were built but not furnished. At CINCPAC, every lieutenant commander and above received not only a well-furnished bedroom but also an adjoining "rumpus room." I made a list of furniture that I thought would bring our commanders' quarters up to Navy flag rank and took it to Nimitz's Executive Officer with a brief sales pitch saying this would improve relations between our commands. He didn't receive me but merely scrawled the word NEGAT across my memorandum. There is a sequel: While his furniture was being built by an Air Force carpenter, a private, Kissner told him how he wished the bar to be built. The private replied with a straight face, "I will build it just as you say, General. I want to do everything I can to win this war."

LeMay's takeover of the 21st Bomber Command did not immediately change the strategy of high-level precision bombing to which he was dedicated as much as Hansell had been. The next attack on February 19, 1945, however—on the Nakajima aircraft factory in Musashino which was still the number one priority target—showed the limitations of such bombing in the unpredictable Japanese weather. The 119 planes were unable to see the target and dropped on the city of Tokyo by radar. The radar operators, being untrained, hit only insignificant targets, causing little damage compared to a low-level Navy attack on Musashino two days earlier. Under Colonel "Monty" Montgomery's prodding, LeMay realized that he was losing two tons of bomb load in getting to 31,000 feet and, because of the unpredictable clouds, could not see the small targets that required the precision bombing. After 2,000 high-level sorties over Japan, not one important target had been destroyed.

LeMay now knew that unless, by taking a chance, he could change the strategy of the bombing, he would probably be relieved as Hansell had been.

Strategic bombing might be given up, and it would be necessary for the United States to launch a mass invasion of Kyushu in November which, it had been estimated, would cost 200,000 American lives. Without telling anyone in Washington for fear of being stopped, LeMay began planning for a low-level night incendiary attack on Tokyo on February 25.

At about the same time, LeMay received the first agents of a brand-new strategy, based on an awesome weapon he knew nothing about—a bomb created by the top-secret Manhattan District Project. Soon, personnel of the 509 Composite Group, most of whom didn't know the nature of their weapon either, started coming into our base on Tinian Island to complete their training. I met with them in LeMay's staff meeting without learning anything about their mission. It was not until actual plans were being made for the drop that I was brought in to plan liaison with the Navy and air-sea rescue for two planes, involving attacks against two Japanese cities that I could see had hitherto been saved from attack.

In the meantime, LeMay's low-level night incendiary attack, which he still had not cleared with Washington, was scheduled for March 9. I was sitting next to LeMay in the vast Operations Room, writing a letter to my wife, Cecilia, as he followed the course of the flight. Since there was little to do while the flight was in progress, almost everyone had gone to bed to be ready for the debriefings the next day. My letter to my wife that evening said, in part:

March 9. It is 2 A.M., but I will still call it March 9. I am in Operations Control with a small group hovered around the General on a platform along one side of the vast room. He is keeping score on a chart before him of radio messages being received directly from the squadron leaders of 350 B-29s (4,200 men) over Tokyo. Each squadron leader is reporting which target he bombed, whether visually, with enemy opposition, did they see big fires, did they get away. Tomorrow it will all be announced, the most valuable of our raids to date, maybe of the war. The guts of Tokyo will be bombed out, hundreds of thousands of people will probably be killed. Everyone here is interested in the number of our planes bombing the primary target (Tokyo) visually and seeing conflagrations. After that will be the problem of getting them all back safely. We have a lot of people standing by to pick them up.

Our air-sea rescue efforts had proved themselves equal to the task. The Tokyo flight was followed by one on March 11 against Nagoya, and on March 12, against Osaka, both highly successful. In the Tokyo attack, we picked up 30 downed airmen, bringing our total rescue to 200. It was a far cry from the severe losses in the 73rd Bomb Wing before we took Iwo Jima, and the morale of the flight crews had improved accordingly.

Back to my next letter to my wife:

March 11. You have probably heard about our first big low level Tokyo strike. I have seen all of the post-strike pictures as they came in and they are appalling. The papers have announced that 15 square miles were burned out of the heart of Tokyo, greater destruction than that created by the big Tokyo earthquake and fire. The loss of life must have been terrific.

All of us were, of course, eager to know the results of the bombing. We sent reconnaissance planes over the next day, but there was so much smoke over Tokyo that we could not get photographs. When we looked at the first good map, we could not believe what we saw. The gray areas on the map corresponding to devastation by fire covered the entire heart of Tokyo, an area of some 44 square miles—an area the size of Manhattan.

After the war, we learned that some 150,000 people had lost their lives in Tokyo that night. This was approximately three times the number killed in the subsequent atomic bombing of Hiroshima. Curiously enough, world opinion never reacted to the Tokyo bombing raid as it did to the raid on Hiroshima. Even to this day, commentators have not inveighed against the tremendous loss of life or criticized LeMay and the U.S. government for this incendiary destruction. This undoubtedly had to do with the sinister future implications of the atomic weapon.

This fire-bombing raid was the beginning of an incendiary campaign against Tokyo and the other cities of Japan that continued until the end of the war. With 850 planes available every other day, no one target could be found that required the entire force; thus, it was necessary to assign our aircraft to a number of missions, three or four of them on some occasions. We suffered few losses as a rule, though on one Tokyo raid, we had a disastrous result. Evidently, the assigned track of our planes was right down the middle of "flak alley," and some 35 planes went down. Not one sent sufficiently clear inflight distress messages to permit air-sea rescue searches to be undertaken. We searched the return routes blindly for several days without finding any trace of downed aircraft. All of the crews, some 385 men, were lost.

On June 29, I departed Guam in an Air Force plane with a small group of intelligence and operational officers of the 21st Bomber Command for the Philippines. Our objective was to plan with General Douglas MacArthur's staff the role of the 21st Bomber Command in the anticipated invasion of the Japanese home islands. After much discussion, a decision was made to invade Kyushu, the southern main island, on November 1. In view of the large number of U.S. casualties expected, we hoped very much that we could force the Japanese to surrender before this would become necessary. Even though the B-29 was not built to assist ground or landing operations, the 21st was expected to do everything it could to help our invasion forces. LeMay, against his better judgment, had been forced to suspend strategic bombing of Honshu to assist our naval forces being attacked by Kamikazes during the bloody invasion of Okinawa. He hoped it would not be necessary again. In addition to naval and air-sea rescue matters, LeMay had commissioned me to bring him some of those good Philippine cigars. Here is another letter to my wife.

July 3. I have now extended my travels a bit more. I can scratch Japan from my must list. You may have read about our record 850 plane strike of July 1–2 in honor of Air Force Day, dropping the largest tonnage ever dropped in one raid. They would not let me fly in one of the attacking aircraft because of the information I know, but since the war is so nearly over, they let me go in one of the "superdumbo" planes that orbit just off the Jap coast looking for planes in distress. I needed to go, for my work, and because I have always wanted to go along on at least one mission.

Actually our flight lasted 22 hours, including a short stop in Iwo Jima on return. We took off at 1710 and flew near the center of the main stream of 850 B-29s, with 10,200 men. I had the bombardier's seat in the nose with excellent visibility. There was a continuous line of planes in both directions as far as one could see. To avoid collisions, which were a greater threat than Jap fighters, all running lights were on. As the sky darkened the very mass of the thousands of lights presented a glorious spectacle.

On the way up my "superdumbo" opened up communications as we passed over the air-sea rescue submarines, which typically had been placed on station at even latitude points on the return routes for the various flights. We called the submarine by VHF radio using the same names that we called other B-29s. "Nelly's Belly" was a favorite name. When we opened up there was an immediate response and communication was terminated.

Past Iwo, we went on alone to our station about 30 miles from the coast east of Tokyo. Another plane joined us; the rest of the 850 B-29s split into separate streams heading for their separate targets, each with its prescribed bomb loads. For a time, we had a grandstand view of a high explosive raid on Kawasaki, just south of Tokyo. We saw all the bombs hit the oil tanks, which were the objectives, burning brightly, saw the Jap searchlights, and heard the anti-aircraft ack-ack bursts.

Later we saw an incendiary attack on Mito, sixty miles north, which created a beautiful fire. We could hear the men in the strike aircraft talking to each other on VHF voice radio, including one poor fellow who was shot down. An erroneous report had been received by us, as rescue plane, that a B-29 was down in our area. As a result, although we were scheduled to start back at 0330, we continued to orbit our position for four hours, till 0730, when our gas was so low we had to return to Iwo to refuel.

It became daylight at 0500, and our search took us up to the Jap coast. It was a beautiful clear day and we could, during our stay of over two hours, see the little coast towns, Tokyo, and Mt. Fuji beyond, dominating everything. It was a tremendously interesting experience. We saw no Jap aircraft. The Japs had too few fighters left to risk them on a single rescue plane. Later we heard that the plane we were searching for got home safely.

After I had rested from the flight, I had a great feeling of pride and appreciation for the pilot, Lieutenant Eugene G. (Bud) Cook, and his crew from the 19th Bomb Group of the 93rd Squadron, who had flown the plane with only one short break for 22 hours over the mostly dark Pacific.

During my stay in Guam, I became aware that a squadron of B-29s was stationed in Tinian under the command of Colonel Paul Tibbets, which had a special mission in the war. The matter was dealt with in great secrecy, and in all of the staff meetings I attended, I never heard any mention of the precise mission of the squadron.

I was finally told that the squadron would conduct a strike on Japan on a particular day. There would be two planes. The primary target would be Hiroshima, and the secondary target, if weather made it impossible to hit the primary, would be Nagasaki. Hiroshima, for some reason hitherto unbeknownst to me, had not been attacked. We had been conducting many missions over Japan and had burned down substantially all of the other major cities of Japan. As I was later to discover, this was because Hiroshima had been saved for this particular raid. Since the Japanese were used to single or double planes seeking weather or photographs for intelligence, it was unlikely that the special planes would be attacked—unless the Japanese knew their secret.

I was told that this raid was of such importance that I must make every effort to rescue the crews in the event they were forced down. Since it was not known which of the two targets would be hit, it was necessary to make rescue arrangements for both. I was told to "shoot the works," that there was no plan that could be too elaborate, so I spared nothing.

I was also told one more bit of information, namely, that I was to advise all U.S. commands in the area that no U.S. aircraft could come within 100 miles of the target within five hours after the raid. To me, as a physicist, this meant only one thing, radioactivity. I had heard a few rumors about an atomic bomb but never before had any inkling that one had been prepared or that the squadron in Tinian was to drop it. I said nothing about this to anyone since secrecy made even the use of the word "nuclear" dangerous. However, it was clear in my own mind that the squadron was carrying an atomic bomb. I did probe, however, to see whether any changes could be made in our advice to the navy, since I could have devised other means to keep American planes out of the danger zone. I was told, however, that it was too late to change decisions made at the highest level. Since I had heard at one stage that if an atomic bomb was ever dropped, there was some possibility that the hydrogen in the atmosphere could combine with the oxygen and detonate all around the world, I had a little apprehension about this on the day and the hour of the drop.

Following my instructions, I proceeded to devise the most thorough air-sea rescue arrangements I possibly could. The problem was compounded by the fact that Hiroshima was on the Inland Sea in the interior of Honshu, and Nagasaki was some 70 or 80 miles from deep water—all of which made it impossible for submarines to come close to either target. If a plane was shot down over Hiroshima or Nagasaki, the crew might have to bail out before reaching deep water. The only possibility for rescue—and this was a long shot but nevertheless one that we had to be ready for—was to have Navy Dumbo flying boats come up from Okinawa, ready to land in the Inland Sea or just offshore at Nagasaki.

Either eventuality had to be prepared for, so planes had to be ordered to both places. And since the time of the drop could not be estimated precisely and the time on station for the Dumbos was only a half hour, several planes had to be ordered up in sequence to relieve earlier planes on station. In the event a plane got into distress over Hiroshima, it might possibly make it to the Bungo Suido, which is the channel south of Hiroshima between the Inland Sea and the deep Pacific Ocean. As a consequence, I also stationed a submarine there and requested 14 submarines on even latitude lines along the return routes the planes would follow coming back to Guam from either target. This made it unnecessary to put the coordinate points on paper. I also placed destroyers on the line of return at the maximum distance north of Iwo Jima that they could expose themselves. Similar arrangements were made on the return from Nagasaki.

The day of the strike was a momentous one for me. All of the arrangements were in place, and it remained only to direct the search in the event any of the planes were forced down. If in trouble, they would report inflight, and we would repeat the message to the various waiting naval commands and units affected. The coded message from Hiroshima said that they had found the primary target open, had bombed it, and they had gotten away. Actually, the Japanese paid no attention to the flight, because they took it for a reconnaissance aircraft or because they had so few fighters left at this stage of the war.

The planes were not damaged by the explosion on the Hiroshima drop, returning safely to their Marianas base without incident. The subsequent drop on Nagasaki also went according to plan, and air-sea rescue was not required. Although the Nagasaki drop was not as successful as the one on Hiroshima, which took 50,000 lives and destroyed most structures within the city, both of the bombings must be credited with helping accomplish their purpose—to induce the leaders of Japan to surrender.

I could go home. On November 1, the day the Emperor, with LeMay present, signed the papers of surrender on an American battleship in Tokyo Bay, I walked my temporary duty orders to Washington through two headquarters in Guam, hitched a ride on a Navy plane, and landed the next day in Dallas, where I happily joined my family after a year's absence. For me, the war was over.

During its year of operations, the 21st destroyed 65 major cities covering 175 square miles of urban area. Total civilian casualties came to 900,000 killed, 1.3 million injured, and 9.2 million rendered homeless, approximately 50 percent of the population of the cities. The Japanese did, indeed, pay a heavy price for their disastrous miscalculation in starting the war at Pearl Harbor.

In a formal ceremony at the Pentagon shortly after the war, General LeMay awarded me the Legion of Merit with the following citation:

Lieutenant G. C. McGhee, United States Naval Reserve, As Naval Liaison Officer to the XXI Bomber Command from November 1944 to August 1945, planned, organized and directed air-sea rescue activities in support of long range bombardment operations from the Marianas. His efforts resulted in the employment of a network of submarines, destroyers, surface craft and aerial observers that rescued hundreds of airmen from ditched craft that contributed materially to the success of strategic bombardment.

I also received three battle stars to adorn the Legion of Merit.

7

The Tripartite Declaration of 1950

Control of Palestine has been a source of conflict since the days of King David and the beginning of Judaism. The Romans ruled the land at the time of Christ, but Islam prevailed after the Arab conquest in the seventh century, only to be followed from the eleventh to twentieth centuries by non-Arab empire builders. The last of these, the Ottoman Turks, ceded control when they were defeated in World War I, and the victorious British pledged support of a Jewish national homeland. In 1920, a British Palestine mandate was recognized.

Jewish immigration to Palestine was swelled in the 1930s by refugees from the Nazis, and an influx of Arabs from Syria and Lebanon also occurred. In 1947, the United Nations General Assembly voted to partition Palestine into Arab and Jewish zones, and as Britain withdrew on May 14, 1948, Israel was declared an independent state. Rejecting partition, the armies of the Arab League—Egypt, Jordan, Syria, Lebanon, Iraq, and Saudi Arabia—invaded, and U.N. mediation was required to end the hostilities. Israel and the Arab nations signed armistices in 1949, but no peace settlement was reached.

Such was the situation in the Middle East when I returned to Washington in March 1950, having ended my African tour in Saudi Arabia. There was concern over certain problems that had remained after the Arab-Israeli truce arranged by the United Nations, one in particular having to do with arms. The United Nations had embargoed the shipment of arms to the entire Palestine area, and while the ban was lifted on August 11, 1949, the United States and the British had strictly limited shipments to those arms required for internal security and self-defense. But the Arab-Israeli war had created a vacuum, and a large quantity of arms was arriving, much of it from Czechoslovakia. The Middle East was vulnerable in the Cold War, and we felt that the flow of arms from Eastern Europe might result in increased Communist influence, possibly even total control. We therefore wanted to assure an orderly supply of arms for internal security and defense.

British authority in the Middle East was on the wane, as evidenced by a stalemate in negotiations with Egypt over troops and bases. We were now left with a dilemma. Although we wished to see the Middle East grow militarily and contribute to defense of the area, we worried about nationalistic trends. We also did not want to resume a substantial arms supply without giving assurances to people at home and abroad, especially those with concerns for the embattled state of Israel. And we wanted to emphasize that we would prevent an arms race or any aggressive use of the arms we furnished.

We were also concerned about the often conflicting hopes and aspirations of the immediate parties to the conflict. While a full mutual defense treaty with Israel was not likely to gain approval in the Senate, we wanted to assure the new government and its citizens that we would not condone Arab aggression. We also wanted to allay Arab concerns that Israel might use increased arms supplies to satisfy an interest in more territory, possibly that lying west of the Jordan River. In addition, we bore in mind that the leaders of the Arab states also feared aggression by other Arabs. During my recent visit to Saudi Arabia, for example, I had learned that King Ibn Saud was apprehensive about the territorial designs of King Abdullah of Jordan and the Regent acting for young Faisal II in Iraq. Later, Abdullah told me of his desire to reshape the Middle Eastern boundaries in his favor.

We intended to put to rest all suggestions of aggression, so that the nations of the region could concentrate on internal problems—the refugee problem, in particular—and seek a lasting peace. We sought the cooperation of Britain and France in shipping arms, because we did not wish to be Israel's principal arms supplier (as we would ultimately become). In addition, we were determined to insulate the potentially explosive issue from our domestic politics.

How to achieve these myriad objectives occupied me as I sat at my desk at the State Department on a day late in May 1950. The Department had been pondering the problem for some time. In late March, Secretary Acheson had received a group of congressmen who feared that large-scale shipments of arms by Britain to Egypt would upset the precarious military balance. At the same time, the National Security Council sent over a draft report, "U.S. Policy Toward Arms Shipments to the Middle East," which essentially supported the proposition of Anglo-Egyptian military cooperation and emphasized that we would not oppose U.K. arms shipments, but President Truman found it to be one-sided. Acheson suggested that the problem could be solved by nonaggression declarations by the Middle East countries, and this idea appealed to Truman.

In the formulation of foreign policy, there are seldom any really new ideas; almost every possible course of action has been thought of before. Break-throughs occur only because the world changes. The altered scene permits something to succeed at a given time where it would have previously failed. The art of foreign affairs is to sense an opportunity and move accordingly, adapting to changing circumstances. I vividly recall the moment when all the pieces of the puzzle began to fit together in my mind. I got up from my chair and burst into the office of my deputy, Raymond Hare, unannounced.

Ray, I have it. The administration can't get Congress to approve a Middle East treaty, but the three powers can, if we're firm and get together, enforce our views on the states of the area. We are the "big boys." The Middle East states are the "little boys." All we have to do is set the rules and say, "Look here you little boys. If you don't behave yourselves, we're going to take care of you." We don't have to say precisely or under what conditions. If we are really "big boys" we don't have to. They will mind us. Moreover, they are all so concerned just now about what might happen that they will welcome our assumption of responsibility. I believe Britain and France will be happy to join us in such a move.

Ray and I began drafting the Tripartite Declaration. Cleared drafts were submitted on April 3, then in revised form on April 20, and again on April 28. On May 4, the Joint Chiefs of Staff (JCS) suggested adding that "the U.S. neither suggests nor approves a declaration regarding the security of the Middle East, which implies employment . . . of military enforcement measures." The JCS exception was inserted into the final draft.

On May 17, the National Security Council (NSC) recommended the Tripartite Declaration to Truman. The new elements were: (1) the United States would solicit British and French support for public declarations by all three governments; and (2) the shipment of arms to any Middle East country would be prohibited unless the purchasing country submitted to the supplying country assurance that it would not engage in aggression. We would continue to stress to the British and French the importance of avoiding a renewal of hostilities over Palestine. We would also seek their agreement to issuing parallel public statements of resolve to take vigorous action both in and out of the United Nations, should any country appear to want to renew hostilities. Such action would not, however, involve U.S. military forces.

Fortunately, the task of negotiating the Tripartite Declaration with our British and French allies was given to Ray Hare, who as my deputy had made a major contribution to its formulation. (An extremely able career officer, Ray would go on to be Ambassador to Turkey and Assistant Secretary for the Near East, South Asia, and Africa, both positions that I also had held.)

A conference of the Foreign Ministers of Britain, France, and the United States in late April had provided an excellent opportunity for accepting the new policy contained in the Tripartite Declaration. The U.S. delegation was headed first by Ambassador Philip C. Jessup and then by Acheson. Truman offered the judgment that it was "the most successful international conference since Potsdam." With my strong support, Ray Hare was made Delegate for Middle Eastern Affairs. Our proposals were taken up with the British on May 1, and one of Hare's first assignments was to persuade the British that the French ought to be invited to the meeting. The French were potentially significant arms suppliers—they still wielded considerable influence on such countries as Syria and Lebanon—and if excluded, they would be offended and likely to oppose Anglo-American initiatives.

In preliminary meetings, Hare was able to convince the British that the French merited a seat at the conference, and he quieted British fears that the declaration would foreclose future boundary changes or would not be taken seriously by the Middle East nations. In the meeting itself, the British agreed to our draft, and after a perfunctory display of hurt feelings over not being consulted earlier, the French also approved the draft.

The Foreign Ministers—Acheson, Earnest Bevin of Britain, and Robert Schuman of France—sent the Tripartite Declaration to their respective governments, and it was announced on May 25. It read as follows:

The Governments of the United Kingdom, France, and the United States, having had occasion during the recent Foreign Ministers' meeting in London to review certain questions affecting the peace and stability of the Arab states and of Israel, and particularly that of the supply of arms and war material to these states, have resolved to make the following statements.

1. The three Governments recognize that the Arab states and Israel all need to maintain a certain level of armed forces for the purpose of assuring their internal security and their legitimate self-defense and to permit them to play their part in the defense of the area as a whole. All applications for arms or war material for these countries will be considered in the light of these principles. In this connection the three Governments wish to recall and reaffirm the terms of the statements made by their representatives on the Security Council on August 4, 1949, in which they declared their opposition to the development of an arms race between the Arab States and Israel.

2. The three Governments declare that assurances have been received from all the states in question, to which they permit arms to be supplied from their countries, that the purchasing state does not intend to undertake any act of aggression against any other state in the area to which they permit arms to be supplied in the future.

3. The three Governments take this opportunity of declaring their deep interest in and their desire to promote the establishment and maintenance of peace and stability in the area and their unalterable opposition to the use of force or threat of force

between any of the states in that area. The three Governments, should they find that any of these states was preparing to violate frontiers or armistice lines, would, consistent with their obligations as members of the UN, immediately take action, both within and outside the UN, to prevent such violation.

The New York *Herald Tribune* on May 26 hailed the three powers for acting in concert for the first time to prevent renewal of Arab-Israeli warfare and for pledging to take immediate action against any state planning aggression:

Common foreign policy action to some real effect. . . . The great powers have in effect agreed to underwrite the peace in Palestine. . . . The guaranty resolves the dilemma which the arms problem presented from the first. It makes it possible to fortify the Middle Eastern states as a bulwark against Soviet expansion without at the same time subsidizing or encouraging a resumption of the war between them. As such it may seem a rather simple act of statesmanship. But it is also a bold one; for neither France nor Britain nor America would have dreamed, a year or two ago, of pledging its men and resources to the guarantee of any kind of peace in Palestine. . . . The joint statement is a good omen for peace and advancement in the Middle East—and on a greater stage as well.

The *New York Times* also voiced approval of the Tripartite Declaration:

The three-Power declaration on peace and stability in the Near East is another great and welcome step in that "total diplomacy" which must be the goal of the West. It means much to Israel and the seven Arab states to which it specifically refers, but it means even more to the democratic world. The supremely important conference in London had one more link in the strong chain binding the free nations together and holding them safely against the onslaughts of the totalitarian world. . . .

From our own American point of view this is truly an historic move. In 1946 and 1947 the British taunted us for our willingness to give advice about the Near East while we refused to commit ourselves to any decided intervention. Now we are a co-guarantor of the status quo. We pledge ourselves to take immediate action "both within and outside the United Nations" to maintain peace and stability in the area. In the process we and the other two great Powers have redressed an inequality, for it was disturbing to the balance of forces that Israel should have been at a disadvantage in acquiring arms and jet planes. The new move is just and wise, and it will strengthen the West in the global struggle.

The declaration slipped into place in the stream of Middle East policy with little opposition. The states concerned made some pro forma objections that they had not been consulted, which was part of our plan. In private, the Middle East states welcomed the declaration, which had the desired stabilizing effect. A three-power committee on arms sales was set up in London to administer the implementation of the declaration.

The first setback to the declaration occurred in 1955 when Egypt became dissatisfied over its allocations and purchased arms from Czechoslovakia through the USSR. A more serious weakness developed as a result of the ill-fated Anglo-French-Israeli invasion of Egypt in October 1956. The British, in their confusion and ineptness, took the absurd position that the invasion had been pursuant to their obligations under the declaration. Furthermore, a British claim that we had been consulted implied that we made no objections. Actually, we had told them that we considered the invasion in violation of the declaration.

Although the declaration was weakened, subsequent U.S. Presidents from Eisenhower to Carter used it as a basis for actions in the Middle East. I have often cited it as an example of the usefulness of a venerable and ambiguous treaty that can at will be revived or ignored. In the end, the Tripartite Declaration did, I believe, have a stabilizing effect in the Middle East. It relieved apprehension about local wars; it provided the most specific U.S. assurances to protect Israel; it improved a regional arms policy among the three declaratory powers; and, through the London Committee, it provided a continuing mechanism for avoiding an arms race through a fair distribution of arms. Regrettably, however, the plan has not been applied more widely.

8

Anglo-Iranian Oil Negotiations in 1951

While I was in Pakistan in early March 1951, Ali Razmara, the Prime Minister of Iran, was assassinated, and I was instructed by Washington to proceed to Teheran and assess the situation. I was to pay particular heed to the National Front campaign to induce the government to nationalize the Anglo-Iranian Oil Company (AIOC) oil concession.

World attention was focused on events in Iran, a pivotal country in the Cold War whose alliance with the Western powers was of critical importance. With the Soviet Union looming across the northern frontier, the Communists had a foothold in Iran in the form of the outlawed, yet active, Tudeh party. As it hoped for an oil concession of its own in Iran, the USSR was not in favor of total nationalization, but it sponsored demonstrations against the British.

Accounts of my mission to Iran preceded me. On March 17, the day of my arrival, the *London Daily Mail* ran a banner headline: OIL ENVOY SENT TO PERSIA. The article reported that I was to renegotiate the British concession by urging Iran to accept a 50–50 profit-sharing plan being offered by the AIOC; or failing that, I was to obtain assurances that Iranian oil would continue to flow to Western markets. The *New York Times,* in a report on the progress of a nationalization bill in the Majlis, the Iranian Parliament, also noted that I was in Teheran. (By a vote of 41 to 1, the bill had been referred to a committee by the Senate, which was expected to approve it.)

As I read the press reports en route to Teheran, I thought about my futile efforts to convince the AIOC that it must moderate its position toward Iran if it hoped to forestall nationalization. My initial contact with the British oil company dated back to the mid-1930s, when as a Rhodes Scholar at Oxford, I met the daughters of Sir John Cadman, the Chairman of the Board, and visited the Cadman family at their country home. Sir John had explained to me one Sunday why the company, even though a majority of its stock was owned by the government, had refused to comply with the League of Nations' sanctions against Italy for its aggression against Ethiopia. He'd asked his friend Walter Teagle, the Chairman of Standard Oil, what he planned to do, and Teagle said Standard Oil had been selling oil to Italy for 70 years and would keep on selling oil to Italy. "What else could I do?" said Cadman. His anecdote taught me that the AIOC could act independently of the government.

While working on my doctorate in geophysics, I did the first reflection seismic research in southern England and shared the results with the AIOC, since the company planned to drill in the area. When I got my D.Phil.(Oxon) degree from Oxford in 1937, the AIOC offered me a job in Iran. I turned it down, preferring to return to the United States after having been away three years, but I was gratified by the show of interest.

As Assistant Secretary of State, I began my dealings with the company in January 1950, meeting with Richard Seddon, the AIOC manager in Teheran, and W. D. Heath-Ives of the company's New York office. I had just visited Iran and observed that what appeared to be a minor item—a difference of opinion over the allocation of reserves in the company's books—was blocking ratification of the Supplemental Agreement to the oil concession signed by Britain and Iran in 1933. The Supplemental Agreement, awarding the Iranian government a modest increase in royalties plus a lump-sum payment, had been agreed to in 1949 but was never formally ratified by Iran.

Heath-Ives replied that additional payments would leave "nothing in the till" for AIOC, to which I replied that the company's latest annual report indicated considerable profit. The situation in the Middle East had changed, I said. It was time to recognize the legitimate demands of the oil-producing states, and in that regard, I pointed out that better terms had already been granted by American companies in Venezuela and were under consideration in Saudi Arabia.

On August 31, the State Department advised our Embassy in London that the Board of the Arab-American Oil Company (ARAMCO) had authorized renegotiation of its 1933 concession, as Saudi Arabia had demanded. Since it was clear that ARAMCO would go well beyond the Supplemental Agreement in payments to the Saudis, I felt it was only fair to warn the British, so the AIOC would have an opportunity to improve its offer to Iran. I did so in a meeting with the Foreign Office in London on September 21, after first conferring with officers of ARAMCO and its parent companies, Standard Oil Company of New Jersey, Socony-Vacuum Oil

Company, Texas Oil Company, and Standard Oil Company of California, and with Everette L. DeGolyer, a leading oil industry consultant.

The meeting considered a report from Henry F. Grady, the U.S. Ambassador to Iran, who warned that continued delay in getting Iranian approval of the Supplemental Agreement could result in the collapse of Iran or the confiscation of the AIOC concession. Grady reviewed the four points Razmara was demanding to assure ratification of the agreement by the Majlis: a 10-year Iranization program; agreement on Iran's right to examine the AIOC books to determine its share of profits; the setting of oil prices in Iran that were related to their cost to the AIOC; and full information as to the destination of exported oil.

All present at the meeting said that their company would, if presented with such demands, find ways to meet them. In light of the 50–50 profit-sharing grant to Venezuela, the ARAMCO parents also agreed with the ARAMCO officials that the financial terms of any new agreement must represent a large increase over the existing meager royalties. The British government was also said to be sympathetic to Razmara's Four-Point Program, but the AIOC Board was represented as feeling that to accede to demands would only result in new demands. The AIOC apparently believed that a wiser tactic would be to pressure the Iranians into ratification.

When I got to London for the discussions, I realized soon enough that it would be tough going, as the AIOC position transmitted by the Foreign Office stiffened on point after point. To Razmara's request for increased Iranization of company personnel, the AIOC's response was preclusive: the company was already 97 percent Iranian (laborers largely), and qualified Iranian executives were hard to find. As to Iran's right as a participating partner to inspect the books, the AIOC said that Iran's right would extend no further than that of any other shareholder. The AIOC thought it might yield on Razmara's last two points—for a competitive price of oil on the market in Iran and on knowing the destination of Iranian oil.

I advised the British that in the interest of ratification of the Supplemental Agreement, in light of the conclusion the ARAMCO parents had reached in our meeting in Washington, they might wish to reconsider their position on all four of Razmara's points. I then made clear a development to come in a few months, which would be known as "McGhee's bombshell." ARAMCO was on the verge of an agreement with Saudi Arabia that would result in an unprecedented concession. I did not divulge the precise 50–50 split, since ARAMCO had not finally decided on it. The 50–50 split would be approved in November 1950, after the two meetings in my State Department office and negotiations with the Saudis were concluded in December. I indicated, however, that it would involve such a large concession that after the deal was announced, the AIOC could forget about Iran signing the Supplemental Agreement.

At the insistence of Michael Wright, my opposite number in the Foreign

Office, I went to a meeting of the AIOC Board. He had urged me to tell the Board what I had told the Foreign Office. I had wanted to attend, but I was reluctant to suggest it; I was glad that it was the Foreign Office that had suggested it. I was disappointed that Sir William Fraser, the AIOC Chairman, was not there. He was off hunting in Scotland, and I did not know if he had purposely avoided me. Presiding in his place was Neville Gass, who had negotiated the Supplemental Agreement.

I decided to make my position clear from the beginning, urging the Board to make generous concessions to Iran before it was too late. They should consider the expected new ARAMCO agreement with Saudi Arabia as an example to follow. I added that we, the British and the Americans, had helped put Razmara in office, and we were counting on him to shepherd a new agreement through the Majlis. The least we could do, it seemed to me, was to try to meet his four-point set of demands. I said I had discussed the demands with the heads of the ARAMCO parent companies, who all found them to be reasonable. I also made it very clear that ARAMCO's decision on the financial terms of any new agreement would be in the area of 50–50. Razmara was opposed to nationalization, I noted, but to remain in power, he had to show that he was looking after the best interests of the Iranian people.

The AIOC Board, in effect, told me to mind my own business. They knew more about Iran than the Americans did; if the Iranians were given an inch, they would take a mile. The AIOC's tragic failure to act led to the crisis in Iran in March 1951. Although the AIOC would claim it was not advised in advance of the ARAMCO 50–50 agreement with the Saudis, I had indeed warned them three months before the agreement was reached and five months before Razmara was assassinated. Later, I would come across evidence that the British eventually gave in and told Razmara in February that they were ready to offer 50–50 profit sharing. Razmara, who had withdrawn support of the Supplemental Agreement when the ARAMCO-Saudi deal was announced, did not know what to do. In a speech to the Majlis on March 3, he came out against nationalization, and he was shot four days later in a plot by Islamic terrorists to get rid of the "British stooge."

When I landed in Teheran, I was met by my old friend Henry Grady, a highly respected economic expert, and his engaging wife Lucretia. Grady and I had worked together when he was Chief of the Greek Aid Mission and I was Coordinator of Greek-Turkish Aid, and sending him to Iran had been my idea. We had a long and thorough discussion. He had had difficulty in dealing with the British, who were engaged in a losing battle to retain their powerful political and economic influence in Iran.

Shortly afterward I met with the British Ambassador, Sir Francis Shepherd, who described the situation as he saw it. I assured him of the U.S.

hope that the AIOC would not be nationalized and our willingness to help avoid it. I told him candidly, however, that in the U.S. view the company had been too rigid and too slow to recognize that a changing situation in Iran required a new approach. Although the British government owned a controlling interest in the AIOC, I remarked, it permitted Sir William Fraser, AIOC Chairman, to dictate its policy on Iranian oil. American companies were privately owned, I added, but we guided them, at times rather firmly. (Later I was not surprised to learn that when he cabled London about our meeting, Shepherd reported that I had made a "spirited attack" on the Anglo-Iranian Oil Company.)

I took issue with a particular comment attributed to Sir Francis, to wit, that the ARAMCO 50–50 agreement had "thrown a wrench into [the] Persian oil machinery." I recalled that I had personally warned the AIOC Board of the impending ARAMCO agreement. Nevertheless, the AIOC had been unwilling to learn from the ARAMCO experience. I then shifted to a more constructive tack and offered the British Ambassador a bit of advice. I pointed out that the history of oil concessions did not encourage reliance on the sanctity of contracts. I urged that the AIOC engage in a rear-guard action to the extent possible without endangering its control over its oil operation. When I asked Shepherd if he regarded nationalization as inevitable, he said no, but he conceded that the principle had "come to stay."

The next morning, I met with Hussein Ala, a friend from the years he had spent as Iran's Ambassador to Washington. An intimate of the Shah, Ala had been named Prime Minister to succeed Razmara. It was clearly a caretaker role, since Ala was nearing retirement age, and he had been unable to form a cabinet because prospective members were fearful of meeting Razmara's fate. I had a brief discussion with Ala about Mohammed Mossadeq, the National Front leader who seemed to be gathering power, and then he took me to see the Shah. I had last seen Mohammad Reza Shah Pahlavi on his official visit to Washington in November 1949, and I remembered him as a proud, erect young man who insisted on being taken seriously, word for word. Now, in Teheran 16 months later, I was received in a darkened audience chamber by a dejected and all but broken man, in the deepest fear of assassination.

I told the Shah that we were depending on him to make the best of a critical situation, and that we and the British would support him against the National Front's effort to nationalize the AIOC. When I asked him whether he believed that our support could help him stave off nationalization, he replied that he couldn't do it. He even pleaded that we not ask him to do it. He then emphasized that he couldn't even form a government because his followers were afraid of unseen enemies everywhere.

I then suggested alternative courses of action that would pay lip service to nationalization while still being workable. The key provision of a new agreement between the AIOC and Iran would be a 50–50 split of profits, which the AIOC was apparently now willing to offer but which was not generally understood, or, if so, believed. If the Iranian people had been told of the AIOC's intentions, authoritatively, perhaps the National Front would have accepted it, for ownership was less important than operating control and a fair share of the profits. However, the Shah was in no condition to think positively about a strategy, and I was convinced that without his support the prospects for AIOC were very poor. Soon after our meeting, the Shah fled the country for Switzerland.

On my way home from Iran, I stopped in a number of Middle Eastern capitals—Baghdad, Beirut, Amman, and Cairo—and finally in London, having been advised by Washington that the British wanted to discuss with me the crisis in Iran. While in Jordan on March 26, I mapped out a plan in which the AIOC problem might be solved by a revised U.S.-U.K. strategy for dealing with all Middle Eastern oil production. I proposed, first, that oil income to the major producing nations—Saudi Arabia, Iran, and Iraq—be based on a 50–50 split of profits and that the lesser producing states (with lesser needs)—Kuwait, Bahrain, and Qatar—be allowed to gradually catch up. I stated that over time the production rates in each of the countries should be based on a formula that would take into account both productive capacity and financial need.

Finally, I recommended that once the United States and Britain (after consultation with oil industry representatives) had agreed to a joint Middle Eastern oil policy, the policy should be announced. In a public statement, we would affirm that Middle East oil was the natural heritage of the people of the region and that they should benefit from its exploitation. Since the production of Middle East oil would continue to be the responsibility of private companies with the requisite expertise, capital, and access to markets, the issue of nationalization would be irrelevant.

When I arrived in London on Sunday, April 1, a cable from Washington was awaiting me. Referring to my telegram on oil policy, which I had sent to the State Department from Amman, the comments on my plan were favorable. I was authorized to explore with the British this and all other possible courses of action with regard to Middle East oil. On April 2, I met with representatives of the Foreign Office, Treasury, and Ministry of Power and Fuel, and on April 3, accompanied by U.S. Ambassador Walter Gifford, I paid a call on Herbert Morrison, the Foreign Secretary. My meeting with Morrison was of sufficient importance to the British that a transcript was sent to the British Ambassador to the U.S., Sir Oliver Franks, which was available to me in the British Archives. It read as follows:

1. Mr. George McGhee, Under-Secretary of State for Eastern Affairs in the State Department, called on me today accompanied by the United States Ambassador. He told me that he was on his way home after making an extensive tour, in the course

of which he had visited many of the Middle East capitals, as well as Karachi, New Delhi and Colombo.

2. I asked Mr. McGhee to give me his impressions of his tour. He told me he had found the whole area much unsettled. The old discipline imposed by British imperial power had been removed and had not been replaced by stable national Governments cooperating among themselves. The struggle between Russia and the Western Powers and the growing spirit of nationalism provided further causes of unrest. In Mr. McGhee's view the principal problems in the area were Kashmir, the oil question in Persia, Arab-Israel hostility and the Anglo-Egyptian issue. All these problems prevented co-operation between the countries of the area and the Western Powers. The situation could be re-established when the United Kingdom and the United States had built up their strength. During the next eighteen months we should be facing a critical situation in the whole area, especially in Persia, and in Mr. McGhee's view we should do all we could to hold the position during that critical period. With these considerations in view, Mr. McGhee said, the United States Government had decided to adopt a new policy towards the Middle East. Hitherto, they had concentrated mainly on the countries on the periphery, Greece, Turkey and Persia. Now they appreciated that the countries behind the outer line, though none of them of considerable individual strength, could nevertheless provide stability in depth. The United States Government proposed, therefore, to supply those countries with arms on a limited scale and to invite them to accept military missions. The object of this new policy would be to build up a more stable structure in the Middle East. This policy would be carried out in close co-ordination with the United Kingdom.

3. I asked Mr. McGhee if he had any criticisms of United Kingdom policy in the Middle East. He said that there had been periodical talks about the Middle East between the State Department and the Foreign Office, which had resulted in close co-operation. Only in Persia had this co-operation been absent. The State Department were very critical of the Anglo-Iranian Oil Company who, in their opinion, subordinated broader political considerations to purely commercial interests. The State Department felt, moreover, that His Majesty's Government had failed to exercise sufficient control over the company's policy.

4. In reply to my enquiry whether Mr. McGhee had anything to say about Egypt, he told me that during his visit to Cairo, the Egyptian Ministers had explained their position very forcibly to him. They made it clear that they feared that His Majesty's Government had receded somewhat from the position which had been adopted by Mr. Bevin. They told him that they must stand firm on a planned evacuation to be completed within a defined period and on the close association between the defence issue and the Sudan. Mr. McGhee said that he had done his utmost to defend the United Kingdom's position. He had warned the Egyptians that it was not in their interests to remove United Kingdom forces from Egypt at this critical moment. He had pointed out that there was no longer any element of Colonialism in British foreign policy, and that the Egyptians would do well to appreciate the formidable dangers of the new imperialism of Russia. To me Mr. McGhee expressed the hope that we should find it possible to reach an agreement with Egypt; that His Majesty's Ambassador at Cairo would be given enough latitude for the purpose, and that talks with the Egyptians would be resumed as quickly as possible. He also expressed the view that it would be unwise to link the question of Egyptian restrictions on the passage of oil through the Suez Canal with the defence issue.

5. Referring generally to the United Kingdom's present difficulties in Persia and Egypt, Mr. McGhee said that as long as they remained unresolved they would hinder the implementation of the United States' policy in the Middle East.

6. Commenting on Mr. McGhee's remarks, I recalled that we had a long experience of the Middle East and of the difficulties of dealing with the various countries in the area. The hostility between Israel and the Arab countries increased our difficulties considerably. We were traditionally friendly to the Arabs, but we also wanted to be friendly to Israel. The new States which had grown up in the Middle East were nominally democratic, but there were dangerous contrasts between rich and poor, and enmity between political parties prevented the establishment of strong Governments. The Nationalist Parties, particularly in Persia, were using "nationalisation" of oil not on its merits but as an instrument of foreign policy. The Anglo-Iranian Oil Company had put money, brains and skill into the development of the oil industry, which the Persians could not run themselves. The Company had a pretty good labour record in Persia. His Majesty's Government were very ready to talk to the Persian Government, and to deal with the present crisis, on imaginative lines, but they must take care to protect their essential oil supplies. As regards Egypt, I said that Mr. McGhee should appreciate the serious trouble which His Majesty's Government have recently had in Parliament. There was very strong feeling on both sides of the House of Commons that we should not facilitate the supply of oil to Egypt as long as the Egyptians were preventing the passage of our tankers through the Canal. But in all this it was profoundly important that United States officials should not adumbrate policies in regard to the Middle East until we had had time to consult together. I hoped that the United States Government would take special care to ensure that there was no crossing of wires. We were always ready to confer with the United States about Middle East policy in relation to our joint interests.

7. Mr. McGhee repeated again that he felt there was no divergence of view between us on the Middle East, except as regards Persia.

8. I am sending copies of this despatch to His Majesty's Representatives at Cairo and Tehran.

I am, &c.
HERBERT MORRISON

In my talks with the British, I said we appreciated the importance of oil rights, but from our point of view the top-priority objective in Iran was internal political stability and the preservation of Iran's independence. The loss of Iran to the Communists would be a setback of incalculable proportions to the Free World, and it obviously would also mean the loss of Iranian oil. Therefore, any solution to the oil crisis must take nationalization into account, since it was ardently desired by the Iranian people, though hopefully the British would not lose AIOC operating control. In the policy statement I had cabled to Washington from Amman (with copies to London and other capitals), I had suggested a joint statement by the United States and Britain, affirming support for a fair profit-sharing arrangement, such as a 50–50 split, as the basis for oil concessions throughout the Middle East.

I observed that the AIOC, by continuing to pursue its own commercial policy in Iran, was increasing tension rather than relieving it.

My policy plan was taken up at the Ministry of Fuel and Power on April 4, and Sir Peter E. Ramsbotham of the Foreign Office offered up the opinion that the profit-sharing principle was "here to stay." None of the objections that had been raised by the Treasury Department were insuperable, he said, although there were practical difficulties to be overcome. Ramsbotham also pointed out that a joint U.S.-U.K. action would provide the AIOC with a new negotiating basis, and he recommended joining the United States in a statement supporting "the principle of a profit-sharing arrangement," as well as some of my other proposals. I appreciated the backing of Ramsbotham (who happened to be a good friend of mine, my opposite number in the British Foreign Office twice), but there was resistance from other quarters. Some at the meeting were still opposed, for example, to public acceptance of the 50–50 formula.

Sir Roger Makins of the Treasury invited me to lunch with Sir William Fraser on April 4. It was our first meeting, but Fraser knew all too well that I had spoken critically of him to British officials, and there was tension in the air. I reviewed the issues separating Iran and the AIOC, and then Fraser replied in his gruff Scottish-accented voice: "The trouble with you, Mc-Ghee, is that you are operating on the basis of the wrong information." He then launched into a long harangue in defense of the AIOC record in Iran, and while appealing for cooperation in the Middle East, he showed he had not yet learned. "Fifty-fifty is a fine slogan," he said, "but it seems to me to be of dubious practicality."

After leaving Britain, I learned that I had caused a small furor at the upper levels of the British government. The following secret message was sent on April 6 by Foreign Secretary Morrison to Ambassador Franks in Washington:

In his talks with us McGhee was so free with his criticisms of His Majesty's Government's and the Anglo-Iranian Oil Company policy in Persia and of His Majesty's Government's policy in Egypt that we were not altogether convinced by his assurances that he had "not given anything away" in his conversations with the Persians and the Egyptians.

While I do not want to appear to be going behind Mr. McGhee's back I should like you, if you see no objection, to convey tactfully to the Secretary of State that Mr. McGhee's approach to some of our Middle East problems struck me as being a little light-hearted and that I thought it was well to tell him when he called on me that it was profoundly important that United States officials should not adumbrate policies in regard to the Middle East until we had had time to consult together and that I hoped that the United States Government would take special care to ensure that there was no crossing wires.

In his reply Franks said: "I found opportunity to convey to Acheson, while talking to him yesterday about the Persian situation, the sense of paragraph

2 of your telegram under reference. Acheson listened to what I said, but made no comment."

Upon returning to Washington, I immediately entered into formal talks with the British on developing a common policy toward Iran. They began on April 9, and the Chairman of the six-member British delegation was Ambassador Franks, who by chance had been my moral tutor at Queen's College, Oxford. The American delegation, of which I was Chairman, had 13 members, including Harold Linder, Assistant Secretary of State for Economic Affairs, and William Rountree, who was in charge of Greek-Turkish-Iranian affairs.

It was soon established that there was a large area of agreement between the United States and Britain: on the importance of Iranian oil and refining capacity to both countries; on the AIOC's special role as a source of oil and foreign exchange to the United Kingdom; and on the fact that the U.S.-U.K. response to Iranian nationalization would set a historic precedent. The British had good reason for vehemently opposing nationalization, since the AIOC concession in Iran supplied 30 percent of Anglo-Dutch oil and 100 million pounds annually to the British balance of payments. Although the United States did not have a direct stake in Iran, our sympathies were all the more sincere for having been forced to accept nationalization in Mexico, where American oil companies were paid only $14 million for their vast oil reserves.

We explained, however, that our priorities in Iran appeared to differ from those of the British. Our first concern was for the loss of Iran from the Free World, and we believed there was no hope of retaining Iran in the democratic fold without accepting at least the principle of nationalization, which the Iranians considered a fait accompli. We encouraged the British to proceed with negotiations in order to assure AIOC operational control and a suitable share of the profits. But our experience in Venezuela and Saudi Arabia had shown that a 50–50 split offered the best hope of success.

The talks were partially successful and bridged part of the gap between the two sides. The British agreed to a 50–50 profit sharing for their operations in Iran, and they made a small accommodation to nationalization. We learned in due course that at midpoint in the talks, Franks had telephoned Sir Roger Makins of the Treasury Department in London and pleaded for "imaginative latitude" in his instructions. Franks did not believe that the Foreign Office member of his delegation had made a constructive case, and he wished to show an interest in nationalization, even if it amounted to only a bow. Franks then advised us that in future oil negotiations with Iran, Britain would be represented not by the AIOC but by a British government representative.

In our final meeting on April 18, I had to inform Ambassador Franks that regretfully the accommodation to nationalization he had proposed did not meet our requirements for success. We agreed to a noncommittal communiqué terming the talks "satisfactory" to both governments, while recognizing that the issues needed to be aired elsewhere by the parties directly involved. (The Iranians had shown increasing resentment at being left out of the discussions.) The press assumed that we were at odds with the British over nationalization—not because of a leak, as the British suspected, but because the issue had been present for so long without being settled. (It was settled in Iran on May 1, 1951, when the Shah signed the nationalization law.)

The failure of the talks was a great personal disappointment, for it meant we had failed to resolve a problem that posed an imminent threat to world peace. In order to clarify our position on Iranian oil nationalization, which was being widely misinterpreted, the State Department issued a statement to the press on May 10. It read in part:

The United States is deeply concerned by the [AIOC-Iranian] dispute and the terms of arrangements which might be worked out.

In our talks with the British Government, we have expressed the opinion that arrangements should be worked out with the Iranians which give recognition to Iran's expressed desire for greater control over the benefits from the development of its petroleum resources. While the United States has not approved or disapproved the terms of any particular British proposal, it is pleased to note a sincere desire on the part of the British to negotiate with the Iranians on all outstanding issues.

We fully recognize the sovereign rights of Iran and sympathize with Iran's desire that increased benefits accrue to that country from the development of its petroleum. In talks with the Iranian Government, we have pointed out the serious effects of any unilateral cancellation of clear contractual relationships, which the United States strongly opposes. We have stressed the importance of the Iranians achieving their legitimate objectives through friendly negotiation with the other party, consistent with their international responsibilities. This would have the advantage of maintaining confidence in future commercial investments in Iran and, indeed, in the validity of contractual arrangements all over the world.

Iran has been urged, before it takes final action, to analyze carefully the practical aspects of this problem. In this connection, we have raised the question of whether or not the elimination of the established British oil company from Iran would in fact secure for Iran the greatest possible benefits. We have pointed out that the efficient production and refining of Iranian oil requires not only technical knowledge and capital but transport and marketing facilities such as those provided by the company. We have also pointed out that any uncertainty as to future availability of Iranian supplies would cause concern on the part of customers which might lead to shifts in their source of supply with a consequent decrease in revenue to Iran.

Those United States oil companies which would be best able to conduct operations such as the large-scale and complex industry in Iran have indicated to this Government that they would not in the face of unilateral action by Iran against the British company be willing to undertake operations in that country. Moreover, petroleum technicians of the number and competence required to replace those presently in Iran are not, due to extreme shortages of manpower in this specialized field, available in this country or in other countries.

The United States has repeatedly expressed its great interest in the continued independence and territorial integrity of Iran and has given and will continue to give concrete evidence of this interest.

One day, on gathering information for my memoirs in the British Archives, I ran across the following letter from Lord Franks. He later gave me permission to publish it.

British Embassy
Washington, D.C.
19th July, 1951

Dear Bowker,

I had George McGhee to dinner by himself the other night. I asked him deliberately when there was no immediate business to transact so that we could have a general talk. George, as usual, talked a good deal and left me with several pretty clear impressions which I think may be of sufficient interest to send on to you.

First of all, I have no doubt of George's own basic friendliness to Britain and support of our position in the Middle East. His support for our position springs in part from sentiment but more substantially from his belief that the United States in the foreseeable future can not and will not be ready to take over any position such as that we enjoy with the Middle East, even if on other grounds it were desirable that an attempt should be made. He is still firmly within the general lines established in the earlier conversations between Michael Wright and himself.

At the same time, George is clearly deeply impressed with the power and violence of the Nationalist movements which have grown up in the major Middle Eastern countries. He sees them as examples of a much wider movement in men's minds which affects virtually the whole of Asia apart from the Soviet-controlled countries. He believes this narrow, heady nationalism is something which has come to stay and which is very seriously to be reckoned with in any broad approach to policy in dealing with the Middle East. In this George is reflecting much more than his own personal view. I should judge that he speaks for the general opinion of the State Department.

At present George has no very clear ideas about how to deal with the countries of the Middle East, save in one respect. He believes that somehow or other we have got to get our relations with these countries on a basis of equality and do it in such a way that it is recognized by these countries that they are being treated as equals and partners. George would relate this view not merely to the rise of nationalism in the Middle East but also to the position we have all taken up in the United Nations which makes some more old-fashioned ways of dealing with these countries very difficult or impossible. Apart for [sic] this it is much more of a business to make the use of force effective. We have both been sending arms to these countries and an army with some modern guns and tanks is a much harder proposition to deal with. In all this I think George speaks for a wider body of opinion in the State Department than his own.

I think he is deeply worried about our own policies and methods of approach in the Middle East. He sees that we are much more deeply involved in the area than the Americans. He sees that what happens there matters far more to us than to them. He sees that we are in the lead and he wants to preserve that relation between the

Americans and ourselves. But he thinks if we are to preserve our interests and our position we have got somehow to be able to put a convincing new look upon our relationships with Middle Eastern countries. At present they do not feel that we come to them as equals and partners however wise and helpful we may be as guides and advisers. Without a convincing new look he fears an explosion, and in this, of course, he worries particularly about Egypt.

In the particular case of Egypt I think members of the State Department have really begun to ask themselves whether there is not a limit to the extent to which they can go along with us. For the time being they see no alternative. They do not want to have to find an alternative. But they have a depressing fear that the present course of events may lead to a situation in which they have to choose between diverging from us and losing any influence they may have on Egypt when ours is gone.

I expect that these impressions, when written down in words, are rather sharper than the state of mind they are intended to reflect. But I do not doubt their existence nor their power, if left unmodified, in the long run to affect American policy. And they have not been made less lively, though possibly more confused, by recent history in Persia and our various exchanges about the Persian oil situation.

Yours sincerely,
OLIVER FRANKS

There was yet one more postscript to the meetings over which Franks and I presided in May 1951. Alex Danchev, in his biography, *Oliver Franks, Founding Father* (1993), gives his own analysis.

In April 1951, at a relatively last stage in the protracted crisis, a series of Anglo-American talks were held in Washington in an effort to find a common platform and a decent way out. Franks, whose involvement thus far had been only peripheral, led for the British. The American side was led by George McGhee, the Assistant Secretary of State for the Near East, South Asia, and Africa, a domain he called the Middle World. To all outward appearances, the dauntless McGhee was perfect for the part of the new Roman. Just 39, oil-savvy and oil-rich himself, the Assistant Secretary's impregnable self-assurance and sharp tongue were enough to give British officials convulsions. In the privacy of their correspondence they called him, scathingly, "that infant prodigy." . . . A former Rhodes Scholar, he had spent three years as a graduate student at Queen's College, Oxford, completing his doctorate in 1937. . . . In McGhee's case, one aspect in particular left its mark. At Queen's, as at most Oxford colleges, each student has a "moral tutor" whom he would see regularly, if infrequently, and to whom he could go in case of need, moral or otherwise. McGhee was allocated to an energetic philosophy don hardly older than himself, and yet, as it seemed, infinitely knowledgeable and infinitely wise. This paragon was Father Franks. The central point about the re-encounter between Franks and McGhee over Anglo-Persian was that, of the two, it was McGhee who knew better. In reality McGhee matched none of the stereotypes for which he was so eagerly fitted in London: he was not anti-British, he was not a simple-minded anti-colonialist, and he was not (as Sir William Strang charged) an "appeaser" of Iran. He was merely the expert. Perhaps the Americans could be Greeks to their own Romans after all.

The re-encounter demonstrated something else, equally chastening for the British. By April 1951, after many months of havering by Anglo-Persian—characterized as "confused, hidebound, small-minded and blind" by their Labour Adviser, Sir Frederick Leggett—there was no decent way out.

9

Meetings with Mossadeq in 1951

Prime Minister Mossadeq of Iran (the "crying premier," as he was called, for he tended to be tearful in public) arrived in New York on October 8, 1951. He was to appear before the United Nations Security Council to answer a complaint by Great Britain on the issue of oil nationalization in Iran. But first, the tall, gaunt statesman with the enigmatic smile was taken to New York Hospital for treatment of an undisclosed ailment; it was obvious that his health was poor, and I suspected he was in a generally run-down condition. Anxious to meet Mossadeq, I came up from Washington and went straight to the hospital the evening he arrived, accompanied by Ernest Gross, our U.N. representative. With me was Lieutenant Colonel Vernon A. Walters, an accomplished linguist who would be my interpreter during 80 hours of interviews with the Prime Minister. (Mossadeq had been educated in France and Switzerland and knew French, but he spoke Farsi in our talks.)

Nearly six months had passed since the Anglo-Iranian Oil Company concession was nationalized and Dr. Mossadeq had been named premier of Iran. A month earlier than that, in March, I had visited Teheran and had begun our government's effort, made on British request, to bring about an agreement between the British and the Iranians. I had not met Mossadeq at the time, but I was given a full account of his erratic behavior by the caretaker Iranian premier, Hussein Ala, whom I had known in Washington. Ala's vivid description of the man who had led Iran in revolution against the monarchy sparked my interest in learning more.

When Mossadeq left the hospital after several days, we moved to his hotel room for our talks, first in New York and then in Washington. Most of the time, just Walters was present, with the two of us sitting on opposite sides of the foot of the 70-year-old Prime Minister's bed. I never did see him cry, possibly because when meeting with me, he was not in the public eye, but I did notice a display of emotion from time to time. What I remember best, however, is his convulsive laughter in response to his own countless jokes. I could not help but like him, for he was an intelligent man, essentially an Iranian patriot whose reasoning was somewhat warped by age and his deep suspicion of everything British. There was no way that I, an acknowledged Anglophile, could influence his attitude toward the British.

Mossadeq was quite stubborn and, as I learned from my later talks with him, his attitude probably foreclosed any bettering of British-Iranian relations and any oil agreement. No matter how hard I tried, I could not make him understand the few basic facts of life I tried to teach him about the international oil business. At the end of my lessons on economic or technical matters, he would invariably say with a smile, "I don't care about that. You don't understand. It's a political problem." He thought Britain needed both Iran and his cooperation so much that they would pay any price.

Some observers felt that Mossadeq had allied himself with the Soviet Union, as my friend Kermit Roosevelt argues in his book, *Countercoup* (which also gives an account of how Mossadeq was ultimately overthrown). There is no doubt the USSR, through the Communist Tudeh party in Iran, capitalized on the political disorder caused by the Iranian oil rebellion, and certainly the Mossadeq-led National Front was glad to accept Tudeh support. Mossadeq, however, was well aware of the Soviet threat, and as a member of the Majlis in 1947 he had courageously forced cancellation of a Soviet oil concession in northern Iran. He was first and foremost, however, a loyal Iranian. Unable to sell oil because of legal threats by the AIOC, and refused aid by the United States, he was desperate and willing to accept help from wherever it might come. He was not willing, however, to sell Iran.

Walters was more than an interpreter. (The Colonel, later General, describes my conversations with Mossadeq in his book, *Silent Missions.*) He had first met Mossadeq while a member of the mission to Teheran led by W. Averell Harriman in 1951, and he acted as a catalyst. I once told Walters I thought I might have gone a bit too far on a certain point, and he replied, "I thought so too, so I didn't translate it that way." When Mossadeq was in Washington, and we were meeting in his suite at the Shoreham Hotel, I invited him out to my farm near Middleburg. Paul Nitze, the director of the Policy Planning Staff, who participated in some of our meetings, also came along. With Walters interpreting, the Prime Minister had a spirited conversation with my farmer, a dignified, elderly gentleman whom everyone called Mr. Lloyd. Mossadeq owned a large farm in Iran, and they compared notes on crops and animals.

The British had decided that talking to Mossadeq was a hopeless exercise and were reconciled to waiting until a more amenable successor emerged. Many Americans shared this view, which probably turned out to be right, but I thought we would be remiss not to try. My task was further complicated by the fact that we could expect no firm British reaction to our compromise proposals until after a parliamentary election on October 25. I thought our best course of action was to keep Mossadeq in the United States until then, to try to educate him and be able to discuss with him any counterproposals from the new British government. This meant killing time, which the Prime Minister understood; there were endless rounds of meetings, and an invitation from President Truman to have a thorough physical exam at Walter Reed Army Medical Center. (The doctors found nothing wrong with him, other than the natural debilities of age.) Our talks continued at Walter Reed and at the Shoreham, and I finally realized that Mossadeq worked in bed because he liked to.

My talks with Mossadeq got off to a good start in New York with his appreciation for being invited to Washington. He was happy with the idea of an extended visit to the capital, preferring a delay in the pending debate before the Security Council. He preferred negotiation in an informal setting; otherwise, he would be forced to excoriate the British publicly for endangering our negotiations. We then got down to the nitty gritty of the negotiation, with Mossadeq taking the lead. On the question of oil, Mossadeq would accept an oil executive with adequate authority to run the Iranian operation, and would consider an outside firm to assure Iranian access to industry technology. However, he was anxious to start talking about nationalization with me the next morning. As I left the hospital, I felt that the weight of the world was on my shoulders.

In our first business meeting on October 9, Mossadeq offered compensation for AIOC properties equal to the aggregate market value of the company stock before nationalization. He then volunteered that former purchasers of Iranian oil would be guaranteed the same amounts they had been taking for a fixed number of years. He would not, however, answer my proposal that an existing international oil company or a consortium of companies similar to one in Iraq operate the Iranian oil industry on a fee basis. I assured him that American oil companies did not seek to replace the AIOC, since that would encourage "concession jumping" on their own properties. Besides, our government could not permit it in view of the disastrous effect it would have on U.S.-British relations. The British were our closest allies.

The climax of our talks, however, came late one evening when I noted the complications that nationalization of the AIOC's refinery in Abadan, the largest in the world, might cause. I had made the point that refineries were too complex to be run by a government agency with hired technicians. Throughout the world they were run by companies with a full range of technical competence. Mossadeq's rejoinder left me dumbfounded.

"But the refinery hasn't been nationalized."

"What do you mean?" I asked insistently. "The world thinks the Abadan refinery was in the nationalization package."

"You can't quote me," he said, "but you can take my word that it wasn't."

"If this is the case," I told Mossadeq, "there is a real possibility of coming to an agreement." I would protect his position, I assured him, but would he agree to the two of us initialing statements that the refinery had not been nationalized? He would. Walters then prepared identical affidavits in longhand, one in English and one in French, and we both initialed them. I could scarcely contain my excitement. Here in a hotel room, late at night, with only Walters present, Mossadeq had given back, via *me,* the largest oil refinery in the world. My hopes for a British-Iranian agreement soared. Later that evening, I took Walters out for the best dinner we could order at Chambord, one of New York's finest restaurants. When he voiced concern over the expense, I told him to think nothing of it. This was an evening I would never forget. I had the Abadan refinery in my pocket, and I was elated.

The next day, Mossadeq leaked word to the press that he intended to nationalize the Abadan refinery, but I took this to be his way of ensuring against being shot by an Iranian nationalist. I never doubted that he would try to live up to his commitment to me, which I kept secret except for letting the British know, orally and highly confidentially, since Mossadeq's life was at stake. He later tacitly confirmed his promise. The papers with Mossadeq's and my initials on them were put in a top-secret file in the State Department and have never been made public.

The Prime Minister addressed the U.N. Security Council on October 15, the day a British resolution to block nationalization was considered. He reviewed Iran's dealings with the AIOC, attacked the competence of the Security Council to adjudicate the issue, and offered to negotiate for oil and compensation. The debate continued for days over such issues as the jurisdiction of the International Court of Justice. It began to appear that the U.N. proceeding would be bogged down by technicalities, and Mossadeq came to refer to the Security Council as his jail.

Meanwhile, our talks in New York continued, and I flew up and back from Washington each day. By mid-October, the Prime Minister was agreeable to a compromise. It called for a National Iranian Oil Company (NIOC), a state-owned entity that would sell to consumers through any intermediary, including the AIOC. The NIOC Board would consist of three Iranians and four neutrals (but no British), and the NIOC would contract with an outside company (Shell, an Anglo-Dutch company, was acceptable) for access to technology and technicians. The NIOC would choose its technical director from a neutral country (not Britain), and payment for oil would be in either sterling or Swiss or Dutch currency. Iran would borrow the required capital from the World Bank.

On October 23, having come to Washington, Mossadeq had lunch at Blair House with President Truman, Secretary of State Dean Acheson, and Secretary of Defense Robert A. Lovett. Walters and I were present along with other State Department officials, the Iranian Ambassador, and members of his staff. Truman assured the Prime Minister that he only wanted to help Britain and Iran reach a fair settlement, and Acheson observed that AIOC operations may have constituted an interference with internal Iranian affairs. When Mossadeq complained that the United States had given little in the way of financial aid to Iran, the President said that while our total foreign aid allotments were limited, American assistance to Iran would have considerable long-term significance. Mossadeq replied that he was forced to seek financial help to prevent a situation in Iran that would endanger security and threaten world peace. Poverty and unrest were widespread in Iran.

Truman likened Iran's situation to the Great Depression in America, when 12 to 13 million people were unemployed. But owing to the programs of Roosevelt and Truman, conditions eventually improved. If Iran could settle its differences with Britain and take the necessary measures to utilize its enormous oil assets, we'd be happy to help, said the President. Acheson added that the settlement between Iran and Britain must be based on a formula that would not destroy the pattern of oil agreements around the world, and the Prime Minister agreed.

Acheson met again with Mossadeq the following day at Walter Reed Hospital, where the Prime Minister at our invitation was undergoing more tests. (Again, the doctors concluded that his problem was nothing more than advancing age.) I was also present, as were Colonel Walters and Paul Nitze. Acheson said he was soon to attend a foreign ministers' conference in Paris, and would have an opportunity to discuss an Iranian settlement with the British. He reviewed the proposals Mossadeq had submitted to me, ignoring as best he could an outburst in which Mossadeq decried the 1933 Anglo-Iranian oil agreement, which he maintained Iran had signed under duress.

Acheson commented that if, as Mossadeq had affirmed in his talks with me, the Abadan refinery could be turned over to a non-British company that would compensate the AIOC, the remaining claims and counterclaims might cancel out. Mossadeq offered not to demand payment of back revenues, if the AIOC would release Iran from further claims, and he agreed to extend the contract with the AIOC's purchasing organization to 15 years. No progress was made, however, on the price of oil. Acheson argued that, to be competitive, Iran ought to charge about $1.10 a barrel, but Mossadeq insisted on the Persian Gulf posted retail price of $1.75. Acheson lectured Mossadeq on the difference between wholesale and retail markets. He illustrated his point by citing the difference between the price of beef on the hoof at his Maryland farm of 25 cents a pound, with the retail butchers' price of 90 cents. But the Prime Minister was adamant. It was on this unfortunate note that his meeting with the Secretary ended.

In his book, *Present at the Creation,* Acheson had an amusing anecdote about Mossadeq:

> He had, I discovered later, a delightfully child-like way of sitting in a chair with his legs tucked under him, making him more of a Lob character than ever, with many and changing moods. I remember him sitting with the President and me after lunch in Blair House, his legs under him, when he dropped a mood of gay animation and, suddenly looking old and pathetic, leaned toward the President.
>
> "Mr. President," he said, "I am speaking for a very poor country—a country all desert—just sand, a few camels, a few sheep . . ."
>
> "Yes," I interrupted, "and with your oil, rather like Texas!" He burst into a delighted laugh and the whole act broke up, finished. It was a gambit that had not worked.

The terms on which we had reached agreement left a lot to be desired, but they spelled progress, particularly in light of Mossadeq's private assurance to me on the Abadan refinery. Journalist Elmer Davis, commenting in a column on my many meetings with the Prime Minister, said I should be awarded the Nobel Peace Prize if I succeeded in reaching an agreement. Unfortunately, I didn't.

Briefly, our proposed settlement stipulated that Iranian oil management would be placed in the hands of the National Iranian Oil Company, which would be responsible for the exploration, production, and transportation of crude oil. The Abadan refinery would be sold to a non-British company, which could be the Anglo-Dutch Shell Oil Company, and which could use either its own technicians or those supplied by Iran. The refinery would be run on a cost-plus basis, with the profit or fee established by Iran and the AIOC purchasing organization. A smaller refinery at Kermanshah would be owned and operated by the NIOC for the Iranian market.

Marketing would be the responsibility of the AIOC, which would establish a purchasing unit to supply Iranian oil to customers who requested shipments in writing. The contract with the purchasing unit would be for 15 years and a minimum of 30 million tons annually. Iranians would be entitled to up to 1 million tons of oil a year at cost plus a reasonable profit. The NIOC could market oil in excess of that required by the AIOC purchasing unit, at prices that would not prejudice the unit's long-term contracts.

The price of oil would be set by the Iranian and British governments, assisted by our government, with an understanding that periodic adjustments be made to stay abreast of changing world prices. Payments would be in sterling, with the NIOC paying all costs of production and transportation. All claims and counterclaims left over from past operations would be canceled, and the price paid by the purchasing unit for oil would not exceed

$1.10 a barrel. (Mossadeq's final willingness to concede on price was considered a major breakthrough.)

I and my State Department colleagues had been optimistic about the prospect of approval until we encountered the attitudes of the new Conservative government in Britain. Neither Prime Minister Winston Churchill nor Foreign Secretary Anthony Eden, who had been out of government for a while, was familiar with the Iranian issue. Since they had been critical of the Labour government's attempts to compromise with Mossadeq, it was politically difficult for them to do so. In any event, the British leaders decided they could never reach a suitable deal with Mossadeq, and that an unsuccessful effort would only serve to strengthen him. So they decided to await his fall in the hope that his successor would be more tractable.

Eden gained experience in dealing with Iran as Under Secretary of the Foreign Office in 1933, when the Anglo-Iranian oil agreement was signed. Having visited Iran in 1948 as a member of the opposition, he warned Sir Stafford Cripps, the Chancellor of the Exchequer, of possible trouble because of decreased oil payments to Iran. When Eden returned to power, he said he was determined to reach an accommodation with Iran but one based on "fixed principles." These principles, which he proposed to Acheson when they met in Paris on November 4, 1951, included fair compensation to be agreed upon between the parties or by arbitration; security for the payment of compensation, which he understood could only be paid in oil; denial to Iran of any more favorable terms than those accorded concessionary governments who respected their contracts; and refusal to negotiate on the basis of discrimination against U.K. nationals.

During five discussions, Acheson urged Eden to accept the compromise he and I had reached with Mossadeq as the basis for further negotiations, but Eden stood firm, refusing to accept the argument, as he wrote in his memoirs, "that the only alternative to Mossadeq was communist rule." He would not accept the exclusion of British technicians in Iran, and he opposed handing over a valuable asset on the basis of "confiscation without compensation." For his part, Acheson rejected Eden's proposal that American oil companies participate in Iran. Both Acheson and Eden agreed that Mossadeq should not be encouraged to remain in Washington any longer.

Paul Nitze and I, along with others involved in the negotiations, were waiting in the State Department communications room when Acheson returned to our Paris Embassy from the final luncheon discussion. Eden wouldn't buy it, Acheson said succinctly. The Foreign Minister had thanked us for our efforts; he sent me a personal message of thanks. But, he could not accept our proposal and didn't want to negotiate any further. He asked us to tell Mossadeq that the deal was off. My associates were silent, knowing I was crestfallen.

I requested an appointment with the Prime Minister, and when I entered his bedroom at the Shoreham, he said, "You've come to send me home."

"Yes," I said. "I'm sorry to have to tell you that we can't bridge the gap between you and the British. It's a great disappointment to us as it must be to you."

He accepted my message quietly, with no recriminations.

On November 13, the State Department issued a statement admitting our failure in breaking the stalemate in Iran: "While progress has been made, no new basis has emerged on which a practicable solution could be reached." The next day, Mossadeq announced in a speech at the National Press Club that he was asking the United States for a loan to keep his country from being paralyzed, and a State Department spokesman said his request would be given every consideration. On November 18, the Prime Minister left Washington for Teheran.

Only a miracle saved Iran from the disaster that had threatened since the assassination of Ali Razmara in March 1951. With all oil revenues cut off by the AIOC, economic ills caused erosion of Mossadeq's support, and his authoritarian ways alienated many members of the Majlis. In August 1953, when the Shah attempted to replace him, Mossadeq responded by deposing the Shah and forcing him into exile. After several days of chaos, the army rallied in support of the Shah and arrested Mossadeq. He was convicted of treason and sentenced to prison. He served three years before being allowed to return to his farm; he lived in banishment until his death at the ripe old age of 90.

Mossadeq failed because of his own limitations; he did not take advantage of his success in freeing Iran from foreign domination. Largely because he was prevented by AIOC from selling Iranian oil, he was unable to improve the economy and establish the base for a democratic society. However, Mossadeq will, I believe, always be revered by Iranians as the "father" of their country.

The author with Willy Brandt, mayor of Berlin, 1963

President John F. Kennedy during his visit to Berlin for his "Ich bin ein Berliner" speech, with the author, General Lucius Clay, and General James Polk, 1963

Chancellor Konrad Adenauer at a reception in the American Embassy in Bonn with the author, Mrs. McGhee, an aide, and Vice Chancellor Erich Mende, 1967

The author and Mrs. McGhee welcome SACEUR of NATO General Dwight D. Eisenhower during a visit to Ankara, 1952

The author overlooking the Berlin Wall, 1963

The author inspecting a German brigade with General James Polk on his right, 1964

General Curtis LeMay awards the author the Legion of Merit with three Battle Stars, 1945

The author at his desk as Ambassador to Bonn, 1963

President John F. Kennedy confers with the author, 1962

The author with Emperor Haile Selassie of Ethiopia in Addis Ababa, 1950

Prime Minister Jawaharlal Nehru with the author in New Delhi, 1949

10

Ambassador to Turkey:
1951–1953

My appointment as Ambassador to Turkey had come in December 1951, when Ambassador George Wadsworth announced his retirement and President Truman named me as his replacement. I also succeeded Wadsworth as chief of the U.S. Aid Mission to Turkey. It represented a most interesting challenge for me, which I had requested. Although I regretted leaving my post as Assistant Secretary, the idea of complementing my Washington experience with a mission of my own was appealing. Given my close involvement with Turkey during the preceding four years, Ankara was a welcome posting. I looked forward to assisting Turkey in its accession to NATO and to doing everything possible to facilitate U.S. assistance in building up Turkey's military contribution to NATO and Middle East defense.

Soon after my arrival, I was present in the visitors' balcony of the old Turkish Parliament building when the Majlis voted unanimously, with one abstention, to accept the invitation to join NATO. I often wondered what happened to the member who abstained. The vote was more remarkable in that 18 U.S. senators had opposed America's entry into NATO, including Robert Taft. I was, of course, jubilant. My tour as Ambassador had been given a good start. The Turks were very much aware of my efforts as Assistant Secretary to help them gain entry into the select organization they had coveted so ardently.

My first Turkish contact was with President Bayar when I presented my credentials. Already in his late 60s, Bayar was one of Turkey's most respected elder statesmen. He had been a close associate of Ataturk. In 1946, with President Isiner Inonu's approval, he formed the opposition Democratic party and, with the party's victory in 1950, was elected President. I had been greatly impressed by Bayar's sincerity, friendliness, and sound judgment during my meetings with him during earlier visits and was to enjoy a close association with him. Bayar was a neighbor in Cankaya, a suburb of Ankara, where his official residence was next to the Embassy residence. There were friendly greetings as he walked in his garden. Through his interpreter, he often spoke with our children when they were playing nearby.

On one very pleasant occasion which provided an interesting insight into his personal life, he invited my wife and me to join him for a convivial weekend cruise on a private yacht on the Marmora Sea. We were the only foreign guests. Present also were his daughter, Prime Minister Adnan Menderes, and President of the Grand National Assembly Refik Koraltan, with whom I had a number of interesting conversations. Our host for the cruise was a political supporter of the President, who provided pleasant amenities, drawing the group together at drink and meal times. I particularly enjoyed the opportunity for informal talks with Menderes, who spoke excellent English. On one occasion when the boat was anchored, Menderes, who was in a bathing suit, plunged into the sea without any announcement and swam with a strong breast stroke the considerable distance in a choppy sea to a nearby deserted beach. Feeling challenged, after appraising the distance with no little apprehension, I followed him and we continued our conversation lying comfortably on the sand.

Soon after my arrival in Turkey, I had also called on Menderes, for whom I had developed a high regard over the past few years. A wealthy landowner from western Turkey, Menderes had attended an American college and had served in the Grand National Assembly under Ataturk before joining with Bayar in founding the Democratic party. At 51, Menderes was a handsome, articulate, and confident leader; unfortunately, he would become a victim of the revolutionary colonels during the 1960 coup.

Finally, I made a brief courtesy call on the official who would be my normal point of contact as ambassador. Foreign Minister Mehmet Fuad Koprulu, then 61, had begun his career as a distinguished intellectual, serving as professor of history and writer at the School of Political Science and the Academy of Fine Arts in Istanbul. Turning to politics in 1935, Koprulu was elected to the National Assembly; he was a founding member of the Democratic party and had come to the Foreign Ministry following the 1950 election.

A short, wiry man with graying hair and a friendly smile, Koprulu was still very much the scholar, possessing a keen mind and articulate views on any important issue touching on Turkish or Middle Eastern history and politics. I had particularly looked forward to doing diplomatic business with Koprulu and learning from his vast store of knowledge of the region. During our meetings I inconspicuously took copious notes, which permitted me to reconstruct our conversations nearly verbatim.

I began my first official meeting with Koprulu on January 8, 1952, by expressing my hope that we could develop close and early consultation between our two governments and coordinate our actions regarding major world events, particularly in the Middle East. I mentioned the usefulness of the consultations our governments had held on Iran, the Middle East Command, and Korea, telling Koprulu that I hoped this type of consultation could take place on a regular basis. He expressed agreement and said he would welcome a more consistent exchange of information and analysis between the United States and Turkey.

I also suggested that we broaden our cooperation beyond the field of security. I noted that the broader the base of our relations, the better the chance that any unforeseen difficulties that might arise could be overcome. To this end, I suggested cultural and information exchanges and a closer working relationship between the large number of American personnel working in Turkey and the Turkish government, institutions, and people. Again, the foreign minister expressed full agreement with my formulations.

My talk with Turkey's foreign minister also covered the evolution of thinking regarding U.S. aid programs. I explained to him that the new emphasis in the U.S. Mutual Security Program was on military rather than economic aid. Congress had placed importance on short-term and military projects, making it more difficult to justify such long-term projects as dams, whose impact on the economy could not be felt for several years. I mentioned to Koprulu that I was aware of talk in Turkey that the level of U.S. economic aid was unsatisfactorily low, and I suggested that he and others in the government might point out to critics that Turkey was the only European country to receive large-scale development assistance, for Marshall Plan aid had been conceived to help economies devastated by war. I also assured him that the United States would provide Turkey with as much aid as possible to help achieve our common objectives. He requested that I return the following week, so that we could discuss economic questions in more detail with Secretary General Fatin Zorlu present.

Koprulu suggested we focus on ways to encourage American capital to invest in Turkey, on the policy and organizational aspects of the new Mutual Security Program, and on the means to make current U.S. economic aid more effective. I began the meeting by explaining that I understood that, although unfettered free enterprise worked successfully in the United States, in some countries, at various stages of development, state initiative might be useful or even necessary. I was aware of Ataturk's initial use of etatism in the development of the Turkish economy. Since his original efforts to solicit private investment had failed, it could be said that he had no alternative. Turkey's Democratic party had come to power on a platform of encouraging free enterprise, and I told the two Turkish leaders that the progress that had been achieved thus far was heartening. I felt that Turkey, with its great resources of arable land, minerals, and energetic people, stood a good chance of developing a free-enterprise market system in which the country as a whole could prosper. However, certain steps needed to be taken.

Along with resources and people, another important variable was the extent to which the government created a framework for economic freedom. In the past the Turks had not been great traders or industrialists, but, I noted, this trend seemed to be changing in recent years. I told Koprulu that in order to encourage American investment in Turkey, the government should demonstrate the importance it attached to success in business, perhaps by passing legislation that would further liberalize the business environment or by bringing successful businessmen into key government positions.

Another requisite, of course, was the availability of capital—which was one area in which the United States might be able to play a role. With the exception of the Soviet Union, I observed, no country had developed a large industrial plant without the assistance of foreign, private capital. Although loans from governments could play a certain role, they were never sufficient to meet the needs of industrializing countries. Since the war, I explained, private American capital had been available mainly from companies that invested their surplus funds in foreign ventures in their own field. However, an advantageous pattern of partnership between American companies and local business groups had developed and had brought capital, management skills, and technology into the country.

The United States, I pointed out, was itself the strongest competitor for American capital, for it was still developing, and great profits could be made at home without considering foreign investment. Nonetheless, I noted that several American firms had recently invested in Turkey and others had expressed an interest, such as the Anderson and Clayton Company, a leading cotton processing and sales organization. As U.S. firms began to enter Turkey, if their experience was positive, other firms would follow.

Koprulu, who had at various times during the conversation indicated approval of my remarks, spoke up at this point to say that the Democratic party was in agreement with the analysis I had laid out and was doing everything in its power to free up the business environment, including a law passed to encourage foreign investment. There was virtually no competition from the government in the form of state firms, although he acknowledged that some members of government, particularly in the government investment banks, still held on to notions of etatism. He asked what else I thought could be done to encourage foreign investment.

Turkey could take a number of measures that had proved successful in other countries, I suggested, and I gave the following examples: the United States and Turkey could conclude a Treaty of Friendship, Commerce, and Navigation; exchange visits of leading industrialists could be arranged on invitation by the two governments; a joint commission of Turkish and

American industrialists could be formed; and a publicity effort could be made in the U.S. media. The Turkish Ambassador in Washington could make speeches on business in Turkey, and I could make similar speeches or write articles about opportunities there. Koprulu agreed that such steps should be taken. Later, U.S. firms in Turkey made considerable progress in the pharmaceutical and electric light bulb industries and in petroleum production, refining, and marketing.

During May 6–8, 1952, I had the opportunity to discuss a broader Turkish role in Middle Eastern affairs and development of Turkey's economy with President Bayar, when I was invited to travel with him on his official train to observe the military exercises at the Cankari Infantry School. The trip provided a pleasant atmosphere for the informal discussions that developed naturally.

I began by suggesting that Turkey should be able to play a leadership role in the Middle East analogous to that of the United States with Latin America. I pointed out that, whereas these countries had previously distrusted the United States, we had now developed an important degree of cooperation throughout the inter-American system. Turkey, I said to Bayar, should, in light of its historical role, military strength, political stability, economic development, and membership in NATO, consider pursuing a Good Neighbor Policy in the Middle East, as we had in Latin America.

In our meeting the next day Bayar told me that he believed my arguments might have some merit. He acknowledged that Turkey had in recent years largely ignored the Middle East, as the country put efforts into strengthening ties with the West and joining NATO. The Middle Eastern countries were militarily weak, and he spoke of them with a certain degree of disdain. He agreed, however, that now that Turkey had achieved its main objectives, it might be time to put some effort into its relations with the states of the Middle East.

When we came to the matter of the development of Turkey, I suggested that Turkey had great economic potential because of the country's high ratio of undeveloped land and mineral resources to population (at that time 21 million). In my judgment, only Brazil offered similar possibilities for development.

The President agreed. He believed that Turkey's development could best be achieved by increasing its agricultural production and its value through processing to as advanced a degree as possible. It was on this policy that he had based the Democratic party's economic program, in contrast with the previous government, which had artificially encouraged the development of industry.

I pointed out that U.S. development had been based largely on agriculture, particularly in the South, where the cash crop had been cotton. Industry had developed naturally out of consumer demands created by the agricultural income. I commented, however, that I believed the time had also come in Turkey for light consumer industries to help fill the rising demand for such goods, combat inflation, and save Turkey's scarce foreign exchange. I mentioned the new Squibb pharmaceutical plant and the General Electric light bulb plant, in which cases U.S. capital had participated along with Turkish capital. I expressed the hope that other U.S. firms would make similar investments.

How many people, I asked the President, did he think Turkey could ultimately support? He replied, 50 million. (Turkey's population is currently over 70 million.) If so, this would put Turkey's resource base on a bar with that of any country in Europe, except a united Germany. If Turkey's current rate of agricultural production and industrialization were to continue at about 8 percent annually, its economic potential by the time its population reached 50 million would correspond to that of the major Western powers (whose populations have increased little compared with the larger increase in their economies).

The strengthening and broadening of ties between Turkey and the United States that was occurring in 1951 continued. On several occasions I had casual discussions with high-level Turkish officials on how Turkey might develop its stagnant oil industry. One day President Bayar mysteriously mentioned that he would like to invite me to discuss a "certain matter." Finally, on May 28 he asked me to tea at the Marmara Kiosk of Cifik Farm, an experimental farm originally established by Ataturk. When I arrived, I found not only Bayar but also Menderes and Koprulu—the three highest Turkish officials—and an interpreter. I had never met with all three together; I was very surprised—and apprehensive. I was not certain what the matter in question would be. Perhaps I had made some gaffe, or they wished to bring up some urgent and serious problem in U.S.-Turkish relations. I guessed it might have to do with petroleum, and as it turned out, I was right.

President Bayar opened the meeting by recalling that Turkey had been exploring for oil for nearly 30 years, with relatively little success. Petroleum deposits had been found in the Ramandag area, near the border with Syria, but the other two areas where oil was believed to exist had proved too difficult for the Turks to explore. He said the government believed it to be in the country's national and strategic interest to seek the assistance of U.S. oil companies to ensure that Turkey would have access to indigenous oil. He acknowledged that Turkey possessed neither the capital nor the technical knowledge to discover its oil and said that the country was willing to allow foreign companies to enter the market, even if this meant their earning large profits.

Having already given the matter some thought, I told Bayar that I would like to respond to his inquiry in two different capacities—first as an oil man, which I was, and a friend of Turkey, and second as the U.S. Ambassador. As an independent oil man in Texas, I had had no ties with the U.S. international oil companies with whom I had competed, and hence no conflict of interest. It was certainly true that Turkey needed to have access to its own supply of oil if the country hoped to continue on its path toward industrialization. Petroleum had become one of the sinews of the modern state; the United States had been able to develop rapidly in part because of the availability of cheap oil. At present, oil imports were costing Turkey some $50 million a year of its scarce foreign exchange. If the country continued to grow and develop at the rate Bayar foresaw, its petroleum requirements would become an even greater drain on the economy.

Developing a petroleum industry, however, is quite different from developing other mineral resources. Usually, mineral deposits can be quantified, and the quality of the deposits can be evaluated before the expenditure of large amounts of capital is required. With oil, that is not the case. Most commercially viable deposits are found only through heavy capital investment in exploration and exploratory drilling. Although the large international oil companies, mostly U.S., British, and British-Dutch, have access to these large sums, most countries find it difficult to obtain the necessary capital. Even then, there is the further question of whether a country is justified in spending public funds on such a risky undertaking as oil exploration.

In most countries that were then enjoying a large income from oil, such as Venezuela (which earned $360 million a year), Saudi Arabia (which earned $150 million), and Kuwait and Iraq (which earned $100 million), production was in the hands of private international oil companies, which generally had been able to work quite well with the host country. In countries such as Chile, Argentina, and Brazil, which for political reasons had attempted to develop their own oil industries, the operations had been unsuccessful. All of those countries continue to be oil importers, despite excellent prospects.

I shared with Bayar, Menderes, and Koprulu my own geologist's opinion of Turkey's prospects for oil exploration. Turkey was largely mountainous, which was not favorable for oil. The two oil fields that had been discovered in the Ramandag area were not strong producers, and the oil that was produced there was of low quality compared with the oil from other Middle Eastern countries. The Adana-Iskenderun area, however, showed much more promise; seepages contained good quality, high-gravity petroleum, and a location desirable from the standpoint of sea transport to consumption centers. I myself and, as I believed, U.S. companies also would be interested in exploring in the Adana-Iskenderun area, as well as in the other areas where geological conditions, though requiring more exploration, appeared favorable.

Finally, in my capacity as U.S. Ambassador to Turkey, I told them that if the Turkish government approached me formally with President Bayar's proposal, my government would do all it could to help Turkey develop its oil resources. We would expect Turkey to do this by inviting competition among all qualified companies, regardless of nationality. Indigenous oil production not only would assist Turkish economic development but might also be available for export to other countries, ensuring that Turkey would not be cut off from petroleum supplies in time of war.

I informed the group that the normal procedure under the circumstances would be for Turkey to pass the necessary legislation (called a petroleum law), as other nations had done, prescribing conditions under which private companies could acquire rights to explore for, produce, refine, and market oil in Turkey. Broadly speaking, I said, the basis for foreign participation, starting in Venezuela and spreading to Saudi Arabia and other countries, would be on a 50–50 division of profits with the host country.

If their law was competitive with those in other countries, I was sure that many oil companies, including the major U.S. companies, had a favorable enough view of Turkey's oil prospects to seek participation. The first step the Turkish government must take was to hire one of the international consulting firms specializing in petroleum laws. We would be happy to furnish a list of reputable firms, which could be checked and augmented by their own embassies and experts. Once such a law was passed, I believed the oil companies would be knocking at their door.

At the end of the conversation, President Bayar declared that I could consider that he had approached me about this matter in my capacity as U.S. Ambassador and that he had made his proposals in order that they be communicated to the U.S. government. Although it was several years before the Turkish Majlis passed a suitable petroleum law, based on the recommendation of a Denver-based consulting firm that had drafted the corresponding Israeli law, there was an immediate response from the world's oil companies.

The first wave of exploration involved private investments of more than $100 million. Unfortunately for Turkey, the results were not as favorable as had been anticipated. Mobil Oil made a sizable find near Adana in southeast Turkey, but only Shell Oil discovered enough resources to make appreciable net profits. At the peak of production only about 30 percent of Turkey's requirements were met. Nevertheless, Turkey saved what it would have spent in exploration, and the funds expended by the companies for this purpose were much greater and were more expertly applied. The results did alleviate, if not eliminate, Turkey's oil-shortage foreign exchange drain.

Around this time, members of Turkey's administration were invited to take a cruise with units of the U.S. Sixth Fleet in the interest of increasing good will on their part and demonstrating the striking power of the Sixth Fleet and the support it could give Turkey in the event of war. The party boarded the aircraft carrier *Wasp* on August 6, and President Bayar was given a 21-gun salute by all units of the Sixth Fleet.

As it turned out, the visit provided the setting for some important top-level discussions regarding Turkey's role in Middle East defense. I began the informal talks with Bayar and Menderes by volunteering my opinion that Turkey had a strong tendency to underplay its position in the Middle East—in relations to the countries of the region and with outside powers as well. President Bayar responded immediately, agreeing that Turkey had been "timid" in its relations with other nations. He explained that this stance had resulted from the foreign policy inherited from the Republican party which, through its embarrassment in not having lived up to its commitments during World War II, had not wanted Turkey to assert itself in foreign policy since that time. Even recently, Bayar pointed out, the Republicans had opposed some government initiatives, such as the decision to send troops to Korea.

Nonetheless, Bayar said, the Turkish government had taken steps to improve relations with other Middle Eastern countries: some of their leaders, including King Abdullah of Jordan, had accepted invitations to visit Turkey. Many of the visits, however, including that of the foreign minister of Egypt, had not materialized. The Shah of Iran had at one point shown interest in Turkey as a model for progress in Iran, and Bayar had visited the country himself and would be willing to do so again, he added, if it would be useful. According to Bayar, the Shah had not gone as far as Turkey had gone, and in not carrying through, the Shah's revolution had been unsuccessful.

Both leaders agreed that it was important for Turkey to establish closer relations with the Arab states in order to exercise a positive influence over them. However, they said, the government—particularly the foreign minister—was adopting a cautious stance, waiting for the opportune moment. As I knew from previous conversations, Koprulu was also concerned over what he perceived to be French and British opposition to Turkish efforts in the Middle East.

My experience in Middle Eastern affairs, I told the two, had led me to the conclusion that the "right moment" to make any particular constructive move in the Middle East would probably never come. That was why the United States had pursued its initiatives more or less on its own, sometimes in spite of British, and particularly French, reluctance to accept U.S. involvement in what they considered to be their spheres of influence. Although some of our efforts had not been as successful as we would have liked, I felt they had at least facilitated some progress toward stability in the region. I suggested to Bayar and Menderes that Turkey might take the initial step by making some sort of public gesture that would demonstrate Turkish sympathy and understanding for the Arab cause.

On March 4, 1952, Turkey was honored by an official visit by General Dwight D. Eisenhower, in his capacity as NATO commander. Eisenhower displayed his usual friendly and engaging personality. During their talks, in which I participated, Eisenhower and President Bayar focused mainly on

Turkey's role in NATO. Eisenhower told Bayar that his sword was longer and stronger as a result of Turkey's admission to NATO and that he looked forward to working closely with Turkish military authorities. After his earlier conversations, he foresaw no difficulties in Turkey's active involvement in NATO, and he added that he hoped to maintain close liaison between NATO headquarters and the Turks. He assured Bayar that he would be particularly mindful of any logistical problems that Turkey might be facing.

To that end, Eisenhower said, he would request periodic reports on Turkey's economic situation in order to avoid jeopardizing Turkey's military efforts. Bayar paid a tribute to American economic and military aid to Turkey. As a result of the large-scale importation of American tractors, Turkey had for the first time become an exporter of wheat—up to 100,000 tons annually. The visit was a brief one, but Bayar and Eisenhower got on well and the trip further cemented Turkish relations with NATO and the United States.

Despite a grueling schedule, Eisenhower, in his usual thoughtful way, came to the Embassy after an official dinner to meet and chat with the Embassy personnel. This was a great treat for all of us. He was particularly attentive to my young son George and invited him to accompany him on his plane to Istanbul the next day. When he said goodbye to George, he asked for a sheet of paper. "When I get back to Paris I will send you my picture," he promised, writing on the paper, "George, if I don't send you my picture, the next time you see me you can hit me." It was something George will never forget, illustrating the personable quality that so endeared Eisenhower to the American people.

The presidential campaign of 1952 turned out to be one of the most bitter in American history. General Dwight D. Eisenhower, who had retired from the Army after giving up his position as NATO commander, won the presidency with Richard Nixon as his running mate. They scored an easy win against former governor of Illinois Adlai E. Stevenson. The new Secretary of State-designate John Foster Dulles had been particularly critical of the State Department on the issue of anticommunism, threatening widespread dismissals. Although I had entered the Department at the lowest civil service level and had never, after abandoning an interest to run for Congress after retiring from the Navy, played any active role in politics, I voted, as a Texan, Democratic.

When the Republican victory was announced, I wrote a "Dear Foster" letter to Dulles, whom I knew well from his assignment in the State Department and as a neighbor in Washington. I explained that I did not consider myself a political appointee, that I enjoyed and considered Turkey an important post, and that I very much wanted to remain there until I completed a normal tour. In reply I received a short "Dear George" letter stating that since he knew I would like him to be frank with me the policy of the new administration would be to remove all Democrats who were not Foreign Service officers. I was not surprised, but still it was a very hard blow.

As time went on, however, after Eisenhower became president no further word came to me. Hank Byrode, my successor as Assistant Secretary for NEA (Near East, South Asia, and Africa), later wrote me a letter saying he tried hard to save me and at one time thought he would be able to, but he had ultimately failed. I advised him that if I was to be relieved I would like to remain until after my four children's school year ended. Suddenly, one day, I received word that at Nelson Rockefeller's insistence Avra Warren, a career officer who was then Ambassador to Pakistan, was to relieve me. As a last try, I picked up the phone and called my friend Dean Rusk, then president of the Rockefeller Foundation, explaining my situation. He replied tersely as was his custom, that he was lunching with Nelson and would see what he could do. Later Dean told me that Nelson had said that he had given $25,000 to the Republican campaign and that the only thing he had asked for was this post for Avra, who had at personal risk given him invaluable assistance in reaching agreement on the United Nations Charter in the San Francisco preparatory meeting. He had nothing against me.

When the Eisenhower administration came into office in 1953, it undertook a comprehensive survey of existing national security policy, particularly in the Middle East where little progress had been made in building an adequate security system. Pursuant to this review, Secretary of State John Foster Dulles—accompanied by former Governor Harold Stassen, director of the Mutual Security Agency, and a considerable staff—made a visit to the key Middle Eastern and South Asian countries in the Spring of 1953. The group arrived in Ankara in late May 1953. Dulles and Stassen stayed at the Embassy residence, where I and the staff took good care of them.

Since Dulles was in the position of having relieved me and of having criticized sharply the policies of our superiors in Washington and the Foreign Service as a whole, relations between us were rather cool. He agreed rather reluctantly to address our Embassy staff. In his remarks he spent most of the time explaining why he was just the man to be Secretary of State in such a difficult time, both because of his vast experience and his heritage from antecedents in high positions in the Department. Condescendingly, he assured the staff that he did not consider all Foreign Service officers disloyal. The atmosphere in the Embassy auditorium was palpably tense.

I and the staff briefed Dulles and Stassen for their meetings later in the day with Prime Minister Menderes and President Bayar on security matters. Dulles was restive and broke up the meeting after a short time, explaining that he had to cut the meeting short because I had arranged an interview for him with the *New York Times* representative (which actually had not been set for any particular time). In this interview later in the day, Dulles unveiled his "Northern Tier" concept of the Middle East defense. It was obvious that this policy decision had been greatly influenced by his meetings with the Turkish leaders. The *Times* article that resulted from his interview was unfavorable to his proposal, as was the general American Jewish reaction.

Upon his return from the area in mid-June, Dulles announced his overall conclusions regarding the security of the area, some of which were not surprising but others of which implied new directions since his Ankara interview. Dulles recognized the continuing Soviet pressures and threat of aggression to which the Middle East was subject. He concluded that any sound defense of the area must be a result of the wishes of the people and governments of the various countries of the region, most of which were not willing to be associated with the West in a defense organization. The states of the "Northern Tier" (those bordering the USSR), he concluded, that best understood the Soviet threat would be most likely to do something about it and were in the best position to protect the area as a whole. The cornerstone of any such alignment could only be Turkey—the strongest state in the region and the only NATO member.

In accordance with tradition and as part of a general reshuffle of Ambassadors to reflect the sharp differences of the new Eisenhower administration's foreign policy, on June 19, 1953, I resigned my post as Ambassador to Turkey (as I had been asked to) to return to private life. My final telegram to the State Department reflected my views on the state in which the proposed Middle East Defense Organization (MEDO) was left after more than two years of discussions. I emphasized the importance of a prompt clarification of the U.S. position on Middle East defense. Continued uncertainty, I stressed, would lead to growing differences among the sponsoring powers and would fuel speculation that Turkey and the United States had a serious divergence of opinion. The Turks' real concern, especially after Dulles' speech, I pointed out, was that the United States was willing to wait indefinitely for the Arabs to agree to a defense organization. Because they were skeptical that such an agreement would ever be forthcoming, the Turkish authorities wished to move ahead, along with the Americans and the British, in order to close the dangerous security gap in the Middle East as quickly as possible.

Since such an approach could greatly anger the Arab states, however, it would evidently not further the U.S. political objective of collaboration with the countries of the Middle East. Therefore, I suggested, as I had to Koprulu, that perhaps the United States should support covert ongoing talks and planning between Turkey, Great Britain, and the United States—the three powers that actually had military forces in the area. This could help perpetuate the concept of MEDO and thereby calm Turkish anxieties, while at the same time avoiding a direct flaunting of Arab will.

In 1958 President Eisenhower appointed me to two very important posts: member of the President's Committee to Study the United States Military Assistance Program and consultant to the National Security Council. It was a great boost to my morale to return to the top echelons of government, and it gave me hope that I would some day come back again officially, as indeed I would just three years later. Bill Draper, a close friend whom I had seen a great deal of since Marshall Plan days, chaired the Military Assistance Committee, a stimulating two-year project that frequently brought me to Washington from Dallas.

The Committee itself included a number of high officials: Dillon Anderson, Joseph M. Dodge, Alfred M. Gruenther, Marx Leva, John J. McCloy, Joseph T. McNarney, Arthur W. Radford, and James E. Webb. The two committee reports, the second on Economic Assistance which Draper had added to his assignment, laid out a much needed balance to the two related programs, resulting in an increase in the military side to redress a bad name that it had collected. According to the Summary of the Military Report:

The Communist military threat is greater than ever. The Communist economic and political threat and capabilities are expanding. The average level of expenditure needed for military assistance over the next few years is, in the judgment of the Committee, not likely to be less, as an order of magnitude, than that required in the recent past. To reduce the program drastically would imply a strategic retreat. The Committee recommends that approximately $400 million be made available for new commitments, primarily for the NATO area, in addition to the $1.6 billion present request. This should not change significantly the estimated expenditures in Fiscal Year 1960.

The proposed economic assistance program for Fiscal Year 1960 is the minimum needed. In fact, a level of lending for economic development under the Mutual Security Program at a rate of at least $1 billion a year will probably be needed by Fiscal Year 1961. The Mutual Security Program is now and will remain an essential tool of foreign policy. Accordingly, the Committee proposes that the Congress and the Executive Branch take the necessary legislative and administrative steps to put the Mutual Security Program on a continuing basis. Specific recommendations will be made in our final report.

Admiral Arthur Radford and I had been the Middle East Subcommittee of the full Committee. The principal countries that we inspected as we traveled through the Middle East were Iran and Pakistan. The Military Report recognized that:

Our mutual defense effort in less developed countries in direct contact with Communist forces is particularly difficult, though vital to them and to ourselves. Unless these countries have adequate holding forces, they cannot hope for timely help short of the most drastic military action by their allies. Situated on the front line and with examples of recent Communist aggression in mind, their leadership, with which we live on a cooperative basis, wants to have the forces they judge adequate to their particular circumstances. Without the weapons and support we have furnished to the SEATO and Baghdad Pact nations adjacent to the Communist bloc, their own direct defenses and our own position beyond our shores would have little substance short of a major nuclear effort.

In October 1958, General Mohammed Ayub Khan took over power in Pakistan following a coup. I happened to be in Pakistan with Admiral Radford at that time on a visit as the Middle East Subcommittee. Ayub Khan, with whom Radford had had a close association, invited us to join a dinner that turned out to be the first meeting of his new cabinet. Also present was Aly Khan, son of Aga Khan, who was at the time the Pakistan U.N. representative. As we sat down to dinner one of the younger cabinet members remarked jokingly, "Look at us. There are those who say we are dictators. How could anyone possibly believe that who knows us?" Pakistan, however, has never really had a democratic government since.

President Eisenhower did not accept the report's recommendations on the population problem, which Draper had insisted on adding as the key to a successful economic assistance program for the developing world. Draper, who had expected approval, was greatly disappointed. A U.S. policy on this vital question would not be forthcoming until the Kennedy administration, in which I happily played a role. Based on a thorough study by the Policy Planning staff, we persuaded Kennedy, even though he was a Catholic, to get $35 million from Congress as the first expropriation for population planning and to arrange support for the first such effort in the United Nations. I later became an active member of Draper's Population Crisis Committee.

One day in 1960 I received a call in Dallas from Dean Rusk, who had been involved in most of my previous assignments.

"George," he said, "You may not have seen in the newspapers that the President has asked me to be Secretary of State. I want you to come up and help me get the new Department started."

"Well, Dean," I replied, "It's pretty late today. I'll be up tomorrow."

Dean and I started with two adjoining rooms in the basement of the State Department, where he began the longest Secretaryship in modern history, and I started eight more years of diplomacy which would furnish a rewarding climax to my many years of public service.

_**11**_

The Kennedy Administration
Takes Over: 1961–1963

Before the Kennedy administration came into office, I worked with Secretary-designate Rusk, helping prepare him and the new President to assume power. I helped Dean decide on top Department jobs and ambassadors, and briefed him on current U.S. international problems and what might be done about them. As was usual when a new administration takes over, he was besieged by callers seeking jobs and offering gratuitous advice. Gradually he accumulated additional staff.

The country that posed the most threatening problem at that time, to which I devoted particular attention in preparation for Rusk's first meeting with Kennedy and Eisenhower, was Laos. Rusk had organized a "shadow" interdepartmental committee, which I chaired, to make recommendations as to the policy we should pursue there. Our report was presented to the President, and he accepted it in its entirety, with the exception of one relatively important recommendation: As a counterpoise to the intrusions of the Viet Cong into Laos, we recommended sending troops to Thailand. Although this step was later taken, when the situation in Laos became more acute, Kennedy declined to do it at that time. I assumed that he did not wish to take such a provocative step so early in his administration. As a consequence, although we stepped up our effort to assist Laos, we recommended no spectacular changes in policy.

I was not deeply involved in the President's early consideration of our policy in South Vietnam, which had not yet reached crisis proportions. The program for Vietnam was considered a routine one of military assistance; no one foresaw it as the breeding ground for one of the most disastrous wars in American history. One morning I got a call from Kennedy's office asking me to prepare, for a meeting to be held shortly, a summary of lessons from the Greek guerrilla war, insofar as it might be applicable to the South Vietnamese–Viet Cong guerrilla war. At this meeting, I produced a paper giving eight reasons why we were successful in Greece. The President immediately saw one point that I had considered very important—the elimination of Yugoslavia as a sanctuary for guerrilla forces, who when pursued could easily cross over the mountainous Greek border to safe haven. The President used this to prove his point, at the meeting, that we faced grave difficulties until Laos could be removed as a sanctuary for the Viet Cong in South Vietnam.

One of Kennedy's first acts after his inauguration was to ask Dean Acheson to study NATO policy in general. I participated as a member of Acheson's supporting committee. One of our particular recommendations concerned the removal of the MRBMs (Medium Range Ballistic Missiles), the Jupiters, from Turkey and Italy. At one of the meetings dealing with this problem, the President asked me, because of my experience as Ambassador to Turkey, whether I thought the Turks would permit us to take the MRBMs out. I replied that I doubted it, but that we would look into the matter thoroughly and see what could be done. As a result, we studied the problem and sought the advice of the Embassy in Ankara.

When Secretary Rusk and I were in Ankara shortly thereafter, at a CENTO (Central Treaty Organization) meeting, we talked with the Foreign Minister of Turkey about the MRBMs. He was firmly against their removal. The Turks had poured a good deal of money into installing the Jupiters, which had just come into place, and the Foreign Minister said that it would be difficult for the Turkish people to understand their removal without any compensating additions to their security.

As a result, I had to report to the President that, in my opinion, the Turks would not agree to removal of the MRBMs without some compensation or stronger pressure than I believed would be justified at that time. Much later, the Jupiters were removed, but only when we were able to put Polaris submarines into the Mediterranean. It would have been preferable if the President's original wish could have been carried out, since the removal of the MRBMs at the later date was widely, though wrongly, interpreted as a consideration we paid for the Soviets' removal of offensive missiles from Cuba in 1962.

Another incident from the early days of the new administration occurred when Kennedy asked me to stay behind after a meeting. "How is it," he said, "that the oil men in Texas can avoid paying income tax?"

I replied that I assumed he was referring to the recent articles that had been written about the Dallas Hunt family's tax avoidance in oil. This was indeed true, I said, but probably entirely legal. Because of their influence in Congress, Texas oil men received favorable tax treatment through the so-called depletion allowance. No Texas oil man paid taxes because he could legally deduct up to 27.5 percent of his gross income, which was limited to half of his net income, in calculating his tax. This let him drill up his taxable income and use the rest for nontax avoidance expenses. This, I rashly volunteered, is what your father does through a drilling syndicate in San Antonio, giving its name. Kennedy did not seem offended and asked nothing more.

I also became deeply involved in our policy toward the Dominican Republic and the dictatorial regime of Rafael Leonidas Trujillo. As Kennedy took office in 1961, great concern was voiced about Trujillo. The CIA had mounted a major effort in the Dominican Republic, the objective of which was, I'm sure, Trujillo's removal. A contingency plan had been prepared in anticipation of this eventuality. The man in charge of anti-Trujillo strategy at that time was Richard Goodwin, a White House Special Assistant. I had nothing to do with the plan and don't know to what extent the State Department was consulted.

When Trujillo was assassinated in June 1961, a series of meetings were held at the Department to decide a course of action. Goodwin wanted us to act immediately on his contingency plan that would put U.S. troops in the Dominican Republic to assist the Freedom Fighters who had, he assumed, assassinated Trujillo. The discussions culminated late one morning when President Kennedy was away. Vice President Lyndon Johnson came to the State Department with Attorney General Robert Kennedy and Goodwin to consult with George Ball, Under Secretary for Economic Affairs, and me. Kennedy and Goodwin strongly urged that we intervene with force. "We're doing nothing but sitting here," said Kennedy. "We should be helping those people in the Dominican Republic." Others spoke in a more temperate vein, but I took the strongest position against intervention.

First, I said, we did not know who had killed Trujillo and who would end up in power. We suspected that it might be an Air Force General; he appeared to have the greatest backing. If we went into the Dominican Republic, we would have to take over and run the country, probably in opposition to the military. I also pointed out that our intervention in an affair that did not directly involve our interests would provoke adverse reactions not just in Central and South America but worldwide. Ball also urged moderation but he did not take as strong a line as I did. The final decision was not to intervene, and I am convinced that as a result of this confrontation Robert Kennedy became unfriendly to me.

On October 5, 1961, Ball said he wanted me to go to the Dominican Republic to negotiate with Ramfis Trujillo, the son of the late dictator, along the lines he would explain. The plan Ball outlined for me had been recommended to the President by John B. Martin, a publisher and Dominican expert, who the President had sent to the Dominican Republic to analyze the situation and recommend action, which was as follows:

Several choices were open—all bad. We could simply do nothing. The Dominicans kept saying, "If you don't help we'll kill each other," and one might be tempted to reply, "Go ahead." But we could not, nor could we support the [existing] Balaquer-Ramfis regime, recognize it, vote to lift the sanctions, and send an Ambassador. That would . . . be turning our backs on the people. As our final choice we could help establish a broad-based provisional government until free elections could be held with OAS help, negotiate Ramfis out of his economic power at once, and later negotiate him out of the country, [help the Republic borrow enough to get the economy going, send out civil and military missions to help, and gradually lift the existing sanctions.]

Martin's recommendations, with some modifications, became the basic strategy that would be adopted. Ball, in discussing it with me, indicated that the first objective was to establish contact with Ramfis Trujillo (Trujillo's son), try to obtain his confidence, and negotiate with him for the return of the sugar properties and miscellaneous industries held by the Trujillo family. At the same time, it was recognized that we needed Ramfis Trujillo and that we should say nothing about his removal. On the other hand, we should not give him the impression that we would back him indefinitely. We had concluded that we badly needed Trujillo to help keep Sanchez, a powerful Air Force general, from taking power. We also wanted very much to get his support in removing his two uncles, Hector and Arismendi Trujillo, who were plotting with various groups for power and who constituted a threat to the development of democratic government in the Dominican Republic.

Balaquer, a puppet President under Rafael Trujillo, who together with Ramfis Trujillo ran the country, was at the United Nations in New York. Ball and I went up and spent an evening with Balaquer, explaining our basic strategy with which he agreed. Balaquer impressed me as a broad-gauged leader on whom we could rely. He had been foreign minister before being named President, and after Trujillo's assassination, he was widely suspected to have been a co-conspirator in the plot against Trujillo. On the other hand, most people had real confidence in him, and, as later events showed, he was quite capable of being elected President of the Dominican Republic by popular vote. In any event, he offered his full assistance in the negotiation I was to undertake in his country.

Before leaving Washington, I met with President Kennedy to get his final instructions as to the proposal I was to make to Trujillo. Kennedy said to me: "Now you negotiate, George, just like this was your own purchase. Keep your price low." The President knew that we would be criticized if we sanctioned paying Trujillo too much for his properties. After making the necessary arrangements to meet with Ramfis Trujillo through our Chargé, John Hill, I flew to the Dominican Republic.

When I arrived, I was met by Hill and briefed at the Consulate General. My meeting with Ramfis Trujillo was arranged at the San Isidro Air Force base. Ramfis had been made a full general by his father at the age of nine, and the Air Force had been created largely as his plaything. Ramfis, who by this time was in his early 20s, had been a notorious playboy. He had been expelled from the U.S. Military Command College at Fort Leavenworth after widely publicized affairs with various movie actresses. He was a tall, handsome young man with a mustache, and he met me wearing an elegant uniform, well-shined boots, and dark glasses, carrying a pistol in a holster. The office in which we met was large and well furnished, with dark mahogany paneled walls and closed blinds. It was so dark that it was nearly impossible for me to see the man I was dealing with.

Our conversation began along general lines. I expressed appreciation for the cooperation he had given our government and Consul General Hill. I said he had a great opportunity to help restore his country and to lead it ultimately in becoming a democracy. I suggested that he could thereby become the father of democracy there, which would enhance his family's reputation. I pointed out that there were sinister elements lurking in the Dominican Republic, but I felt sure that he would continue to cooperate in preventing them from seizing power.

I noted the great importance of the properties held by his family, consisting of tens of thousands of hectares of sugar-producing lands, some of which were not being tilled, as well as a large share of the country's sugar-refining industry. It was unlikely, I said, that he would ever be able to gain full control of these properties. He obviously was already a wealthy man. What a fine thing it would be for his country, if he would establish a trust under his name, place these properties in it, and allow the proceeds to be used for the benefit of his country. I would bring an expert down from the United States who could advise him on how to set up such a trust. He had plenty of properties left of his own on which to live a comfortable, useful, and influential life.

Ramfis Trujillo essentially replied: "I'm not an angel. I'm not going to give these properties away. I would have to receive some compensation before I release them." I did not pursue the matter further but instead talked about his uncles, Hector and Arismendi, pointing out the trouble they were causing him and the country. Would he help us persuade them to leave the country? He promised that he would see to it that they left, a promise he actually carried out, alleviating a tense situation.

In the meantime, I had long talks with Hill and his staff as well as officials of the Dominican Republic about the value of the Trujillo properties. I had heard that Thomas Pappas, a successful businessman from Boston whom I knew, was in fact in the Dominican Republic attempting to buy the properties. I had no evidence that he was in a position to offer cash, but was instead attempting to obtain an option on the properties at a greatly reduced price, which he hoped to sell at a considerable profit. Pappas and his brother, whom I also knew, had gotten their start in a Boston racetrack, among other businesses. Tom later became quite wealthy when he fronted for a refinery built in Greece by Standard Oil Company of New Jersey. As well as I could determine, the free-market value of the properties could well be in excess of $100 million. Pappas, I heard, was offering Ramfis Trujillo $35 to $40 million.

I sent a message to Pappas asking him to come and see me, and I talked very bluntly to him. I said I had come to the Dominican Republic on a mission for the President involving the sugar properties. I couldn't tell him precisely what we had in mind, but his efforts to buy the properties were standing in our way. As an official of our government, I asked him to abandon his efforts to purchase the properties. I must say I admired Tom Pappas for his quick reaction to my request. He said that if I put it to him that way, he would quit his efforts and go home. Later, I got President Kennedy to write him a letter thanking him for his patriotic response. Coming from Boston, I felt sure that Pappas would welcome a letter from Kennedy, even though he was a Republican. Later he expressed to me his great appreciation for Kennedy's letter.

In any event, I decided that I would make an offer to Trujillo for his properties. This would not be paid by the U.S. government, but by the Dominican Republic with our sanction. Since we were supporting the Dominican government on a large scale, we obviously were interested in how much it paid Trujillo out of its meager funds. Hill and I had a meeting with Balaquer, who agreed that I could make an offer of $15 million in behalf of his government. It was a low figure, and I did not expect it to be accepted. However, I thought it was attractive enough that it would not be spurned out of hand and would lead to a counterproposal by Ramfis that we might be able to accept.

I then met with Ramfis again in the Presidential Palace—Balaquer was also there—and offered him $15 million. He deprecated the figure, pointing out that the properties were obviously worth a great deal more. I repeated that he was not in a good position to sell and that his ultimate ability to retain the properties was much in question. For the reasons I had mentioned to him earlier, as well as his own desire to get something for the properties, he should seriously consider my offer. Later, Trujillo sent back word that he would not accept my offer, but that he was making a counterproposal of $25 million. I replied that there was no point in further direct discussion at this time and that I would return to Washington and advise him of our decision. In that final conversation, Ramfis said something quite interesting. "I can always be counted on to do the right thing," he said.

Personally, I believed that we should accept the $25 million. It was only about 25 cents on the dollar of real value and was, I estimated, no more than the value of what had been spent to create the present crop. Others in Washington were quite ready to accept the $25 million, and I communicated this to Ramfis. In keeping with my promise we dispatched a lawyer, a specialist in trusts from the Ford Foundation, to advise him.

But on November 15, Hector and Arismendi Trujillo returned to the Dominican Republic. Air Force General Echiverra emerged as a strong man, and Balaquer feared a coup. On November 19, U.S. Navy ships appeared on the horizon. The President asked me to return to the Dominican Republic and talk with Ramfis again to see if he couldn't stabilize the situation. I put through an immediate request for a meeting with Ramfis, and in order to facilitate getting there, I proceeded to Miami where I stayed in a hotel room awaiting a reply. At this juncture, Ramfis was apparently taking narcotics and living on his yacht, the *Elita,* with a group of his friends, playboys and playgirls. He seemed to have gone completely to pieces. When he got my message, he replied rather incoherently to the effect, "No, there's no use in McGhee's coming. I've already given him everything."

Thereupon, Ramfis got a number of his friends to join him and, taking some $14 million in Dominican currency, set sail. He was seized in Guadalupe, his first port of call, where his money was impounded. Before he left, he had personally shot all six men suspected of killing his father. Since he had not carried out his promise to remove his uncles or to stay and maintain stability, we considered that he had forfeited his $25 million. The remainder of Ramfis Trujillo's short life was tragic. The family had created sufficient assets abroad to enable him to live in luxury in Madrid; however, he was killed in an automobile accident while he was still a young man.

Balaquer went on to become a highly respected President of his country. On one occasion when he feared his enemies, he sought asylum in this country, which was granted on the understanding that he would not engage in any political activity. When we had received evidence that he was becoming active again, I called him on the phone as Under Secretary of State for Political Affairs and admonished him in a stern but friendly way, telling him that if he did not quit his political activity, we would force him to leave the country. He replied, rather meekly, that he would quit. But he later returned to the Dominican Republic, again rose to power, and is still, at this writing, even though he is over ninety, the President.

12

Covert Intelligence in Cuba, Iran, and Vietnam: 1961–1968

Covert intelligence operations have long been a subject of controversy. Widely used during the Second World War, when any means was acceptable if it would help defeat the enemy, the same methods were continued into peacetime, often without proper consideration of whether they were appropriate from either a moral or practical point of view. To begin with, the term *covert intelligence* is a misnomer, since in its application it has little to do with intelligence. No one questions the collection of information by governments, whether done openly or secretly—using American agents and recruited foreign nationals, engaging in counterintelligence activities, and so on. Intelligence of this sort is accepted, although when caught, spies may be prosecuted and imprisoned, unless the governments involved agree to an exchange.

Covert operations, on the other hand, involve the use of "dirty tricks," which range from rigging an election to assassinating a head of state, and are a different matter altogether. When covert operations are revealed they can result in retaliation, broken relations, and even armed conflict.

From my own experience, almost all covert operations are eventually exposed, by accident or by self-seeking parties. The reaction to an exposed covert operation is almost always more adverse, being open ended, than an initial gain. One of the few touted covert operations resulted in the Central Intelligence Agency's (CIA) overthrow of the Communist-backed reformist government of President Jacopo Arbenz in Guatemala in 1952. But the action only led to a more damaging countercoup. Even today this incident remains an embarrassment for the CIA and the United States.

Since I was in the military service, I have never questioned wartime use of covert operations, and I could also make exceptions of certain projects during the Cold War, In peacetime I could accept such innocent methods as secret CIA control of newspapers and magazines, as well as bribes to individuals and contributions to political parties. But when I entered the State Department after World War II, many covert operations were revealed to me that I could consider neither useful nor moral. They seemed to be the product of minds still dominated by wartime operations, making a fetish of a secret, conspiratorial approach to international problems. Many of the countries that were targeted had not been lost to communism, and as a result of our own covert overreaction, as in Iran, they turned against us.

When I first joined the State Department in 1946, I was not exposed to covert operations. As Coordinator for Aid to Greece and Turkey, I was aware of CIA activities related to the Greek guerrilla uprising that had the earmarks of wartime. As Assistant Secretary for the Near East, South Asia, and Africa, I knew of a few relatively insignificant cases—I even participated in some—of giving innocuous aid to influential individuals and groups because we wanted to keep them "on our side." But I do not recall any actions aimed at overthrowing a government or assassinating a leader.

The situation changed abruptly during the Eisenhower administration, as a result of the Foster–Allen Dulles combination as recreated in a recent book, *The Very Best Men,* by Evan Thomas (1995). A plethora of daring covert actions all around the world date from that period, including one in Iran in 1953, which led to the overthrow of Prime Minister Mohammed Mossadeq and the return of the Shah. Kermit Roosevelt, the CIA officer who, with the British intelligence, ran Operation Ajax, wrote a book about this incident (*Countercoup,* 1979), despite CIA efforts to block it. The book's first edition, a copy of which I obtained despite the publisher's attempt to withdraw it, cites the Anglo-Iranian Oil Company as having conceived the idea of deposing the Iranian Prime Minister. The AIOC, according to Roosevelt's account, sold the project to British intelligence, and the CIA agreed to it at Roosevelt's urging. This book, as well as a public award to Roosevelt presented by President Eisenhower, confirmed for the Iranians that we had played the key role in overthrowing their constitutionally elected leader. Mossadeq had freed Iran from AIOC-British control without loss of blood and was considered a national hero. His overthrow led to anti–United States attitudes in Iran. We became the incarnate of evil, the Great Satan of the Khomeini era.

When I returned to government with the Kennedy administration in 1961 as head of Policy Planning, I was asked to chair a committee to investigate the record of the Eisenhower administration in covert intelligence activities. We found that during this era there had been a major expansion of such activities all over the world, including the overthrow of Mossadeq. Deeply concerned by something so contrary to my own experience and point of view, I reported this finding to Rusk. The entrenched power in the clandestine services of the CIA that carried over from one administration to another resulted, I am sure, in the termination of my assignment to evaluate covert operations.

Evan Thomas's book *The Very Best Men* charts the rise and fall of an era starting in 1951 when Frank Wisner became the chief of covert action for the CIA, which had been formed out of the intelligence residue from the wartime Office of Strategic Services (OSS). For 10 years Wisner, together with Desmond Fitzgerald, Tracy Barnes, and Richard Bissell, with little higher supervision, fought the widespread covert actions of the Cold War. All were Ivy League graduates who, as close friends, lived and socialized within a narrow circle in historic Georgetown. All were intelligent, charming activists dedicated to stopping communism wherever it appeared in the worldwide battles of the four-year-old Cold War. The result was an inbred outlook among successive leaders sharing the same basic point of view. This included the willingness that they had rationalized to incite mass uprisings resulting in human losses and to use any means available in attempts to assassinate Castro in Cuba and Lumumba in Zaire. They were, at the same time, loyal Americans who were willing to risk their own lives while achieving few successes.

The first major effort after the overthrow of Arbenz was the Hungarian revolution against Soviet rule on October 23, 1956. Three hundred thousand Hungarians marched on the Parliament demanding free elections and Soviet withdrawal from Hungary. The CIA controlled Radio Free Europe, which broadcasted a "call to arms" through small stations in Hungary. During an invasion by 200,000 Russians, 30,000 Hungarian lives were lost. It is a controversial matter whether U.S. aid had been offered; however, none came. Starting in 1955, the CIA had stored papers in Indonesia to influence elections against Communist-leaning ruler Sukarno, with indifferent results. In August 1957 with Allen Dulles's approval, $10 million was advanced to a group of revolutionary colonels to spread the rumor of an affair between Sukarno and an airline stewardess. This effort failed, as did others to drop supplies to the lawless colonels, and so Dulles disengaged from Indonesia.

Richard Bissell rose in power through his highly successful U-2 spy plane which could fly at 70,000 feet for 4,000 miles. The quality of its photography revolutionized the science of photographic intelligence. The loss of a U-2 over Russia on May 21, 1960, and the capture of the pilot led to a heating up of the Cold War. Nikita Khrushchev, who was scheduled to have a very important meeting with Eisenhower, denounced the United States in the Supreme Soviet, and the meeting was canceled. The Cold War was accelerated.

Bissell eventually succeeded Wisner as head of covert intelligence. However, in 1961 he was held responsible for the fiasco of the Bay of Pigs.

Although the new President John Kennedy accepted blame, both Bissell and Dulles had to go—and their era of CIA covert action was over. Largely because of the relentless Robert Kennedy, the CIA spent enormous sums trying unsuccessfully to kill Castro, which could have led to the Missile Crisis or, as some still believe, the assassination of President Kennedy. This last era was not a good one for the CIA.

I was not consulted on the top-secret CIA project inherited from the Eisenhower administration: the Bay of Pigs invasion of Cuba in 1961. I knew about it from bits of information circulating in the State Department and from leaks to the *New York Times* that secret preparations supported by the United States were under way at various points around the Caribbean for a surprise invasion by Cuban expatriates. I did not see any authentic information regarding details, and I did not ask for any. I was particularly interested because I had spent a considerable time in Cuba as a young man supervising oil exploration with seismic crews.

One day I was walking to my office at the State Department when a door opened beside me and a large group poured into the hall. From the composition of the group, I knew it had to be the one considering the secret Cuban project. A friend walking beside me probably thought I had also been at the meeting, for he was mumbling to himself, "They won't make it. They're not going to have enough protection." This confirmed my general evaluation of the Cuban situation and further aroused my opposition to such covert operations.

I said nothing, but I immediately put in a request to see Rusk. "Dean," as I called him only when we were alone, "you haven't asked me for my opinion, but I have surmised from what I have gleaned from several sources that we are planning an invasion of Cuba."

Rusk replied without any confirmation of what I had said. "George, you probably know that we have been giving this more consideration since we came in than any other problem."

"I know, but from what I have heard, we may be making a very serious mistake. Some of those involved feel that plans do not provide enough protection for your Cuban volunteers. If they are captured, I believe Castro will put them in jail, torture them for confessions, and put them and the U.S. up for trial before the whole world. The captives will feel that we abandoned them and will, in exchange for leniency, make the worst possible case they can against us. We will be deeply embarrassed. Our new government will be discredited before we get started." Rusk made no reply.

A few days later, Under Secretary of State Chester Bowles was unable to go to a scheduled meeting of what was called the Committee of Ten on the Cuban project, and I went in Bowles's place. Without being asked, when the committee opened, I blurted out exactly what I had told Rusk. No one said a word. The Chairman passed to the next subject. Later, the Committee passed a resolution that in the future it would not again admit substitutes for full members. Years later, McGeorge Bundy recalled what I had said at this meeting, adding "You were right. We should have listened to you." But I would not escape the aftermath of the fiasco when it came. Rusk was in Atlanta making a speech, and George Ball had just left for a Bilderberg meeting in Canada which I was also scheduled to attend. I was preparing to leave when the phone rang. The President was on the line.

"Where is everybody?" Kennedy shouted, in a voice that seemed to me almost hysterical. "You're the policy planner. We need some plans. Where are your plans?" I didn't think I should point out that, although I had not been included in the operation, I had opposed it privately with those who were. "Here," said Kennedy, "here's the Vice-President." Johnson, when he came on the phone, seemed even more hysterical. "We need help here. Why is no one trying to help us? Everyone has gone." I was shocked by their seeming loss of control and began seriously to doubt their ability to govern.

I could only reply, "It's difficult at this stage to plan. I would call it damage control. Maybe we can get some of our friends in the hemisphere to help us. I'll talk with our Latin American people and see what we can do." There was, in fact, little else that could be done. Thus, of the three covert operations described here—Guatemala, Iran, and Cuba—two were originally considered a success, which I now deem failures, and the other was a preordained failure.

This leads us to Vietnam, perhaps the greatest mistake the United States, or any other modern nation, has ever made. I am embarrassed that what I say puts me in another "I told you so" position. Even so I was myself just as much a failure in not helping my superiors to avoid the failures.

When I assumed my post as head of Policy Planning under Kennedy in 1961, Vietnam did not pose a serious problem. As in Korea, which the successful allies had also artificially divided into two separate areas, the North and South Vietnamese were engaged in a civil war. Disregarding France's advice not to get involved, which Eisenhower accepted, the Kennedy administration adopted a positive role in supporting the Southern forces under President Ngo Dinh Diem. The area was not, however, expected to give us any serious trouble. For us in Policy Planning there seemed to be nothing that we needed to do.

Seeking a way to bolster the South, Kennedy sent Walt Rostow, then a White House assistant, and the highly regarded General Maxwell Taylor to Vietnam in October 1961 on a fact-finding mission. On their return, they recommended sending out 10,000 American troops to stem the Viet Cong advances. Although Kennedy did not accept this recommendation at the time, he later started a secret buildup of troops under a cover of irrigation specialists, which were later gradually increased to 25,000.

Without my knowledge, my friend John Kenneth Galbraith, then U.S. Ambassador to India, wrote to Kennedy on November 3, 1961, when the serious question of whether we should help overthrow Diem was under intense consideration. Galbraith suggested that I be sent to replace Frederick Nolting as Ambassador to South Vietnam. He said he believed I would be capable of "holding my own with Diem and the United States military" and "would insist once and for all for government reform and would understand the United States political implications of developments there."

On November 15, McGeorge Bundy, Kennedy's Special Assistant for Security Affairs, wrote to Kennedy: "I would still consider McGhee. For one thing, if he thinks it won't work after a good look, he'll tell you, and he has the authority of the Victor of Greece." Kennedy seemed receptive. If a general military command was set up in Vietnam, he wrote, he "wanted to be sure that someone like George McGhee headed it; in fact it might be good to send McGhee." Copies of Kennedy's message went to Rusk and McNamara on November 19. But JFK didn't, fortunately for me, make a final decision. As a surprise, on November 26, he gave me a double promotion to Under Secretary of State for Political Affairs.

The President, having not yet made his decision on Saigon, had at the last minute decided that he would name George Ball to replace Chester Bowles as Under Secretary and me to replace him as Under Secretary for Political Affairs, third man in the hierarchy. JFK would have realized that it was better than naming me Ambassador to Saigon, if he had known the opinion I gave Rusk on Vietnam the day after my appointment as Under Secretary was announced. The record is that I said to Rusk:

I would like to raise Abe Chayes' memorandum to you of November 16 on the subject of Vietnam. There is one consideration bearing on the introduction of U.S. forces into Vietnam which is not mentioned in that memorandum and which seems to me worth noting.

Domestic U.S. dissatisfaction with what would surely be the prolonged involvement of American soldiers in these indecisive anti-guerrilla operations would mount and give rise to growing demands that we attack the source of the aggression in North Vietnam. . . .

If we gave into these pressures and attacked North Vietnam, we would be propelled into a widening conflict which might be hard to terminate. . . .

In short, once we committed combat troops to Vietnam we would tend to lose control of subsequent events—either in that theater or more generally—by reason of the popular reactions that our continued involvement would likely trigger.

This gratuitous advice to the Secretary reflected the basic decision I had made in administering Greek-Turkish Aid in 1947—that under no conditions would our 36,000 armed forces or advisers expose themselves in combat or fire weapons. The reasoning behind this advice was that until we engaged in combat we could always pull out. As a result, we had not lost a man. Once we shot or got shot at, it was "our war." The Greek government had been informed of this policy.

The potential danger in Vietnam became more real to me after I became Ambassador to Bonn on August 25, 1964, after the visit of Henry Cabot Lodge, who was then our Ambassador to Saigon, the post I had escaped, and would later succeed me in Bonn. In discussions with Chancellor Ludwig Erhard, which I had arranged, Lodge deprecated the danger of any major war developing in Vietnam. It was costing us only a paltry $1.1 million a day, and we had lost only 200 men over two and a half years. In light of my experience in Greece, however, I was concerned to learn from Lodge that U.S. personnel in Vietnam were in combat to the point of occasionally taking command. I feared that Vietnam might become "our war."

In *Robert Kennedy in his Own Words,* in answer to a question by interviewer John Martin, Robert Kennedy is quoted on the subject of why President Kennedy had felt there was an overwhelming reason for the United States to pursue victory in Vietnam. Kennedy's answer was: "[Because of] the loss of all Southeast Asia if you lost in Viet Nam. I think everybody [in the administration] was quite clear that the rest of Southeast Asia would fall—it would have profound effects on our position throughout the world." Four years later, in announcing his candidacy for the presidency, Robert Kennedy pledged to end the conflict. He had changed his position 180 degrees.

At the time President Kennedy was assassinated, we had 25,000 soldiers in Vietnam. Under Johnson at peak, the number was 550,000, and when the war ended, 58,000 had been killed. We had also lost much more. Our failure to raise taxes to pay for the war resulted in U.S. and world inflation. As parents, we lost the respect of a generation of our young, many of whose lives were completely disrupted. The war led to the Nixon Doctrine which now endorsed the abandonment of U.S. leadership in assisting nations threatened by communism. We paid a heavy price for a mistaken analysis of what proved to have been a civil war.

Naturally, as a fellow Texan, I knew Lyndon Johnson well. Our families had enjoyed close relations. Although my own attitude toward American participation in the Vietnam War was well known both to Johnson and to others in high positions in government, I never expressed this view publicly. During my ambassadorship to Germany starting in May 1963, I scrupulously supported U.S. policy in Vietnam publicly and tried to sell it to the German government and people. I had not received any inside information on the fateful decisions made in 1965 that led to the drastic escalation of our involvement.

Personal clashes are unavoidable in foreign policy making. In view of our differences in policy—in Cuba, the Dominican Republic, and in Vietnam—it was perhaps impossible for me to avoid conflict with Robert Kennedy. However, I never lost the support of President Kennedy, who appointed me to my highest positions, including my double promotion to Under Secretary for Political Affairs. As was well known, Lyndon Johnson mightily resented anyone who opposed his Vietnam policy. This was, I believe, additional evidence of Johnson's insecurity, which was becoming increasingly evident to me and which I believe contributed to the failure of his presidency. I had often heard him belittle himself because he had not gone to Harvard as Kennedy had, but just to San Marcos Normal. After Johnson's inauguration as President in 1964, when I was Ambassador to Bonn, I tried very hard to persuade him to make an early visit to key European capitals. But his staff had persuaded him that he should postpone a visit until it could coincide with a successful negotiation. I explained that such successes were few and far between, and if he waited too long, European leaders might conclude that he didn't value them as allies, or even worse, that he was afraid that he couldn't match the successful Kennedy visit to Germany in 1963. He never came to Europe during his presidency except for a brief, unimportant visit for Konrad Adenauer's funeral in April 1967. I was only able to arrange some exchanges on the edges of the funeral with a few important people.

On another occasion, I was visiting Johnson at his ranch. We were sitting on his front porch when all of his cabinet arrived to discuss their various problems. When I got up to leave, he signaled me to stay. "This should be interesting for you," he said. One by one they raised various problems and requests, which I thought he took care of very well. When they left, he turned to me and said, "You probably don't think I'm a very good executive, do you?" This was a most disconcerting question coming from the chief executive of the most powerful nation in the world. What he wanted from me, of course, was a flattering comment about his ability to handle the cabinet, which I did give him. I really thought he had done well.

When I returned to Washington from Germany in June 1968 to assume the position of Ambassador-at-Large, Johnson did not accept my request to call on him, as he always had during my visits to Washington. For the remaining six months of his presidency, I had no personal contact with him, whereas in earlier days he would have called me for advice. Cecilia and I were never invited to the White House or to the ranch. A few years later Cecilia and I were sitting on the terrace of our farm near Middleburg, next to the estate of George Brown of Houston, whom Lyndon and Ladybird often visited. Suddenly I sensed a towering figure standing behind me. It was Lyndon. He and Ladybird, without calling, had walked over the half-mile for a neighborly visit. They sat and we had a friendly chat, like many we had had before. Lyndon died just two months later. I have always felt that before he died he wanted to make peace with me.

13

The Congo Crisis in 1962

In November 1961, when Chester Bowles resigned as Under Secretary of State and was replaced by George Ball, I became Under Secretary for Political Affairs. Holding down the number-three job in the Department kept me busy enough, but I had gained considerable experience as a troubleshooter, and in July 1962, on orders from President Kennedy, I became responsible for policy coordination for the crisis-torn Congo. For 10 months, until I became Ambassador to West Germany in May 1963, I devoted much of my time and thought to the Congo.

My initial assignment was to mediate the differences in views between the two State Department factions involved: the African Bureau, headed by Assistant Secretary Mennen Williams, tended to sympathize with the newly independent Congolese government, whereas the European Bureau, under William Tyler, often took the side of Belgium, whose interest in the region did not end entirely when the Congo was freed in 1960. Valuable copper mines and facilities were still owned by a Belgian company, Union Minière, in mineral-rich Katanga Province.

Although I had visited the Union Minière properties in Katanga in 1950 when I was Assistant Secretary, I had not been directly concerned with the Congo problem before becoming Under Secretary for Political Affairs. As head of Policy Planning I had followed the area generally, but since the Congo had become mostly an operational U.N. matter, I had not gotten deeply involved. The Kennedy policy toward the Congo, as the President explained it to me when he put me in charge, was very clear. He strongly supported the U.N. effort to end the Katanga secession pursuant to a Security Council Resolution of February 21, 1961, which directed the U.N. Command to use force if necessary to prevent civil war in the Congo. However, the principal point Kennedy made to me was to avoid by every means possible an outbreak of hostilities.

Later, the President backed strengthening the U.N. military position in Katanga against the mercenary-led forces loyal to Tshombe. On December 21, 1961, we sent an additional support of 21 cargo planes, despite opposition by Great Britain and other European allies. The African nations widely saw this as proof of our sympathy to their anticolonial aspirations. Kennedy feared, however, that if we permitted hostilities to break out in the Congo, the Soviets, who had been building up native forces in areas adjacent to the Congo, would seize the opportunity to come to the aid, either directly or through surrogates, of those opposing our interests. The President reasoned that this could create the threat of the first shooting war of the Cold War between us and the Soviets, which he believed should be avoided at all costs.

The President remembered that the Congo had been a principal issue when Kennedy and Khrushchev met in Vienna in June 1961. It was then that the Soviet leader made an impassioned defense of the speech he had given in January pledging support for wars of national liberation. Kennedy had no basis for regarding the Soviets as anything but an "enemy" in the Congo.

Pursuant to my instructions from the President, I made every effort to avoid an outbreak of hostilities. My strategy was to try to hold the situation together and "play for the breaks," as in a poker game. As long as the stakes were low, we should continue to play even when holding low cards, hoping to draw higher cards. By being patient, we hoped to achieve our objective without risking a major conflict. Those in the Department who had favored resorting to force to bring Tshombe into line—Bowles, Williams, and Gullion—had never quite been able to persuade President Kennedy against Rusk, Harriman, and later myself, who had opposed action that would risk war. My mission to the Congo represented a final effort to avoid a war.

By the time I became involved in the Congo, the impasse between the African and European bureaus, which was perhaps inevitable, had become acute. Accordingly, I met daily with officers of the two bureaus and the International Organization Bureau until we agreed on a course of action in what came to be called the U Thant Plan (after the Secretary General of the United Nations). All of my later work in connection with the Congo was also in close cooperation with Belgian Foreign Minister Paul Henri Spaak. I communicated frequently with Spaak through our Embassy in Brussels, and I visited him a number of times. We were in agreement on most Congo issues, and he was helpful in achieving the objectives we both sought.

The U Thant Plan had been initiated by President Kennedy's request for an "action plan" for the Congo, based on previous proposals by Ball, Williams, and our Ambassador to the Congo, Edmund Gullion. Largely drafted in my office, the plan was presented to Kennedy in August. It called for a series of complementary actions by the Congolese government of Prime Minister Adoula and the Katanga government of President Tshombe. These actions, among others, were directed toward specific accomplishments: a federal constitution, a plan for 50–50 sharing of tax and foreign exchange revenues, a reunified currency system, and an integrated army.

The overall objective of the plan was a unified and independent Congo, and after many revisions it was approved by Kennedy and the Belgians (but only partially by the British and not at all by the French). On August 9 it was presented to Ralph Bunche, the U.N. Under Secretary for Political Affairs, and by late August Gullion had persuaded Adoula to accept a watered-down version. On September 5, Tshombe qualified his approval by calling the plan a basis for an "acceptable settlement," while the Soviet Union denounced it as a "conspiracy hatched by the Western Powers."

Copper production usually resulted in cycles of overproduction. Copper was then in plentiful world supply, and it was of particular importance as a source of revenue to the Congo. But if Katanga, which was producing about 10 percent of the world's copper, was shut off, there would have been a temporary shortage. This would not have resulted in a world crisis, however, since copper production could have been increased in the United States, the USSR, Chile, Canada, and what is now Zambia, all of which produced more than the Congo. There were also many substitutes for copper, the one most used being aluminum.

We had taken a conciliatory approach with Union Minière because we wanted to make use of its influence in persuading the secessionist Tshombe to return to the fold and to make at least some of Katanga's copper revenues available to the Congo as a whole. Spaak and I were eventually able to obtain an agreement by Union Minière for direct payment of copper royalties to the central government in Leopoldville. This did not mean, however, that we approved its actions in general. I personally considered Union Minière a greedy, narrow-minded company, interested only in holding on to its copper concession for the greatest possible profit. I also believed that Union Minière had played a key role in the Katanga secession.

I would like to emphasize that I became a great admirer of Spaak. I worked very closely with him for over a year and found him consistent and loyal in his undertakings. This wasn't easy for him because Union Minière was very powerful in Belgium and could easily have hurt him politically. But this consideration never seemed to worry Spaak. He was always candid, and he arranged for me to meet with Union Minière without his being present. "Tell them whatever you want to," Spaak said. For my part, I felt obligated to keep Spaak informed of our thinking, and on the average of once a month I flew to Brussels to spend a day or two with him and his associates in the Foreign Office—Baron Robert Rothschild and Count d'Avignon. (D'Avignon later became the head of the Common Market.) After the Congo crisis,

I still kept in touch with Spaak until his death, and I'm still in contact with Rothschild and d'Avignon.

One particular incident shows how Spaak and I worked together. Following a meeting between Kennedy and British Prime Minister Harold Macmillan in the Bahamas in December 1962, I learned from an in-flight message from Kennedy's plane that without consulting the Belgians or anyone else, they had agreed to send a mission to assess U.N. military supply needs in the Congo. Without waiting to clear it with Rusk, I caught a plane for Brussels. Spaak fortunately had not heard about the mission when I arrived the next morning, and I tried to explain it as best I could. It had come as a surprise to all of us in Washington, I said. However, it had been worked out at the highest levels in the Bahamas, I told him, and we were committed. I promised to keep him posted on the mission's activities, so we could take his views into account. Although the existence of the mission gave the U.N. forces in the Congo a boost, when the mission presented its report, the equipment it was considering was no longer needed.

Over time, considerable criticism of President Kennedy's Congo policy developed. The President asked me to try to placate some of the leadership of the opposition—Senator Richard Russell of Georgia, Chairman of the Armed Services Committee; Senator Thomas Dodd of Connecticut; and former Vice President Richard Nixon. Much of this dissent had been stirred up by Michael Struelens, Tshombe's U.S. representative, who issued pro-Tshombe press releases from the Katanga Information Service in New York. It was my job to convince the powerful politicians opposing the President's policy that the Kennedy administration was not anti-Tshombe. We did not want to eliminate the Katangan President, I assured them; we merely wanted to encourage him to reach an agreement with Adoula so that the Congo could be reunited. I also pointed out that we were trying to enlist Union Minière's support.

I practically lived with Dodd during this period, conferring with him at his home and taking him to my club for lunch. He responded reasonably, and in the end, I believe he helped the President's cause. I then flew to Georgia to meet with Senator Russell, who had come under the influence of missionaries from his state who, while serving in Katanga, had become favorably disposed toward Tshombe and were telling Russell that we were trying to unseat him. Russell also seemed receptive to my assurances that this was far from the truth.

I was unable to see Nixon, but I phoned him in California and made the same case I had presented to Dodd and Russell, emphasizing that the anti-administration propaganda with regard to Kennedy's Congo policy was false and misleading. Nixon, who had been Kennedy's opponent in the 1960 election, was noncommittal. President Kennedy, who was aboard a Navy cruiser in the Atlantic, called me at the State Department to ask how my conversations had gone. I said I believed I had done well with Dodd and

Russell, but I was not sure about Nixon, and when I was pressed by Kennedy, I elaborated candidly. "Nixon gave no indication," I said. "I can't say he promised to support us, but he did not indicate he was against our policy or that he would do anything about it."

The next day, the press carried a statement by Nixon that was sharply critical of Kennedy's Congo policy. Since it had been written prior to our telephone conversation he had deliberately deceived me, perhaps so that he wouldn't lose the impact of his statement if there was a leak.

The purpose of my trip to the Congo—between September 26 and October 29, 1962—was to meet with Tshombe and try to convince him of the wisdom of the U Thant Plan. (Whenever I talked about the plan with U Thant himself, he would smile and say, "You mean, the so-called U Thant Plan.") The plan had met with general acceptance in both Leopoldville and Elizabethville, but neither government had done much to implement it. It was difficult for Adoula and Tshombe to cooperate on the plan when they were not even on speaking terms. Adoula was also having trouble with obstinate members of his Parliament. On my arrival, I realized that acceptance of the entire plan all at once was too much to expect, and it would be prudent to approach it as a series of minor hurdles rather than one major one.

My strategy was to try to ignite action on enough of the plan to create momentum in other aspects, and eventually all of it. I was later to hear criticism of my willingness to accept some initial concessions by Tshombe. They were so limited, it was said, that they might ultimately weaken the plan by relieving him from giving more. However, I could see no way to get both sides to agree on acceptance of the whole plan in one fell swoop. Certain aspects of the plan could, in fact, only be achieved in seriatim. I believed that if Adoula responded to some of the concessions I obtained from Tshombe, we would be on our way to a step-by-step acceptance of the entire plan.

I found Tshombe to be an intelligent, engaging, and interesting man. I was with him constantly, night and day. He and his young Belgian secretary and I drove out one day to visit his farm on the Rhodesian border, which I realized would be useful to him if he decided to flee the country. Tshombe and I talked while his secretary took notes. I was impressed with how well his office and files were organized. His staff could always produce the right telegram or memorandum. We had many meals together. The only problem arose when at a dinner he gave for me, he criticized Dean Rusk, who was not only the Secretary of State but also an old friend of mine. When I stood up and said that I would not stay there and hear him slander Rusk, he desisted.

In the end, Tshombe did make a number of important concessions. He gave the Adoula government a $10 million advance against future royalty payments. He agreed to initiate telecommunications between Elizabethville and Leopoldville, and to open the key Lulibash Bridge, greatly facilitating the transportation of copper and supplies. I was only disappointed that Adoula failed to recognize publicly his acceptance of Tshombe's concessions and cooperate by offering concessions of his own and trying to obtain more. Adoula was, it must be admitted, under great political pressure not to make any concessions at all to Tshombe in lieu of a complete acceptance of the plan. At first Adoula was even afraid to meet with me when I returned to Leopoldville, because it might appear that he was conceding something. I finally met with Adoula and Foreign Minister Bomboko, with Ambassador Gullion present, on October 18, but I did not succeed in getting Adoula to give Tshombe any credit for his concessions. At the end of my visit I felt that progress had been made in moving the U Thant Plan forward, but success was not in sight.

The Cuban Missile Crisis of October 1962 occurred immediately upon my return from my visit with Tshombe. When normal operations resumed, Kennedy drew even further back from a militant Congo policy. On November 6, he approved a request for two more cargo planes by the U.N. Military Command, and I recommended sending two fighter aircraft, to be deployed only if no progress had been made toward a peaceful settlement. At a climactic meeting with the President on December 14, the hard-liners were joined by U.N. Ambassador Adlai E. Stevenson in support of an almost immediate application of force.

It is interesting that most of those who favored force were people usually identified as liberals. For this group to be called hawks seemed to me to be what the Germans call *umgekehrt,* upside down. I sensed, however, that we were on the verge of a breakthrough in negotiations, with Tshombe's acceptance of Union Minière paying taxes to Leopoldville. Once again I opposed the use of force in favor of urging Adoula to negotiate on the basis of Tshombe's concessions, though I was ready, if this failed, to recommend force on a graduated scale. Kennedy again delayed a decision on force, and deserves full credit.

Our relations with U.N. Secretary General U Thant were in general quite good throughout the negotiations. I met with him several times in New York, and each time I came away believing we shared a common objective, which was called, after all, the U Thant Plan. Of course, the extremists were still to be heard from, including many members of the U.N. staff who opposed anything that smacked of colonialism. By this time, colonialism had been thoroughly discredited as an institution, particularly in the United States, a former colony. The issues now being raised had to do with how rapidly the remaining vestiges of colonialism would be replaced by the governments of newly created nations. Belgium, which had a poor colonial record, left a political vacuum in the Congo when it announced in January

1960 that independence would be granted in just five months. One of the main colonial vestiges left was Union Minière.

As the stalemate continued in the Congo, disturbing reports emerged that the Indian commanders of the U.N. forces were getting restless, and we feared they would precipitate a war in order to end the impasse. I met with U Thant and explained our policy, warning him that if the United Nations started a war that could have been avoided, he could not count on our support, since we were determined that there not be a war. Harlan Cleveland, head of the Department's International Relations Bureau, reported to Rusk that U Thant had complained about my forceful presentation. I found it amusing that I would be criticized for warning the United Nations against starting a war. We were also concerned that the peacekeeping forces might be acting too aggressively, and we wondered whether the Indian commanders were actually under full U.N. control.

In January 1963, however, to our surprise, Tshombe's troops played into the hands of the Ghurkas by rioting on a Saturday night in Elizabethville, providing the opportunity for the U.N. troops to march on Tshombe's redoubt in Sadotville and neutralize it. It was then no effort for the United Nations, in a few days, to take Elizabethville and all of Katanga. Although we had originally opposed the initiation of force, since the United Nations was successful, we made no issue of it. Had we been consulted at the time, we would, under the circumstances, undoubtedly have agreed with the decision of the Indian commanders. The war against Katanga had been won. Victory, for which President Kennedy deserved full credit, had been achieved.

There was an interesting sequel to my encounter with Tshombe. Later, during the brief period when he was Prime Minister of the Congo, he paid an official visit to Bonn, when I was Ambassador to Germany. His embassy gave a reception for him, and we reminisced at length about our time together in the fall of 1962. He flattered me by saying that he remembered everything I had told him and that he had tried to follow my advice to the letter. It was a pleasant reunion. Tshombe went on to Berlin, and I got a call from Washington saying the Belgians had important matters to discuss with Tshombe, but he was being diffident. Would I persuade him to go to Brussels for a meeting with Spaak? I immediately called Tshombe and said that I was sending my plane to Berlin to take him to Brussels. He reluctantly agreed to go, but when he got there, Spaak, who didn't fly, was returning from Paris by train. I later heard that Tshombe was quite miffed by Spaak's being late, but when provided with luxurious guest quarters in an ancient castle, he awaited Spaak's return in a good frame of mind.

My overall impression of Tshombe is that he was an independent Katangan nationalist with a burning resentment over the indignities he faced under Belgian colonial rule. He told me his father, a tribal chieftain, wanted

THE WHITE HOUSE

WASHINGTON

January 21, 1963

Dear George:

Now that the UN Forces have occupied Kolwezi
and Katangese secession is over, I think a little sense
of pride in our achievement in the Congo so far is in
order, even though there is still much hard work to be
done.

I wish to express my appreciation to you for your
hard and devoted work in the year and a half that we
have wrestled with this task. Our problems in the
Congo have been as difficult and as complex as any in
the whole range of our foreign policy problems. The
necessity to operate through the UN and to strike a
proper balance between our own conceptions of what
might be done and the interests and concerns of the UN
and our European allies who are involved in the problems,
as well as the direct interests of the Congolese Government, has made our task extraordinarily difficult.

You have had the direct responsibility for inter-
weaving and balancing all these concerns within the Department of State. In addition, you have carried some
of the burdens of direct negotiation in the Congo, and the
no less difficult burdens of persuasion with the Congress
and the public. Your excellent performance in all these
tasks has made a major contribution to the successful
result.

Sincerely,

Honorable George C. McGhee
Under Secretary of State for
    Political Affairs
Department of State
Washington, D. C.

**Letter of Thanks from President Kennedy to the Author for his Diplomatic
Work During the Congo Crisis.**

him to be educated in Europe, but the Belgians would not allow it. It was clear that he was engaged in a power struggle and that he was adept at playing his adversaries against each other. While some believed there might have been evidence that he was controlled by Union Minière, I did not believe this was the case. He clearly demonstrated his versatility when he was elected Prime Minister of the entire Congo in 1965; later, he was the victim of an Army coup and went into exile. In 1967, he was kidnapped under ambiguous circumstances and taken to Algeria, where he died. Although he had his high points and his low times, he had made his mark on history.

14

Five Years as Ambassador to Germany: 1963–1968

The period May 1963 to April 1968 covers the last six months of the chancellorship of Konrad Adenauer, the three years of Ludwig Erhard's government, and a year and a half of Grand Coalition government under Kurt-Georg Kiesinger. The end of the Adenauer era, which covered the extended period 1949–1963, was marked by the formalization of Adenauer's long-time collaboration with President Charles de Gaulle through a Franco-German treaty of cooperation signed in January 1963. Erhard greatly strengthened cooperation with the United States, focusing on the so-called Kennedy Round of European-American tariff negotiations, East-West relations (particularly German reunification), and the movement toward European unity.

Johnson's abandonment of the multilateral force (MLF) in favor of a common nuclear planning group in late 1964; difficulties over German payments under the military expenses offset agreement with the United States that reached a climax in September 1966; the United States' increasing preoccupation with the Vietnam War; and an apparent U.S. preference for détente with the Soviet Union over reunification of Germany resulted in a shift in German attitudes toward greater independence and self-reliance. Erhard's domestic standing suffered from a mild recession that prompted a tax increase and declined further when Erhard was unable to obtain any relief from Johnson from Germany's offset obligations. Erhard also suffered from the efforts of his traditional rival Adenauer and other German "Gaullists" to undercut him, which led to his downfall in 1966.

Kurt Kiesinger took a strong turn toward a closer alliance with France, distancing himself from the United States. But he too was weakened by the continuing recession and by disagreements between the coalition partners, particularly over an election reform that proposed to substitute majority voting in the English or American style for proportional voting and so threaten the viability of third parties like the Free Democratic Party (FDP). Controversy had also arisen with the United States over the terms of the nuclear non-proliferation treaty consummated between the Americans and the Soviets in 1968. Kiesinger did, however, join the United States in a renewed, though again unsuccessful, effort to overcome French resistance to British membership in the European Economic Community (EEC), more popularly known as the Common Market. The most important German foreign policy initiative under the Grand Coalition was Brandt's formulation of Ostpolitik, which was later realized under his chancellorship.

The U.S. government was fully aware of the special situation created by the division of Germany, especially the isolation and separation of Berlin. We believed that the eventual reunification of Germany was essential for lasting peace in Europe and that the problem of a divided Berlin was inseparable from that of reunification. We wanted to make clear to the Germans our sincere interest in these related issues and our support for a solution based on national self-determination. On the other hand, we did not want to get ahead of them, to be "more German than the Germans." In the meantime, Americans remained committed to defending Germany under the NATO guarantee. To prove this to the Germans, as well as to the Soviets, it was the United States' firm intention to maintain its brigade in Berlin and its force of some 200,000 to 250,000 troops in Germany proper.

The United States also had a fundamental interest in good Franco-German relations. The rivalry between these two key European nations had been a fundamental cause of the two world wars. Despite the grave issues created in the early 1960s by France's reluctance to fulfill its NATO responsibilities and its insistence on dealing with the United States and Europe separately, the U.S. government still wanted to encourage Germany to maintain a close relationship with France.

Despite German vulnerability, the hope of any early progress in German reunification was so slight, and the possibilities of a direct Soviet threat against Germany so great, that the Germans had every incentive to be cautious. Soviet harassment of Berlin access and the imposition of new hardships on the East Germans were always available to the Soviets as policy instruments. The delicate situation created by the division of Europe resulted from a war Germany had started and that principally involved the German people. We could not expect to make progress with the Soviet Union on East-West issues without the full cooperation of the West Germans. We must, I thought, guard against the creation of any German tendency to "throw in the sponge" via a movement toward neutralism. This would decide the fate of Europe in favor of the Soviets. It would no longer be possible to organize a credible defense of Western Europe, and Germany would be at the mercy of the Soviet Union.

The United States also looked to Germany, as one of the leading world trading nations, for help in U.S. efforts to liberalize the world trading system. The impending Kennedy Round trade negotiations were the most important initiative the United States had taken to this end in many years. Because of its heavy dependence on exports, Germany, I believed, shared our goals of reducing tariffs and other trade barriers. As strong supporters of NATO, under whose command the German army of 450,000 troops would fall in the event of war, Americans expected full cooperation in NATO affairs. But I was fully aware of the limitations the Bundestag had imposed on the German military budget and of German reluctance to see a revival of militarism.

I was determined to persuade our country to accelerate the reentry of Germany as an equal member of the family of nations—as long as this status continued to be justified by German performance. If Germany had, indeed, done the best it could to recover from its defeat and help other affected nations complete their recovery, this should be recognized by the international community. Recognition would provide the Germans with the incentive to try to complete their expiation for the Nazi era by making a greater contribution to the unity, well-being, and common defense of Western Europe. To deny Germany this recognition would be a disincentive. Later, in the main auditorium of Heidelberg University, in the presence of Chancellor Erhard, I developed this theme in the most important of the many speeches I made while in Germany.

What was more on our minds when I arrived in Bonn was West Germany's special relationship with France. Like many Europeans, Americans were surprised and concerned by the Franco-German treaty of cooperation signed by de Gaulle and Adenauer on January 22, 1963, during Adenauer's official visit to Paris. Adenauer's great respect for de Gaulle and his desire to use their friendship to bring Germany and France together were well known. On numerous occasions Adenauer had acted as de Gaulle's apologist, justifying French policies that challenged the United States and frustrated Europeans working for greater unity. In a letter to President Kennedy, Nikita Khrushchev compared de Gaulle's influence over Adenauer to the Russian peasant who caught a bear barehanded but could neither bring it home nor make the bear let him loose.

The treaty appeared far-reaching, but it primarily detailed bureaucratic procedures that imposed onerous burdens and were difficult to carry out. Amid widespread criticism of the treaty, particularly from the United States, Foreign Minister Gerhard Schröder and his predecessor, Heinrich von Brentano, were appointed to work out a preamble that specified that West Germany's rights and obligations under its various multilateral treaties with the United States and its West European allies would not be adversely affected.

The preamble also stipulated that the treaty would be implemented in such a way that the Federal Republic would continue to pursue such objectives as strengthening NATO and improving relations between Europe and the United States in cooperation with its allies. Finally, the document made appropriate references to the goal of German unity, the future integration of West German forces in the common defense of Europe under NATO, and the lowering of tariffs as the intended goal of the Kennedy Round negotiations, then in progress.

The Bundestag passed the preamble on May 16, 1963, the day I arrived in Germany. The Federal Republic of Germany (FRG) and its friends breathed easier. On July 3, 1964, de Gaulle weakened the pact by failing to advise the FRG in advance of a major move he had made toward the Soviets. The reduced importance of this treaty took a considerable toll on Adenauer and contributed to his final removal from power in October 1963. It also undoubtedly helped create Adenauer's need to defend de Gaulle, something I would encounter in all of my meetings with him.

During my five years in Germany, I gave attention to the possibility of negotiating with the Soviets to stabilize the situation in Berlin. I approached this question from a number of ways during the regular talks I held with the Soviet Ambassador to East Germany, Peter Andreyevich Abrasimov. At no time, however, did I receive any encouragement. The Soviets remained opposed to any new agreement on the Allied presence in Berlin and complained constantly of alleged illegal West German activities there, such as banned Bundestag committee meetings. Both President Kennedy and President Johnson nevertheless continued their efforts to relieve tensions with the East.

I allocated an official visit to Berlin to fulfill one of my formal responsibilities there. Now nearly forgotten, Spandau prison for Nazi war criminals was one of the last remnants of Four Power rule. Since 1946, each of the occupying powers had run the prison a month at a time, the United States having been allotted April, August, and December. On April 23, 1964, I exercised my right as Ambassador to inspect the prison. The official purpose of my inspection was to determine the state of the prisoners' health and treatment and to see whether they had any complaints or requests. As inspector I was to interview each man separately after examining his cell and personal effects. Under prison rules, the prisoners were supposed to be addressed only by their prison numbers. However, I found this too inhuman, and even though I was accompanied by the British, French, and Soviet commandants, I used their names. By tradition, the inspector did not raise personal or political questions.

Of the three, Albert Speer—who was bucking for early release—was the most forthcoming and ingratiating. His daughter, well known in the Berlin American community, had once approached me in her father's behalf at a reception. Under Secretary of State George Ball once told me that she had also sought his help in obtaining Speer's release. Speer, Hitler's minister of armaments and war production, told me that he was primarily interested in having more books and a better lamp to read by.

Rudolf Hess, Hitler's deputy, had always been accorded particular attention at Spandau because of his senior rank and his spectacular wartime flight to Scotland. At the time of my inspection, he was not permitted a watch because of Soviet objections, his books were censored, and he was not allowed facilities to make tea or coffee. Only in 1966 was he allowed a daily, rather than weekly, bath. Hess was then feigning insanity and said nothing that would hurt his game. He looked gaunt and somber, with deep, dark, staring eyes. Nothing of his personality came through. He had two small rooms, each perhaps 10 feet by 6 feet, in one of which, like the other prisoners, he kept a metal footlocker for his meager personal effects. When he opened it for my inspection, the officer's uniform hanging inside was identified as the one he wore when he parachuted into Britain.

Baldur von Schirach, Nazi Youth leader, made no effort to impress me. His appearance was sullen and his requests, if any, were too trivial for me to recall. All of the prisoners expressed a desire for more time outside, where each had a garden. I was told that, when the prisoners were permitted to go outside, Hess and von Schirach were often together. But they refused to associate with Speer, whom they considered as being from a lower social class, leaving him to garden alone. After the release of Speer and von Schirach, the three Western allies decided Hess should be released as well. Apart from humanitarian considerations, Spandau was too large and expensive a prison to hold open for just one prisoner. The Soviets remained adamant that he remain, however, and so Hess died there.

The high point of my activity during my first weeks as Ambassador to the Federal Republic, of course, was President Kennedy's visit to Germany on June 22–26, 1963. His tour was a benchmark in the history of German-American relations. Presidential aide Theodore Sorensen has said that Kennedy's purpose was "to talk to their publics in the wake of de Gaulle's charges against the U.S." Kennedy was concerned with overall U.S. relationships with Western Europe, which he considered of greatest importance "to us and, I hope, to the people of Europe." On his return, Kennedy felt that he had accomplished this objective, particularly with young people, and that he had placed the United States in a position "to get more done."

It was because of Kennedy's visit to Germany that my own arrival in Bonn had been arranged. The visit had been the subject of intense planning by the Embassy over many months. I was determined, in the short time available, to travel to every place Kennedy would visit and meet with every official he would meet. Kennedy drove himself hard and was known to be a tough taskmaster. Since he was to be in Germany only 91 hours, every moment had to count. In addition to Bonn and neighboring Cologne, Kennedy's itinerary included Frankfurt, Wiesbaden, and Berlin. For security reasons he had chosen to stay in Bonn at the home of the deputy chief of mission and in Wiesbaden at the Von Steuben Hotel, the U.S. Air Force's guest house.

During his visit Kennedy was to meet Adenauer, Vice-Chancellor Heinrich Lübke, Brandt, and Erhard. He was to be received by the mayor of each town he visited, attend a mass at the Cologne Cathedral, address the Bonn Embassy staff, be given a dinner by and give a dinner for Chancellor Adenauer, hold a press conference, visit army units, lunch with U.S. military officials, and make a major address at the Paulskirche in Frankfurt, the site in 1848 of Germany's first democratic constitutional convention. In West Berlin he was to speak at a labor convention, which made Adenauer and Erhard apprehensive. He also was to visit the Wall, speak at the city hall, and address remarks to a select audience at the Free University.

No negotiations were involved in Kennedy's meetings with Adenauer and other officials, only what in diplomatic parlance are called tours d'horizon of current issues. He had met them all before and conversed with them with ease. The key events from the standpoint of policy impact were the speeches at the Paulskirche, the West Berlin City Hall, and the Free University, to which considerable thought had been given both in Washington and Bonn.

The subject of the Paulskirche speech, to which most important German officials and leaders had been invited, was "Partnership with Germany and a United Europe." Kennedy opened with a tribute to German democracy, which he recalled had been cradled in a historic meeting of the Frankfurt Assembly at the Paulskirche in 1848. The European and American revolutions and search for liberty and freedom were parts of one common movement, Kennedy said. The interdependence of our age was reflected in our common efforts within the framework of the Atlantic partnership, the strengthening of NATO, the building of Europe, the expansion of trade, and assistance to developing countries.

The object of our common policy, Kennedy continued, was to create a new social order founded on liberty and justice in which men are masters of their fate and states the servants of their citizens, working toward a better life for all. To achieve these goals, we must seek a world of peace in which people live together in mutual respect and regard. "Let it not be said of the Atlantic generation that we left ideals to the past, not purpose and determination to our adversaries," he declared. The audience responded enthusiastically during the speech and applauded strongly at the end.

Kennedy's address on the steps of the Rathaus in Berlin on June 26 before an audience crowded into the Rudolph-Wilde-Platz—the so-called "Ich bin ein Berliner" speech—attracted the greatest attention. The use of the phrase "I am a Berliner" was a great psychological coup for Kennedy. One of the young Embassy wives had helped the President learn to say the phrase in German at a party in Wiesbaden the evening before he went to Berlin. From my vantage point behind Kennedy, I could clearly see the excitement of his audience, which was estimated at 100,000 to 150,000; they filled every bit of space in the Rathaus square and the streets leading into it. Kennedy held them in the palm of his hand from his opening to the final climax. He was at his oratorical best, his timing perfect. As he repeated in his characteristic manner his expression, "Let them come to Berlin," the crowd roared back in approval. One could feel the tension—the developing bond between the slim figure of the young man and the Berlin citizens of all ages and walks of life who had come to pay him tribute. These people had experienced the ravages of war and knew that their freedom, even their lives, depended on the faraway nation Kennedy represented. They were not disappointed; they came away with greater confidence in their future through confidence in him.

Later that day, speaking at the Free University to intellectuals, Kennedy addressed the subject of "The Defense of West Berlin and West Germany." He characterized the objectives of the Free University as turning out "citizens of the world" who could comprehend the sensitive tasks facing free people and who were willing to commit their energies to the advancement of a free society. Kennedy quoted Goethe as believing that education and culture were the answer to international strife. He applauded the Free University for having maintained its fidelity to truth, justice, and liberty.

Justice required, Kennedy said, that the West keep contact with the East and try to improve the lot of their peoples, to show them how democracy works. The reunification of Berlin and Germany was part of the reconstitution of a larger Europe, Kennedy affirmed. The Eastern states were unable to match the pace of modern society and its intellectual ferment, which required human initiatives and the diversity of free minds. This ferment was apparent in the new Europe of the West and would have an increasing attraction for the East. To succeed, however, the West must increase its strength and unity.

In their bland joint communiqué at the end of the visit, Kennedy and Adenauer expressed agreement on continued close collaboration to develop a genuine community among the nations of Europe in close partnership with the United States; to strengthen participation by the developing nations in world trade; to pursue controlled disarmament and the cessation of nuclear weapons tests to help avoid a dangerous arms race; to strengthen NATO common defense planning and the joint operation of defense forces; and to use their best efforts to create the proposed MLF. They also reaffirmed the right of self-determination under the United Nations Charter and German reunification in peace and freedom, including the freedom of Berlin. Here they would seek to counter the inhuman effects of the Wall and try to reduce the tension it created. Their overall goals remained peace and freedom.

Kennedy's visit to Germany in 1963 has been widely acclaimed as one of the most successful state visits on record. It removed some of his own reservations about Germany, and it endeared him to the German people. He was indefatigable throughout, and he mastered all of his briefing material. Although a hundred key Germans were at the dinner Kennedy gave at the Embassy Club in Bonn, he had some flattering comment to make to each, indicating his understanding of each man's position.

The visit brought a remarkable outpouring of admiration and affection for Kennedy from the German people, particularly the young. This charming, youthful American aristocrat, with his ready smile and wit, provided a sharp contrast to the dour octogenarian Chancellor Adenauer and his chubby successor-to-be, Ludwig Erhard. Kennedy's barrage of inspiring statements embodied his idealism, his unbounded optimism, and his hope for the future. Delivered in his effective staccato tempo with his charming Boston Irish touch, his speeches enthralled his audiences. I was sitting next to Kennedy in an open car as we drove from the airport to Frankfurt. Tens of thousand of Germans of all ages lined the road, waving banners and shouting welcomes. As the car went past, their faces lit up. Individually and collectively, the Germans were having a love affair with Jack Kennedy. He had demonstrated his friendship for the Germans and his appreciation of their postwar efforts at rehabilitation. This success served as a long-lasting lubricant for the subsequent day-to-day conduct of U.S.-German relations and gave me great confidence in the outcome of my tour of duty.

Only five months later, in the aftermath of the President's assassination in Dallas, an unprecedented outpouring of grief swept Germany. The Germans felt that they had lost one of their own. By the thousands they stood by candlelight in silent tribute in churches on dark autumn evenings. For months afterward, I was to spend much of my time attending ceremonies dedicating monuments and structures in his honor all over the Federal Republic—here a bridge, there a road, at another place a statue. Germans of that generation would never forget Jack Kennedy.

Many flashes from the Kennedy visit still come to mind: Adenauer and Brandt in Berlin jockeying for precedence with respect to the President in a contest that Brandt won; my being shoved bodily by General Chester Clifton, the President's military aide, so I would displace the French minister in Berlin, who Clifton thought was hogging the limelight by standing directly behind the President as he began his speech at the Rathaus; Kennedy inspecting an infantry division near Frankfurt with its full complement of troops, transport, weapons, and equipment stretched out in formation behind it and the Brigadier General who commanded it alone out front, receiving the President's salute; Kennedy scowling in defiance at the Berlin Wall; hearing the roar of the Berliners in front of City Hall; and feeling the letdown of the crowds at Tegel airport as the President ended the visit that had lifted the whole German nation to such emotional heights. Words were not needed that evening as I returned to Bonn in a U.S. plane with Chancellor Adenauer and other German officials.

Economic issues loomed large on my arrival in Bonn. Substantial German-

American business ties had antedated World War I. American cotton supplied the Bremen market; American oil companies, particularly Esso, Mobil, and Caltex, furnished petroleum to German refineries and marketed their products; Ford and General Motors' Opel were among Germany's largest automobile manufacturers. IBM had achieved a virtual monopoly in advanced computers. In 1963 American investment in West Germany stood at $1.8 billion, exceeded only by investments in Britain and Canada. Meanwhile, West German investment in the United States, as typified by Hoechst, the large German chemical firm, was rising too. American trade in German manufactured products, led by such firms as Siemens and Krupp, was substantial. Heads of U.S. and German companies had developed a high degree of rapport. Most West Germans showed little interest in socialism, and business proceeded on the basis of classical free-market competition.

The correct relationship between American diplomats and American business abroad is a much-discussed subject. Having come to the State Department from a business background, and having served on the boards of a number of companies other than my own, I felt at ease with businessmen and wanted to help them in every legitimate way. Before leaving for Bonn, I made a point of getting to know the chairmen of important American firms doing business in Germany, assuring them that they and their representatives were always welcome in the Embassy. During my five years in Germany, I regularly participated in the periodic meetings arranged by the Embassy's economic section for top representatives of German subsidiaries of American firms. I found these very effective.

American businessmen and the Embassy economic section usually have a good rapport, but since most political officers, including most ambassadors, have had little business experience, company men sometimes question their judgment in business matters. Embassy economic personnel also sometimes fear that if they help one American firm, they can be criticized by its competitors or blamed if their advice to a company turns out to be wrong and the company incurs a loss, endangering their careers. Unfortunately, businessmen often see the officer's hesitancy to help as representing laziness or indifference.

I always arranged meetings between German officials and American businessmen, or gave a luncheon for this purpose. In one instance, I was able to intervene on behalf of McDonnell-Douglas, the St. Louis–based aircraft manufacturer, and the Boeing Company, both of which were negotiating with Lufthansa, the German government-controlled airline, for intermediate-range aircraft for domestic use. Lufthansa was interested both in what eventually became the Boeing 737 and the Douglas DC-9, neither of which was yet in production. I was in touch with both companies. Meanwhile, the British government was pressing the merits of the BAC-111 made by the government-owned British Aircraft Corporation. The sale was worth $35 million. A rather amusing incident occurred at a dinner given in Cologne by the German Rhodes Scholar Association, which both I and my good friend and British colleague, Sir Frank Roberts, attended. Called to the phone, he came back smiling and chuckling. "I believe this call is for you, George," he said. It was Donald Douglas.

As it happened, the negotiations for the Lufthansa plane were at an acute stage when the Embassy heard rumors that the British were putting pressure on the German government, threatening to withdraw troops. At this point, I called Ludger Westrick, Chancellor Erhard's Chief of Staff and a good friend of the United States, and asked to see him as soon as possible. He received me within half an hour, and I explained the situation. I told him that, although the Embassy had assisted both companies, we had not taken sides, leaving it to Boeing and McDonnell-Douglas to sell their product. No matter who won, we would have accepted any decision Lufthansa made on merit, but we could not accept losing the sale to the British as the result of political pressure. After all we had done for Germany, I said, Americans would never understand this. Westrick picked up the phone and asked for Herman Abs, honorary chairman of the supervisory board of Lufthansa. Westrick explained the situation, making it clear that he was speaking for the Chancellor. The West German government, he told Abs, took no position on the sale but expected Lufthansa to make its decision entirely on commercial grounds. Boeing got the contract in February 1965.

These are examples of how I believe an American Ambassador can assist American companies. Preferential treatment must clearly be avoided. But beyond this, one should give any reputable American firm all reasonable help. The United States' already precarious balance of payments provided full justification. The British, who had experienced balance-of-payments difficulties from the end of World War II, set a good example for Americans in the tenacity with which they supported their firms. American companies deserve no less. At least one aspect of the Embassy effort to help new American companies find business in German markets could certainly not be considered controversial. Working with the economic section of the Embassy, the U.S. Department of Commerce organized many industrial fairs all over Germany to help American firms, which were often represented by husband-wife combinations. I attended these fairs, made speeches, and talked with our exhibitors. One fair earned $35 million for the Americans.

One of my first official acts, only five days after presenting my credentials, was to send a message to the Soviet Ambassador to East Germany, Peter Andreyevich Abrasimov. Although this was a routine matter, I had high hopes that I might develop a contact with Abrasimov that might help work out problems between the Allied authorities in Berlin and the Soviet Union. Abrasimov ranked high in his country and party, as his post in East Berlin confirmed. In a sense, he was the government of East Germany. Since we then had no representative there, I looked forward to receiving some impression of the Soviet role in East Germany through contacts with Abrasimov.

Like other U.S. Ambassadors who dealt with him during his long tour of duty in East Berlin, I found him to be an interesting and engaging individual, frank and open within the limits of Soviet custom. We were to have many productive conversations and convivial luncheons. Although no important agreements were reached, there resulted a relaxation of tension and minor accommodations. I felt that I had developed sufficient rapport with Abrasimov to be able to have immediate access to him in a time of crisis.

On my first visit on August 5, I approached the border in my official Cadillac with its two American flags flying bravely from the front fenders. In the presence of the Soviet protocol officer, the East German guard raised the barrier without approaching my car for identification, and I proceeded to the Soviet Embassy. The discussion on this occasion was not of great importance but might be of interest in shedding light on the problems uppermost in our minds. I went on the assumption that I was dealing with Abrasimov only as the Soviet representative in residual quadripartite German matters. He started by putting the conversation on the basis of broad Soviet-U.S. interests. Was it our opinion, for instance, that the Federal Republic could be persuaded to accept adherence to the impending Test Ban Treaty? I declined to address the question, responding merely that I was confident everyone would eventually sign the treaty except for the few nations whose negative attitude were already known.

He suggested that a successful Test Ban Treaty might presage the settlement of such other issues as the future of Germany and West Berlin. I replied that we were still unconvinced, despite many years of discussion, that the Soviet proposals for Berlin offered sufficient guarantees for vital Western interests there. The United States believed that both the Berlin and the German problem could be resolved only in the framework of reunification, in which the East German people were able to express their free will. In any event, I commented, we were not likely to solve the problem in this meeting.

My major pitch was that Americans and Soviets, together with the French and British, had a serious responsibility for minimizing friction in day-to-day matters affecting Berlin. We two could contribute by seeing that tensions between us were minimized. Would he use his undoubtedly great influence on the East Germans for this purpose? Abrasimov replied by disclaiming any responsibility for East Berlin, the capital of an independent state, recognized by 14 nations. He was only empowered to deal with West Berlin, he said. After more discussion of minor issues we parted on a friendly note, although nothing concrete had been accomplished. I liked Abrasimov. In time, I hoped, we could move on to more important problems concerning Berlin and perhaps even solve them.

In October the East Germans twice detained U.S. military truck convoys traversing the Berlin Autobahn with equipment and personnel. These incidents led to serious confrontations between U.S. commanders and the East German military officials who operated the checkpoints. The incidents originated with disturbing demands by the East German authorities that were new and unprecedented. In the process of checking the number of U.S. personnel in a military vehicle, the Germans now demanded that the tailgate of the vehicle be lowered and that, if there were over 30 in a truck, they must dismount to be counted. The U.S. officer in charge of the convoy refused, saying that past procedures had involved only a visual inspection of the interior of the truck from the outside, with the tailgate lowered only if it was too high to look over. We considered it important to avoid setting new precedents that might serve to justify future delays and increasing harassment.

When the first convoy was stopped, the U.S. military mission in Berlin was informed, and we lodged a protest with the Soviet military authorities in Berlin. But they refused to interfere, saying it was an East German responsibility. We then had a direct confrontation with the East Germans. The accepted procedure at this juncture was for the commander of our convoy to give an ultimatum to the East German officer in charge of the checkpoint. Either the barrier must be raised within a specified short period of time or the convoy would go through anyway. On this occasion, the barrier had not been raised so the driver of the lead truck dismounted and raised it, and the convoy proceeded.

The East Germans then brought out two armored personnel carriers, facing each other, blocking the road ahead, and pointed machine guns at the oncoming lead truck of the U.S. convoy. According to instructions, the U.S. truck proceeded as far as it could without ramming the personnel carriers and stopped. The incident was then referred to Washington to be taken up with the Soviets in Moscow. Eventually agreement was reached, and the convoy was allowed to proceed. I had been in touch with the U.S. military commands during each stage of the negotiations.

This incident might have been dismissed as an accident or a mistake had there not been a second similar stoppage. All negotiations failed, and the situation looked serious, so we decided to bring in other U.S. convoys, sympathetic convoys one might say, that would allow themselves to be stopped. Eventually, the congestion of the East German Autobahn became so great that traffic was completely blocked, and the East Germans were forced to give in. In neither stoppage had we given in on any important point of principle. A number of times, however, we feared that the East Germans would call our bluff, creating a situation in which force might have to be used, which we would not have done except on orders from Washington. Fortunately this did not happen.

Shortly after the Autobahn incident, I had a casual talk with Alfried Krupp, the last of his family to be associated with the great Krupp steel and munitions firm in Essen. The family fortunes can be traced to Arndt Krupp, who founded his firm in Essen in 1857. The family had, however, first entered the munitions business in 1621 and eventually became the exclusive armorer to Germany and arms supplier for the Franco-Prussian War and World Wars I and II.

Alfried's life involved a series of tragedies. His family rejected an early marriage as unacceptable. Alfried had taken title to the firm and the name Krupp only when Germany's defeat in World War II was seen as inevitable. He stood trial in 1946 for war crimes, including the use of slave labor and the confiscation of captive steel mills. In 1948 he was sentenced to 12 years in prison and had his property confiscated. But on February 3, 1951, he was released from prison, and his property was restored in a highly publicized amnesty decision by U.S. High Commissioner John McCloy.

On October 39, 1963, Berthold Beitz, the general manager of the Friedrich Krupp company, invited me to lunch with Alfried at Beitz's residence near Essen. Krupp's only son, Arndt, then in his early 20s, was also present. Alfried, a handsome man with a sober, gaunt appearance, still showed some effects of a recent illness, and he let Beitz do most of the talking. Like Beitz, Krupp took the line that Western action to raise the standard of living in the Soviet satellites would ultimately pay dividends by reducing the risk of East-West confrontations. The Soviets were in trouble, he said, and the Eastern bloc as a whole was "in a sorry state" because of mistakes in economic planning. He believed that the situation offered useful opportunities for Western leverage. In the end, I commented that both "we and the Federal Republic would find it difficult to extend long-term credit to the Bloc in the absence of concrete political concessions by the Soviets." On parting Krupp confided that he would like to meet with me privately in Bonn. I told him I would be pleased to receive him.

On December 13 we lunched alone. We engaged in a desultory discussion of the state of the German steel industry, and Krupp told me that German industrialists did not have a high regard for Erhard in business and economic matters. They thought he talked like a professor, and they had never felt close to him. I then raised the question of his problems in obtaining a visa for the United States, which I knew was the purpose of his visit. He grumbled a bit that it was Beitz who had raised the problem and added that he had no present intention of going to the United States. But if he wanted to go, he asked, why could he not have a normal visa rather than one that required waiver of his war criminal status? I attempted to reassure him that, although a waiver was necessary under U.S. law, this could be done quietly. The notation on the visa would be incomprehensible to nonofficials.

Understandably, Krupp felt uneasy about a visit to the United States, fearing the attendant publicity and possible public confrontations. I attempted to minimize this danger, pointing out that he would be free to travel by private plane and that he could visit many places, including Washington, where he would find less latent antagonism than he might in New York City. In the end he decided not to go, but further disasters were to befall him. Because of the huge debts Beitz had incurred in rebuilding the firm, Krupp was converted to a public company. Alfried himself died shortly thereafter under suspicious circumstances. His son, Arndt, renounced any interest in the firm and became one of Germany's leading playboys. One could scarcely grasp the enormity of the loss and grief that had been incurred by one family and by one man who was destined to bear the brunt. The retribution to the Krupps for having produced to their great profit such a multitude of weapons of mass destruction over so many centuries was slow but complete.

The University of Maryland has for many years operated a European division based in Heidelberg that enables members of U.S. armed forces, mainly in Germany, to complete their higher education. Wilson Elkins, president of the university and a classmate of mine at Oxford, asked me to address their May commencement exercises, scheduled for the Aula, or auditorium, of Heidelberg University, and to receive an honorary degree. Chancellor Erhard had been asked to share the platform. I had long wanted to make a major speech highlighting my conviction that the German people's efforts in the postwar period to redeem themselves in the wake of the Hitler era deserved recognition. I wanted to emphasize how important it was to encourage their continued assimilation into an increasingly unified Europe—and their cooperation with the United States. I discussed this subject with Elkins, and he heartily approved. The fact that Erhard would also be speaking would enhance the importance of what I would say.

The essence of the speech was contained in the first sentence: "The time has come, I say, for the world to make up its mind about the Germans." I added, "I say this because there is evidence that many have not yet made up their minds. I say this because I believe that ample grounds for a decision exist." I then recounted what I considered the evidence to be and made a final appeal to the world to "weigh that case and make up its mind about the Germans." The speech attracted wide publicity, in America as well as in Germany, and its thesis was unchallenged. It was included in an American publication of the most significant speeches of that year.

The origins of Brandt's policy toward the East, known as Ostpolitik, go back at least as far as 1958, his first year as governing mayor of Berlin. In an address that year to the Royal Institute of International Affairs in London, Brandt declared that the free existence of Berlin depended, among other things, on being a "uniting bond between the inhabitants of both sectors of our disrupted land." Berlin should promote an "open-door policy in human and cultural contacts." The only other course was "an unflinching stubborn struggle for a powerful solution by political action." During the 1961 local elections, Brandt had campaigned on pledges to build relations with the Soviet Union and its satellites insofar as the situation justified, while also keeping up a counterpressure against Soviet moves. The SPD (Social Democratic Party) vote rose 4.5 percent.

In 1961 Brandt had been critical of the Western powers, including the United States, for accepting the loss of East Berlin implicit in the building of the Wall. Brandt himself was accused of cowardice for having accepted the Wall. He had said, "The Wall is there now, and cannot simply be over-run." He concentrated on steps that could be taken to make it "permeable." The erection of the Wall has been described as the main reason for Brandt's subsequent policy of Ostpolitik, for bringing Germany together again by "small steps." In my early meetings with Brandt, he often talked in terms of improving ties with the East—East Berlin, East Germany, the other sat-ellites, and the Soviets—through "small steps." He based them on responses to "human" problems created by the Wall: the separation of families and the deep yearning of West Germans for Christmas passes to visit friends and relatives in the East. His faithful associate Egon Bahr encouraged him in developing his Ostpolitik policy.

I reported Brandt's views, as did others, and Washington became inter-ested in finding out just what Brandt had in mind. I urged that we en-courage Brandt to explore further practical applications of his policy, but some in Washington were skeptical. A division arose between those who agreed and those who were skeptical—some feared Brandt and Bahr were going too far too fast. Robert Bowie, head of Policy Planning in the State Department, made a special visit to Bonn at Dean Rusk's suggestion to appraise this issue. From all the evidence, however, the State Department continued to accept the policy I recommended.

During his visit to Washington in May 1964, Brandt had discussed his views on Eastern policy with Dean Rusk and had promised to put some of his thoughts on paper. When I saw him, I encouraged him to do so. In late August he forwarded through the U.S. mission in Berlin a paper entitled "Relations with Eastern European States and Peoples" for transmission to Rusk. It proved to be an interesting document, proposing that the Western states engage the Eastern European states in the largest possible volume of communications. This paper was the beginning. It was not until December 1966, when Brandt took over from Schröder as Foreign Minister in the Grand Coalition, that Brandt had the opportunity to transform what had largely been his own musings into Germany's eastern foreign policy.

I had been in Washington during my home leave in July and had discussed the offset question with both President Johnson and Secretary of Defense Robert McNamara. It was clear that their position had hardened. As the time for the Erhard-Johnson meeting approached, I became increasingly apprehensive. I called Erhard's office to see if he wanted to discuss what position he might take in Washington, so I could help prepare the way. I was informed that he did not want to discuss the matter with anyone until he saw Johnson himself. In a sense, he wanted to "throw himself on Johnson's mercy." Had I seen him, I would have warned him not to expect any.

When I arrived in Washington a few days before Erhard, I requested, as usual, a meeting with Johnson. For the first time, I was told that this would be impossible because the President was spending a few days at his ranch. So I prepared a memorandum for the President on the meeting, which I was later assured he read before he met with Erhard. It read in part as follows:

September 22, 1966
Memo for the President
Subject: Your Meeting with Chancellor Erhard, Sept. 26–27

Your meeting with Erhard next week will be the most critical one you have had with the German leader.

The meeting takes place against the backdrop of deterioration in U.S.-German relations, characterized by a fading confidence on the Germans' part in the firmness of our commitments to them and Europe by a feeling that they are not being given the consideration by us they feel is due them as an important and loyal ally. We should set as our primary goal the restoration of mutual confidence and ease in our relationship.

We must also take into account Erhard's weakened internal political position. This restricts his freedom in making concessions to us. Also, an obvious failure for Erhard in the talks could bring down his government. Rightly or wrongly the Germans— including the Chancellor—believe that he has a special relationship with you. If we let him down now he—or his successor—could draw the conclusion that too intimate a relationship with us is not a political asset—perhaps even a liability. This will not go unnoticed in other countries.

We should, therefore, not press the Chancellor too hard on his vulnerable points, should be prepared without sacrificing vital interests to make accommodation with him, and should try to assume at least the appearance of a successful meeting.

This is, in my judgment, a time to be generous. In so doing we can help assure retaining Germany as a valuable ally.

I predict that he will in private throw himself on your mercy, citing Germany's past performance as a loyal ally.

In my memorandum, I argued strongly that Johnson consider sympathetically Erhard's probable request to stretch out offset payments and substitute debt repayment and purchases of U.S. bonds. In particular, I advised against reducing U.S. troops to meet the offset. I also urged that a joint commission be established to examine these repayment possibilities and recommend specific offset targets and force levels, stating, "If agreement can be obtained on force reductions in this way, they could be made with much less repercussion." I added, "We should not press the Chancellor to accept any public formula which rules out forever any multilateral NATO or European nuclear forces. It would be wise, however, to inform Erhard confidentially we regard the MLF/ANF as unlikely of achievement."

The climax of the ensuing discussions came during an all-day confrontation in the State Department. Secretary of Defense Robert McNamara represented the President, and German Defence Minister Kai-Uwe von Hassel spoke for the Chancellor. Hassel, the perfect gentleman, soft-spoken with a well-modulated voice, was no match for McNamara. McNamara, always confident and quick to respond with the right fact or figure, spoke in rapid staccato phrases. He was able to inject a note of the United States' moral right to offset payments, whereas Hassel, asking for leniency in fulfilling an acknowledged obligation, was disadvantaged. Hassel became increasingly embarrassed and finally appeared to give up.

The crucial issue was whether to allow Germany to buy medium-term U.S. Treasury bonds as a substitute for an immediate cash purchase of military equipment and services. Although it represented an equivalent dollar payment, the purchase of bonds was, of course, not as much help to the United States in its balance of payments problem as was a final, cold-cash sale: the funds invested in bonds would eventually have to be repaid to the German government. The U.S. side was unyielding on this point. The final discussions took place at 11 A.M. on September 26 in a fateful "four-eyes" meeting between the President and Erhard at the White House. The only record is in the informal notes taken by Johnson's interpreter, which are now in the State Department files.

Erhard observed that the two were meeting in arduous times. Both of them were dealing with difficult problems. People were searching to find ways to assess blame, but the two of them were, of course, used to that. They were expecting progress, which he hoped would be possible. He could assure the President that Germany would "stay the course and cooperate with the U.S.," the close ties between the two countries being a stabilizing factor all around the world. The German tendency to "lean toward France" was being pursued by a small but vocal minority, Erhard stated. Reconciliation between Germany and France was important; without it, no progress could be made toward achieving the economic and political unity of Europe. Erhard said that he did not, however, believe that Europe could be built on a bilateral German-French base.

Together, our governments faced two basic problems, he observed—offset payments and U.S. troop levels. The offset payment was due on June 30, 1967. At that time, some new formula had to be found for a followup agreement. American troops were very important to Germany, providing protection and a guarantee of future security, he acknowledged. Confidence in the United States was not lacking, but Germans needed to know where they stood, how they would be protected under a nonproliferation treaty, and what voice they would have in nuclear affairs. It was not just a question of military hardware.

President Johnson said he agreed with the Chancellor's formulation of the problems they faced. He felt affection for Erhard and wanted to help him. Erhard interposed that the Germans appreciated the loyalty of the Americans in fulfilling their commitments in Vietnam and wanted to help us, adding, a little self-servingly, that whoever succeeded him might take a different view of loyalty to the United States. But meeting the current offset obligation put the Germans in a difficult economic situation, Erhard continued. The German economy's growth curve currently had flattened. The necessity to reduce the national budget had required post facto cuts in 30 appropriations. His government had also been forced to enact a special price stability law that was just then taking effect.

Then came Erhard's punch line. It would be impossible to fulfill all of the financial obligations under the present offset agreement. The German government would stand by its promises, but it needed more time. Erhard said that the German Central Bank was helping. (We knew that he was in contact with bank president Karl Blessing, who was in Washington at the time, but reportedly he did not succeed in getting help.) Erhard promised that the Federal Republic would pay the equivalent of an additional $250 million for offset during the remainder of calendar year 1966 against $450 million in U.S. Treasury bills they were to purchase by then under the two-year offset agreement.

This left $450 million due on June 30, 1967. Erhard said that Germany would do all it could to reduce the shortfall, which would then be included in the followup military offset budget. He reminded Johnson that it was customary for businessmen who could not meet all of their obligations to roll the balance over in another loan. In defense of his plea for leniency, he cited recent German efforts to protect the dollar through purchase of so-called Roosa Bonds and engaging in "swaps." The Federal Republic had not sold dollars or bought gold since 1962. He added that Germany currently had an unfavorable trade balance with the United States of $800–$900 million a year and that the Federal Republic had previously paid some outstanding government-to-government debts before they were due.

President Johnson agreed with Erhard that the two principal problems were the offset and the level of U.S. forces in Germany. He explained, however, that his financial problems were greater than Erhard's. He was unclear on the essence of Erhard's remarks. In the past he had always taken the Germans' words for granted. If Germany could not keep its commitments, it would put the United States in a serious situation, one he would have to look at carefully.

Johnson repeated that he understood the Chancellor's problems and wanted to help him as a friend. He did not, however, want to see a situation created that might have regrettable results for both countries. He suggested that they refer the problem to economic and military experts on both sides. Although he undoubtedly had in mind the trilateral committee, he did not spell this out. Erhard could only reply that there was bitterness in hearing the President say that he could not trust the German word. There was no reason to doubt the Germans' sincerity and loyalty, he declared. They would pay all they owed; all they asked was an extension. Erhard acquiesced in the referral of the offset problem to experts. Before he left, Erhard again urged the President to visit Germany in 1966, but Johnson was noncommittal. In the end, Erhard agreed that the final communiqué would obligate Germany to meet the full offset through mid-1967.

As Erhard came out of the meeting, he looked utterly dejected. I felt genuinely sorry for him. No one knew, of course, that Erhard's government would fall within a few weeks and that he would be forced to resign from the chancellorship. When it became known in Germany that Johnson and McNamara had refused to give Erhard the relief he sought despite his strong plea, Erhard suffered a severe political setback. Of what value was the presumed high regard in which he had always been held by Americans, Germans asked? After Erhard had proposed an unpopular tax increase largely to meet the offset payment, the FDP's Erich Mende, Deputy Chancellor and junior partner in Erhard's coalition, withdrew his party from the government. Erhard announced on November 2 that he was ready to resign if another government could be formed. He was not even offered the presidency as a face-saver.

But the mood of Germany's political parties and leaders was changing. People were reacting against the rigid policies of the Adenauer-Erhard era. Some believed they had followed the U.S. line too closely, that they had allowed themselves to be overly influenced by the United States' great power confrontation with the Soviet Union and by its uncertain war in Vietnam. The general feeling was that only something as dramatic as a Grand Coalition could solve the smoldering budget crisis. On November 10 the SPD proposed talks on selecting a new Chancellor. Willy Brandt, leader of the SPD, had gained increasing recognition both for his competence as governing mayor of Berlin and as the exponent of a fresh new look toward the East—Ostpolitik. His advocacy of small humanitarian steps, as exemplified by his successful Christmas passes between East and West Berlin, had increased his popular image. He would be a popular choice as Foreign Minister to succeed the more private Gerhard Schröder.

The coalition ultimately bestowed the post of Chancellor on Kurt-Georg Kiesinger, who had been "in exile" from Bonn since 1958. For many years the leading foreign affairs spokesman for the CDU (Christian Democratic Union) in the Bundestag, he had returned to become Minister-President with great success, proving himself an excellent administrator.

Kiesinger's inaugural statement on December 13, 1967, highlighted Germany's grim economic situation, the principal factor behind the change of government that brought him to the chancellorship. He acknowledged that 700,000 West Germans were unemployed and that 340,000 more were working part-time, the first time in over a decade that employment had been a problem in Germany. He promised a further cut in government expenditures but warned that this would still leave a deficit of DM 3 billion in the coming year. The states and municipalities would be urged to reduce their expenditures, and bank loans would be limited. He called for a controlled expansion of the economy in light of the meager 2 percent increase in national income in 1966, along with a reduction in investment and building activity.

Kiesinger's second theme was foreign policy. He promised to continue the policies toward the Federal Republic's Western allies that had characterized both the Adenauer and Erhard administrations. But, for the first time in West Germany's postwar history, he also emphasized that his government would pursue establishment of diplomatic relations with Eastern European countries "wherever possible." De-emphasis on relations with the United States was a major consideration for the new government. Kiesinger made it clear that his government would no longer be running to the United States to solve its problems.

The Nuclear Non-Proliferation Treaty (NPT), one of the most important accomplishments in the widely supported effort to limit and control the use of nuclear weapons, was a revealing test of the German-American relationship. It was signed on July 1, 1968, by three nuclear powers—the United States, Great Britain, and the Soviet Union—and more than 50 other nations, not including Germany, which did not sign until November 1969. France and China, both of which had conducted nuclear tests and developed nuclear weapons, did not sign; neither did a number of nonnuclear countries, some of which were in various stages in the development of nuclear capability. In 1974 India joined those who had tested a nuclear bomb. By 1985, 192 nonnuclear nations had adhered to the treaty.

Under the terms of the treaty, the nonnuclear countries forswore nuclear weapons and the nuclear signatory powers agreed to share nuclear technology, work for general nuclear disarmament, and "seek to achieve the discontinuance of all nuclear weapons for all times." In view of Germany's role in two world wars and West Germany's reputation in nuclear science, it was clear from the treaty's inception that the Federal Republic was an important potential signatory.

The Germans understood that they could never become a nuclear power, and they had no desire to do so. From a purely practical standpoint, to build a nuclear bomb they would have to conduct nuclear tests, which could be easily detected and could lead to immediate retaliation by the USSR and almost all other nations, who would never tolerate a German "finger on the nuclear trigger." Nonetheless, the Germans sought certain assurances about the treaty's impact on their security, economy, and international status; that it not hinder creation of an MLF or European nuclear force; that it not handicap their participation in nuclear development for peaceful purposes;

and that it not enhance the international status of East Germany, a concern they had already expressed at the time of the signing of the Limited Test Ban Treaty. On January 11, 1967, the United States was advised that the West German cabinet had agreed to the treaty in principle. I knew, however, that this was only the beginning and that many roadblocks lay ahead. Another 18 months went by before the final signing.

During my meeting with Brandt on January 10, he appeared very relaxed about the NPT. He was unconcerned about the effect of the treaty on a European nuclear force or on GDR attendance at a conference pursuant to the agreement. He seemed, characteristically, more concerned about issues likely to be raised by the nonnuclear countries, particularly the neutrals. Could we make some statement that the nuclear powers would not use nuclear weapons as a threat against them, he asked.

On January 17, I sent a report to the State Department, noting that on January 11 the West German cabinet had agreed in principle to join the NPT enterprise. This did not mean, however, that U.S. problems with the Germans on this issue were over. I was concerned by rumors in German political circles that we had already reached agreement with the Soviets and that there were secret codicils and side agreements. The basic weakness of the U.S. position lay in our inability to tell the Germans that we had discussed with the Soviets what effect the treaty might have on a possible European nuclear force in the event of European political integration. This open option had emerged as one of the principal German preoccupations in connection with the NPT. The Germans feared that we wanted to keep them from participating in a nuclear force of any kind.

I recognized that if we were to get a treaty, we had to stick to the principle that what was not prohibited was permitted. I pointed out to the State Department that any unclarity would cost us an increasing price in good relations as we tried to get a German signature. To minimize this risk, I suggested an early statement of how we understood the treaty in a letter from Rusk to Brandt, with the additional assurance that our interpretation would be made public at an appropriate time, particularly if the Soviets should contend that the treaty prohibited a European nuclear force. There was a tendency in the German Ministries to question our explanations and to use them as a basis for new questions.

In my meeting with Chancellor Kiesinger on January 16, I asked him what particular problems he had with the NPT. I pointed out that nuclear explosions were probably not practicable in a densely populated country like Germany and that there were no restrictions on peaceful uses. Kiesinger responded that his principal concern lay in the treaty's possible effect on the development of European political unification. This could, he said, develop in various ways—for instance, as a federation or as a confederation. Former Minister of Foreign Affairs Walter Hallstein, in particular, was greatly disturbed over this factor and had told Kiesinger so in a recent meeting. Kiesinger hoped that this aspect of the treaty could be made clear. I pointed out that in our view the present wording of the draft treaty would not preclude a European nuclear force under the political control of a European federation, confederation, or unitary state.

At lunch at our Embassy on February 21 with Ambassador Swidbeer Schnippenkötter, Minister of Science Gerhard Stoltenberg described the intensive negotiations going on within the German government between the Foreign, Economics, Defense, and Science ministries, not to mention the Chancellery. It was his impression that the principal issues remaining were the potential obstacles to development and use of nuclear energy for peaceful purposes embodied in the safeguards envisioned in the NPT's Article III.

The Germans were concerned not so much with the present international inspection policy and methods under conditions where inspection was voluntary, but with what the constraints would be like under a greatly enlarged responsibility with mandatory inspection. Stoltenberg considered it significant that the nuclear powers excluded inspection of their own nuclear programs for military use. He said it was even more difficult for the nonnuclear powers to accept the nuclear powers' exclusion of their installations for peaceful use. Although Stoltenberg understood that we might accept inspection, we both understood that the Soviet Union would not. He was concerned that the nuclear powers would have a competitive advantage in the development of nuclear reactors and other industrial and commercial applications if we were to join the Soviet Union and reject inspection, too.

Stoltenberg accepted fully the U.S. argument that technical "spinoff" on the weapons side was negligible. He did not raise the question of possible discrimination in the use of nuclear explosions. He clearly saw West Germany as a major potential competitor in the field of nuclear development for peaceful uses. He did not want the Federal Republic handicapped by NPT-engendered espionage—or unnecessary constraints.

I explained to Stoltenberg that U.S. experience with IAEA (International Atomic Energy Agency) on "peaceful uses," which we had put under their inspection, had not given competitiors any advantage. On the basis of data I received, I was able to explain convincingly that the NPT would not adversely affect recent arrangements for fuel supply and reprocessing within the European Community. The United States agreed with the Germans that technological "spinoff" in the nuclear weapons field would not create any problem in the "peaceful uses" field. I pointed out that the United States already complied with proposed NPT safeguards in its current bilateral supply agreements with West Germany, Italy, and the Netherlands. The United States required no information or knowledge of nuclear research and development from the recipient countries.

According to FRG disarmament negotiator Schnippenkötter in my meeting with him on May 23, the general reaction against the NPT had subsided in Germany. The only question remaining was how long the treaty would last. Germany was satisfied with the provisions of the U.S. draft on peaceful uses. There were those—including the Chancellor—who sought a limited duration treaty as a matter of principle, regardless of substance. In essence, Kiesinger's view was based on an unwillingness to commit "future German generations" to a treaty whose full consequences could not now be foreseen and that would exist in a world of changing conditions—that is, the possible termination of NATO. In a sense, limiting the treaty's duration was intended to take care of unforeseen contingencies.

Prospects for German ratification of NPT still remained uncertain, although certain of the large number of German questions raised had been met. Other important issues remained, however, and a general sullen reluctance seemed to characterize the key German actors, particularly Kiesinger. Most of them were genuinely concerned over their pet complaints. No one was willing to start a movement toward accepting the treaty draft as it stood, fearing later criticism. This was the mood of the Germans on the eve of my departure from Germany. The NPT was finally signed on November 7, 1969, by Willy Brandt as Chancellor of two weeks.

Included here are a few statistics to show the scope of the Bonn Embassy, which had a staff of about 1,000. The Embassy was responsible in political matters for Berlin and the U.S. brigade there; for the three major NATO commands and 250,000 American military personnel, with about 250,000 dependents in Germany; and for a large CIA group with responsibilities going beyond Germany. Germany is also a key NATO ally and the leading industrial country of the European Community.

The basic duty of an Ambassador is to represent the President of the United States with the host government. During my five-year tenure in Bonn, I participated in 367 meetings with senior West German officials, including 24 with President Lübke and 94 with the three Chancellors, including 14 with Adenauer, 65 with Erhard, and 15 with Kiesinger. I held 39 meetings with Foreign Minister Brandt, 29 with Foreign Minister Schröder, 64 with Under Secretary Carstens, and 117 with other ministers and their subordinates. A typical meeting averaged an hour.

Official visits occupied much of my time as Ambassador. I made 211 visits outside Bonn, 50 official visits to other German cities, 36 to universities, and 125 for speaking appearances. Of my speaking engagements, 57 could be considered major speeches that averaged perhaps 5,000 words. These speeches usually received wide German and often American media coverage. Nineteen were published in the *State Department Bulletin*. Since internal commercial transport is not well developed in Germany, I traveled primarily by car. Only occasionally did I use the state railway; on a number of occasions I traveled on private trains loaned me by the military. I had access to, and often used, one of the planes assigned to our air attaché, and occasionally I borrowed a jet plane from our NATO air command in Wiesbaden for long trips.

Too much of an Ambassador's time is consumed by business-social activities, but few of these activities are strictly social or personal. My wife and I hosted 526 such affairs involving 14,875 guests. These included 220 luncheons, 95 receptions and cocktail parties, 205 dinners, 2 concerts, and 3 large dances. The Embassy staff, including our excellent cook, who was with us the entire time, and our maitre d', were highly professional and tireless. After preparing for a luncheon for 20, they would not bat an eye if dinner for 30 was added for the same evening.

During our five years in Germany, my wife and I received a total of 3,196 invitations of all sorts, of which we could accept only 671, or about one-fifth. Some refusals represented conflicts, some came during absences from the city, and others were to events of less importance. We regretted that we seldom received invitations for small, informal dinners or from young people of lesser rank. Germans are very rank conscious as concerns both invitations and acceptances. I received 1,228 outside visitors in my office during five years. This, of course, is a small number in comparison with those in larger capitals.

THE ROLE OF DIPLOMACY

I hold a strong belief in the importance of diplomacy—the conduct of relations between governments—which includes not only negotiating treaties, making speeches, and giving dinner parties, but also all exchanges across national borders to relieve tensions by reaching agreements. The ultimate instrument for the conduct of diplomacy is generally considered to be a policy, and governments are often criticized for "not having a policy," especially by those who would not recognize a policy if they ran into one in broad daylight. In its most basic meaning a policy is a strategy for providing overall guidance, including self-reinforcement of the means available to the government in achieving a foreign policy objective. If a group of people was searching for a lost child in the woods, they would not just walk at random, but each would pursue a predetermined grid and have the means of signaling to each other.

The international objectives of a democratic government acting in behalf of its people can only be expressed in general terms, such as "to promote the security and well-being of the people of the United States." To be effective, however, the objective must be broken down into specifics such as: "to contain the expansion of communism," "to increase exports and achieve a favorable balance of trade," or "to help the developing nations strengthen their economies and independence." In achieving these objectives, consideration must also be given to its long- and short-term aspects and the extent to which Congress will approve and the American people will be willing to pay the bill. And the question must also be asked: will there be hostilities resulting in loss of life?

If policies correspond to strategies, lines of action and the ways and means of carrying them out represent tactics, which require operational planning, programming, and costing. Since this also involves thinking ahead, it must include policy planning for the future. Contingency planning concerns future events that may or may not occur and has less scope in foreign relations than in military actions. Foreign relations can best be compared to a game of tennis in that the receiving player can have ready in his mind various strategies but he cannot decide which strategy and what tactics he should use until his opponent hits the ball.

In the past most of the world's diplomatic activity has been conducted quietly between embassies abroad and the host government's foreign office. In recent years more emphasis has been placed on direct exchanges between heads of state and on visits of high officials. These visits can, however, arouse undue public expectations as to results and so lead to later disappointment. In addition, such exchanges are often accompanied by leaks to the press that can hamper negotiations. Direct telephone conversations between heads of state can be effective—even necessary. They do not, however, provide the depth required for full consideration and could lead to hasty, poorly considered decisions.

From my years of experience as Ambassador in Ankara and Bonn, I found that the best results came from private meetings with the Foreign Minister or Prime Minister. Since I saw these officials often, our meetings aroused little curiosity from the press, and so there were no leaks that could have embarrassed either of us. We were left to discuss frankly the problem at hand and reach agreement on its solution in a professional way. The usual need to refer back to Washington for the final decision provided time to avoid a hasty decision. In the conduct of diplomacy, timing is of the essence. There are seldom any new ideas available for the formulation of a successful foreign policy. Almost every possible course of action has been thought of before. Breakthroughs usually result from changes in the world scene, which makes something possible which would previously have failed. The art of diplomacy is to sense such an opportunity and make your move accordingly, adapting to changing circumstances.

Differences between nations can also best be resolved by approaching them as early as possible, before they become hardened or lead to open hostilities. Often such problems can be charted, as two ships on a collision course must be negotiated before the collision occurs. For example, the Dutch, having lost Indonesia, had held onto nearby West Irian as a face-saver. But Sukarno, the ruler of Indonesia, had determined to add it to his polyglot empire, and he was landing troops in West Irian for short forays. As head of Policy Planning, I sensed a collision and initiated a study to determine when it might occur. The Dutch admitted that they were not in a position to protect their possessions, and we made it clear we would not fight for them, which left the way clear for Sukarno. To accomplish this peacefully, we offered to play the role of mediation in the person of Ambassador Ellsworth Bunker. The strategy was to use the United Nations as a fig leaf for the transfer, after which the United Nations would conduct a plebiscite and West Irian would end up in Indonesia. After difficult negotiations, the strategy worked and what would probably have been the last colonial war was averted.

Similarly, we played for time in negotiating with President Tshombe of the Katanga Province in 1962 to end his secession. I sought to persuade him to carry out our so-called U Thant Plan and end his secession. Following instructions given by President Kennedy to avoid hostilities, my strategy was to gain momentum in the negotiations with the Congo while "playing for the breaks." The break came when Tshombe's troops went on a binge in Elizabethville; the U.N. Indian generals attacked them in Jadotville and occupied the city—and the secession was over.

Diplomacy has been proven to be effective in the past and will, I am sure, be just as effective in the future. We must remember the period immediately after World War II, which is accepted as the Golden Age of Diplomacy. Drawn together by common enemies, the Allies won the war and organized the peace. The United States underwrote the Marshall Plan to restore the European economy, financial agreements were reached at Bretton Woods, and when the Soviets threatened aggression, NATO was created and its strength maintained until the Soviets capitulated in 1990 and the Cold War was over.

Bibliography

Abdullah. *Memoirs of King Abdullah of Transjordan.* 2 vols. Vol. 1, Philip P. Graves, ed. New York: Philosophical Library, 1950; Vol. 2. Washington, D.C.: American Council of Learned Societies, 1954.

Acheson, Dean. "The Practice of Partnership." *Foreign Affairs* 41 (January 1963).

Acheson, Dean. *Present at the Creation: My Years in the State Department.* New York: W. W. Norton, 1969.

Adenauer, Konrad. *Memoirs, 1945–1953.* Translated by Beate Ruhm von Oppen. London: Weidenfeld and Nicholson, 1966.

Ahmad, Feroz. *The Turkish Experiment in Democracy, 1950–1975.* London: C. Hurst and Co., published for the Royal Institute of International Affairs, 1977.

Ajami, Fouad. *The Arab Predicament: Arab Political Thought and Practice Since 1967.* Cambridge: Cambridge University Press, 1982.

Ali, Tariq, ed. *The Stalinist Legacy: Its Impact on Twentieth Century World Politics.* London: 1984.

Almond, Gabriel A., ed. *The Struggle for Democracy in Germany.* New York: Russell and Russell, 1965.

Alvarez, David J. *Bureaucracy and Cold War Diplomacy: The United States and Turkey.* Thessaloniki: 1980.

Antonius, George. *The Arab Awakening: The Story of the Arab National Movement.* Philadelphia: Lippincott, 1939.

Bahr, Egon. "Renunciation of Force and the Alliance." *Aussenpolitik* (English ed.) 24, no. 3 (1973).

Balfour, Michael. *West Germany: A Contemporary History.* London: Croom Helm, 1982.

Ball, George. *Diplomacy for a Crowded World: An American Foreign Policy.* Boston and Toronto: Little, Brown, 1976.

Barnds, William J. *India, Pakistan, and the Great Powers.* New York: Praeger Publishers, 1972.

Barnet, Richard J. *The Alliance.* New York: Simon and Schuster, 1983.

Binder, David. *The Other Germany: Willy Brandt's Life and Times.* Washington, D.C.: New Republic, 1975.

Birrenbach, Kurt. "The West and German Ostpolitik: The German Opposition View." *Atlantic Community Quarterly* (Summer 1971).

Blake, Robert. *The Decline of Power, 1915–64.* London: Granada, 1985.

Bohlen, Charles L. *Witness to History, 1929–1969.* New York: W. W. Norton, 1973.

Bowie, Robert. "Tensions within the Alliance." *Foreign Affairs* 42 (October 1963).

Brandt, Conrad. *Stalin's Failure in China.* Cambridge, Mass.: Harvard University Press, 1958.

Brandt, Willy. "Germany's 'Westpolitik.' " *Foreign Affairs* 50 (April 1972).

Brandt, Willy. *Peace: Writings and Speeches of the Nobel Prize Winner, 1971.* Bonn: Verlag Neue Gesellschaft, 1971.

Brandt, Willy. *People and Politics: The Years 1960–1973.* Boston: Little, Brown, 1976.

Braunthal, Gerhard. *The West German Social Democrats, 1969–1982: Profile of a Party in Power.* Boulder, Colo.: Westview, 1983.

Brzezinski, Zbigniew. *The Permanent Purge: Politics in Soviet Totalitarianism.* Cambridge, Mass.: Harvard University Press, 1956.

Buchan, Alistair. "Partner and Allies." *Foreign Affairs* 41 (July 1963).

Bullard, Sir Reader. *Britain and the Middle East.* London: Hutchinson, 1951.

Bullock, Alan. *Ernest Bevin, Foreign Secretary.* New York: W. W. Norton, 1983.

Bullock, Alan. *Hitler and Stalin, Parallel Lives.* New York: Alfred A. Knopf, 1992.

Campbell, John C. *Defense of the Middle East.* New York: Harper and Brothers, 1958.

Carrère d'Encausse, Hélène. *Stalin: Order Through Terror.* London, 1981.

Catudel, Honor O'M. *Kennedy and the Wall Crisis: A Case Study in U.S. Decision Making.* Berlin: Berlin-Verlag, 1979.

Chalmers, Douglas A. *The Social Democratic Party of Germany: From Working-Class Movement to Modern Political Party.* New Haven, Conn.: Yale University Press, 1964.

Clay, Lucius D. *Decision in Germany.* Garden City, N.Y.: Doubleday, 1950.

Cordesman, Anthony. "The Middle East and the Politics of Force." *Middle East Journal* 40:1 (Winter 1986).

Craig, Gordon A. *The Germans.* New York: G. P. Putnam's Sons, 1982.

Crawley, Aidan. *The Rise of Western Germany, 1945–1972.* London: Collins, 1973.

Dahrendorf, Ralf. *Society and Democracy in Germany.* New York and London: W. W. Norton, 1967.

Davies, R. W. *Soviet History in the Gorbachev Revolution.* London, 1989.

Dayan, Moshe. *Story of My Life, An Autobiography.* New York: William Morrow and Co., 1976.

De Rose, François. "Atlantic Relationships and Nuclear Problems." *Foreign Affairs* 41 (April 1963).

Dobney, Frederick J. *The Selected Papers of Will Clayton.* Baltimore: Johns Hopkins University Press, 1971.

Dönhoff, Marion. *Foe into Friend: The Makers of the New Germany from Konrad Adenauer to Helmut Schmidt.* London: Weidenfeld and Nicholson, 1982.

Donovan, Robert J. *Conflict and Crisis: The Presidency of Harry S. Truman, 1945–1948.* New York: Norton, 1977.

Donovan, Robert J. *Tumultuous Years: The Presidency of Harry S. Truman, 1949–1953.* New York: Norton, 1982.

Dornberg, John. *The New Germans: Thirty Years After.* New York: Macmillan, 1976.

Droge, Heinz, Fritz Muench, and Ellinor von Pottkamer. *The Federal Republic of Germany and the United Nations.* New York: Carnegie Endowment for International Peace, 1967.

Dulles, Elanor Lansing. *One Germany or Two: The Struggle at the Heart of Europe.* Stanford: Almquist and Wiksell, 1965.

Eden, Anthony. *The Reckoning.* Boston, 1965.

Eden, Sir Anthony. *The Memoirs of Sir Anthony Eden: Full Circle.* London: Cassell and Co. Ltd., 1960.

Engler, Robert. *The Politics of Oil.* Chicago: University of Chicago Press, 1961.

Eren, Nuri. *Turkey Today—and Tomorrow.* New York, 1963.

Erhard, Ludwig. *Germany's Comeback in the World Market.* Translated by W. H. Johnston. New York: Macmillan, 1954.

Erkin, Feridun Cemal. *Les Relations Turco-Soviétiques et la Question des Détroits.* Ankara, 1968.

Erler, Fritz. "The Basis of Partnership." *Foreign Affairs* 42 (October 1963).

Etzold, Thomas H. "The Soviet Union in the Mediterranean." In *NATO and the Mediterranean.* Lawrence S. Kaplan et al., eds. Wilmington, Del.: Scholarly Resources, 1985.

Feis, Herbert. *Between War and Peace: The Potsdam Conference.* Princeton, N.J.: Princeton University Press, 1960.

Feis, Herbert. *From Trust to Terror: The Onset of the Cold War, 1945–1950.* New York: Norton, 1970.

Fisher, W. B. *The Middle East: A Physical, Social and Regional Geography.* New York: E. P. Dutton, 1950.

Ford, Alan W. *The Anglo-Iranian Oil Dispute of 1951–1952.* Berkeley: University of California Press, 1954.

Frye, Richard N., ed. *The Near East and the Great Powers.* Cambridge, Mass.: Harvard University Press, 1951.

Gaddis, John. *Strategies of Containment: A Critical Appraisal of Postwar American National Security Policy.* New York: Oxford University Press, 1982.

Gatzke, Hans W. *Germany and the United States.* Cambridge and London: Harvard University Press, 1980.

Gibb, Hamilton A. R. *Modern Trends in Islam.* Chicago: University of Chicago Press, 1947.

Gimble, John. *The Origins of the Marshall Plan.* Stanford, Calif.: Stanford University Press, 1976.

Glubb, John Bagot. *The Story of the Arab Legion.* London: Hodder and Stoughton, 1948.

Goergey, Laszlo. *Bonn's Eastern Policy, 1964–1971: Evolution and Limitations.* Hamden, Conn.: Archon Books, 1972.

Goldsborough, James O. "The Franco-German Entente." *Foreign Affairs* 54 (April 1976).

Griffith, William E. *The Ostpolitik of the Federal Republic of Germany.* Cambridge, Mass.: MIT Press, 1978.

Grimmet, Richard. "United States Military Installations in Turkey." Congressional Research Service Report No. 84–221 F (December 12, 1984).

Grosser, Alfred. *Germany in Our Time.* New York: Praeger, 1971.

Grosser, Alfred. *The Western Alliance.* Translated by Michael Shaw. New York: Vintage, 1980.

Haftendorn, Helga. *Security and Détente: Conflicting Priorities in German Foreign Policy.* New York: Praeger, 1985.

Hahn, Walter F. "West Germany's Ostpolitik: The Grand Design of Egon Bahr." *Orbis* 16 (Winter 1973).

Hamilton, Charles W. *Americans and Oil in the Middle East.* Houston: Gulf Publishing Co., 1952.

Hanrieder, Wolfram. *The Stable Crisis: The Two Decades of German Foreign Policy.* New York: Harper and Row, 1970.

Harris, George S. *Troubled Alliance: Turkish-American Problems in Historical Perspective, 1945–1971.* Stanford, Calif.: Stanford University Press, 1972.

Harris, Kenneth. *Atlee.* London: Weidenfeld and Nicholson, 1982.

Haslam, Jonathan. *The Soviet Union and the Struggle for Collective Security, 1933–39.* New York: St. Martin's Press, 1984.

Heathcote, Nina. "Brandt's 'Ostpolitik' and Western Institutions." *World Today* 26 (August 1970).

Henderson, Loy W. "American Political and Strategic Interests in the Middle East and Southeast Europe." *Department of State Bulletin* 17 (November 23, 1947): 996–1000.

Hillenbrand, Martin J. *The Future of Berlin.* Montclair, N.J.: Allenheld, Osmon, 1980.

Hillenbrand, Martin J. *Germany in an Era of Transition.* Paris: Atlantic Institute for International Affairs, 1983.

Hiscocks, Richard. *The Adenauer Era.* Philadelphia: Lippincott, 1966.

Hitti, Philip K. *Lebanon in History.* London: Macmillan and Co., 1957.

Holloway, David. *The Soviet Union and the Arms Race.* New Haven, Conn.: Yale University Press, 1983.

Hoskins, Halford L. *The Middle East: Problem Area in World Politics.* New York: Macmillan, 1954.

Hostler, Charles W. *Turkism and the Soviets.* New York: Praeger, 1957.

Howard, Harry N. "The Development of United States Policy in the Near East, 1945–1951." Reprint from the *Department of State Bulletin* (November 26, 1951).

Howard, Harry N. "The Development of United States Policy in the Near East, South Asia, and Africa." Reprint from the *Department of State Bulletin* (December 15, 1952).

Hurewitz, J. C. *Diplomacy in the Near and Middle East.* Princeton, N.J.: Van Nostrand, 1956.

International Bank for Reconstruction and Development. *The Economy of Turkey.* Washington, D.C.: IBRD, 1951.

Jessup, Philip C. *The Birth of Nations: U.S.A.* New York: Columbia University Press, 1976.

Johnson, Lyndon B. *The Vantage Point.* New York: Holt, Rinehart, and Winston, 1971.

Jonas, Manfred. *The United States and Germany: A Diplomatic History.* Ithaca, N.Y.: Cornell University Press, 1984.

Kaiser, Karl. *German Foreign Policy in Transition: Bonn between East and West.* London and New York: Oxford University Press, 1968.

Kennan, George F. *Foreign Affairs* (Spring 1987).

Kennan, George F. "Polycentrism and Western Policy." *Foreign Affairs* 42 (January 1964).

Kennan, George F. "The Sources of Soviet Conduct." *Foreign Affairs* (July 1947) under the pseudonym "X." Reprinted in *American Diplomacy* (Chicago: 1951).

Kennedy, John F. *The Burden and the Glory.* New York: Harper and Row, 1964.

Khadduri, Majid. *Independent Iraq: A Study in Iraqi Politics Since 1932.* New York: Oxford University Press, for the Royal Institute of International Affairs, 1952.

Kiep, Walter Leisler. *A New Challenge for Western Europe: A View from Bonn.* New York: Mason and Lipscomb, 1974.

Kirk, George. *The Middle East, 1945–1950.* London, 1954.

Kirk, George. *The Middle East in the War.* London, 1952.

Kirk, George. "Turkey." In *The War and the Neutrals.* Arnold Toynbee, ed. London, 1956.

Kissinger, Henry. *White House Years.* Boston and Toronto: Little, Brown, 1979.

Kuniholm, Bruce R. "The Geopolitics of U.S.-Turkish Relations: Implications for the Future." International Security Studies Program, The Wilson Center (June 6, 1988).

Kuniholm, Bruce R. *The Near East Connection: Greece and Turkey in the Reconstruction and Security of Europe, 1946–1952.* Brookline, Mass.: Hellenic College Press, 1984.

Kuniholm, Bruce R. *The Origins of the Cold War in the Near East: Power Conflict and Diplomacy in Iran, Turkey, and Greece.* Princeton, N.J.: Princeton University Press, 1980.

Kuniholm, Bruce R. "Retrospect and Prospects: Forty Years of U.S. Middle East Policy." *The Middle East Journal* 41, no. 1 (Winter 1987).

Kuniholm, Bruce R. "Rhetoric and Reality in the Aegean: U.S. Policy Options Toward Greece and Turkey." *SAIS Review* 6, no. 1 (1986).

Kuniholm, Bruce R. "Strategies for Containment in the Middle East." In *Containment: Concept and Policy.* Washington, D.C.: National Defense University Press, 1986.

Kuniholm, Bruce R. "Turkey and NATO: Past, Present, and Future." *Orbis* 27 (Summer 1983).

Laipson, Ellen. "The Seven-Ten Ratio in Military Aid to Greece and Turkey: A Congressional Tradition." Congressional Research Service Report No. 85–79 (June 15, 1983; revised April 10, 1985).

Landau, Rom. *The Moroccan Drama: 1900–1955.* London: Robert Hale Ltd., 1956.

Landau, Rom. *The Sultan of Morocco.* London: Robert Hale Ltd., 1951.

Landauer, Carl. *Germany: Illusions and Dilemmas.* New York: Harcourt, Brace, 1969.

Laqueur, Walter. *Germany Today: A Personal Report.* Boston and Toronto: Little, Brown, 1985.

Laqueur, Walter. *The Soviet Union and the Middle East.* New York, 1959.

Leach, Barry A. *German Strategy Against Russia in 1939–1941.* New York: Oxford University Press, 1973.

Lenczowski, George. *Russia and the West in Iran, 1918–1948.* Ithaca, N.Y.: Cornell University Press, 1949.

Lewis, Bernard. *The Emergence of Modern Turkey.* London, 1961.

Lewis, Geoffrey. *Turkey.* 3rd ed. London, 1965.

Lilienthal, Alfred M. *There Goes the Middle East.* New York: Devin-Adair, 1957.

Livingston, Robert Gerald. *The Federal Republic of Germany in the 1980's: Foreign Policies and Domestic Changes.* New York: German Information Center, 1983.

Livingston, Robert Gerald. "Germany Steps Up." *Foreign Policy* 22 (Spring 1976).

Longhurst, Henry. *Adventures in Oil.* London: Sidgwick and Jackson, 1959.

Longrigg, Stephen Hemsley. *Iraq, 1900–1950.* New York: Oxford University Press, for the Royal Institute of International Affairs, 1953.

Longrigg, Stephen Hemsley. *Oil in the Middle East: Its Discovery and Development.* London: Oxford University Press, 1954.

Louis, Wm. Roger. *The British Empire in the Middle East, 1945–1951.* Oxford: Clarendon Press, 1984.

Macmillan, Harold. *The Blast of War, 1939–1945.* New York: Harper and Row, 1967.

Macmillan, Harold. *Tides of Fortune, 1945–1955.* New York: Harper and Row, 1969.

Majonica, Ernst. *East-West Relations: A German View.* New York: Praeger, 1965.

Mastny, V. *Russia's Road to the Cold War.* New York: Columbia University Press, 1979.

McGhee, George. *Envoy to the Middle World.* New York: Harper and Row, 1983.

McGhee, George. *The US-Turkish-NATO Middle East Connection.* London: Macmillan Press Ltd., 1989.

Merkl, Peter H. *Western German Foreign Policy: Dilemmas and Directions.* Chicago: Chicago Council on Foreign Relations, 1982.

Merritt, Richard L., and Anna J. Merritt. *West Germany Enters the Seventies.* New York: Foreign Policy Association, 1970.

Merson, Allan. *Communist Resistance in Nazi Germany.* London, 1985.

Messer, Robert L. *The End of an Alliance: Byrnes, Roosevelt, Truman and the Origins of the Cold War.* Chapel Hill, N.C.: University of North Carolina Press, 1982.

Morgan, Roger P. "The Federal Republic of Germany." In *European Political Parties.* Stanley Hening, ed. New York: Praeger, 1969.

Morgan, Roger P. *The United States and West Germany, 1945–1973: A Study in Alliance Politics.* London: Oxford University Press, 1974.

Morris, James. *The Hashemite Kings.* New York: Pantheon Books, 1959.

Myers, Kenneth A. *Ostpolitik and American Security Interests in Europe.* Washington, D.C.: Center for Strategic and International Studies, Georgetown University, 1972.

Noelle-Neumann, Elizabeth. *The Germans: Public Opinion Polls, 1967–1980.* Westport, Conn.: Greenwood Press, 1981.

Noelle-Neumann, Elizabeth, and Erich P. Neumann. *The Germans: Public Opinion Polls, 1947–1966.* Allensbach: Verlag für Demoskopie, 1967.

North, Robert C. *Moscow and the Chinese Communists*. Stanford, Calif.: Stanford University Press, 1953.

Peterson, Maurice. *Both Sides of the Curtain*. London, 1950.

Polk, William. *The United States and the Arab World*. 3rd ed. Cambridge, Mass.: Harvard University Press, 1975.

Prittie, Terence C. F. *The Velvet Chancellors: A History of Post-War Germany*. London: Frederick Muller, 1979.

Ramazani, Rouhollah K. "The Autonomous Republic of Azerbaijan and the Kurdish People's Republic: Their Rise and Fall." In *The Anatomy of Communist Takeovers*. Thomas Hammond, ed. New Haven, Conn.: Yale University Press, 1975.

Ramazani, Rouhollah K. *Iran's Foreign Policy 1941–1973, A Study of Foreign Policy in Modernizing Nations*. Charlottesville: University Press of Virginia, 1975.

Rees, David. *The Age of Containment: The Cold War, 1945–1965*. New York, 1968.

Rich, Norman. *Hitler's War Aims: The Establishment of the New Order*. New York: Norton, 1974.

Roberts, Frank. "The German-Soviet Treaty and Its Effects on European and Atlantic Politics: A British View." *Atlantic Community Quarterly* 9 (Summer 1971).

Roberts, Geoffrey. *The Unholy Alliance: Stalin's Pact with Hitler*. London, 1989.

Roosevelt, Kermit. *Arabs, Oil and History*. New York: Harper and Brothers, 1947.

Roosevelt, Kermit. *Countercoup: The Struggle for the Control of Iran*. New York: McGraw-Hill Book Co., 1979.

Rustow, Dankwart. "Foreign Policy of the Turkish Republic." In *Foreign Policy in World Politics*. R. C. Macridis, ed. Englewood Cliffs, N.J.: Prentice-Hall, 1958.

Rustow, Dankwart. "Turkey's Liberal Revolution." *Middle East Review* (Spring 1985).

Ryder, A. J. *Twentieth-Century Germany: From Bismarck to Brandt*. New York: Columbia University Press, 1973.

Saunders, Harold. *The Other Walls: The Politics of the Arab-Israeli Peace Process*. Washington, D.C.: American Enterprise Institute, 1985.

Schlesinger, Arthur. *A Thousand Days: John F. Kennedy in the White House*. New York: Greenwich House, 1965.

Schmidt, Helmut. *Perspectives on Politics*. Boulder, Colo.: Westview Press, 1982.

Schweigler, Gebhard. *West German Foreign Policy: The Domestic Setting*. New York: Praeger, 1984.

Seton-Williams, M. V. *Britain and the Arab States: A Survey of Anglo-Arab Relations, 1920–1948*. London: Luzac, 1948.

Slesser, Sir John. "Control of Nuclear Strategy." *Foreign Affairs* 42 (October 1963).

Smuts, J. C. *Jan Christian Smuts*. London: Cassell and Company Ltd., 1952.

Sorensen, Theodore S. *Kennedy*. New York: Harper and Row, 1965.

Spaak, Paul-Henri. "Hold Fast." *Foreign Affairs* 41 (July 1963).

Stehlin, General Paul. "The Evolution of Western Defense." *Foreign Affairs* 42 (October 1963).

Talbot, Phillips, and S. L. Poplai. *India and America*. New York: Harper and Brothers, 1958.

Thayer, Philip W. *Tensions in the Middle East*. Baltimore: Johns Hopkins University Press, 1958.

Thomas, Evan. *The Very Best Men*. New York: Simon & Schuster, 1995.

Thomas, Lewis V., and Richard N. Frye. *The United States and Turkey and Iran*. Cambridge, Mass.: Harvard University Press, 1951.

Thornburg, Max, et al. *Turkey: An Economic Appraisal*. New York: Twentieth Century Fund, 1949.

Toynbee, Arnold J. *The Western Question in Greece and Turkey*. London: Constable, 1922.

Trevor-Roper, H. R. *The Last Days of Hitler*. 2nd ed. London, 1950.

Truman, Harry S. *Memoirs*. 2 vols. Vol. 1, *Year of Decisions;* Vol. 2, *Years of Trial and Hope*. Garden City, N.Y.: Doubleday, 1955.

U.S. Congress. *Aid to Greece and Turkey*. Report of the Committee on Foreign Relations, 80th Cong., 2d Sess., on S. 2358. Washington, D.C.: Government Printing Office, 1948.

U.S. Congress. *Assistance to Greece and Turkey*. Hearings before the Committee on Foreign Affairs, U.S. House of Representatives, 80th Cong., 1st Sess., on H.R. 2616. Washington, D.C.: Government Printing Office, 1947.

U.S. Congress. Testimony of Ambassador Parker T. Hart, *Security and Development Assistance*. Senate Committee on Foreign Relations, Hearings (S. Hrg. 98–908), USGPO. Washington, D.C.: 1984.

U.S. Congress. Testimony of George McGhee and Dean Acheson, *The Middle East, Africa, and Inter-American Affairs* (Historical Series). Vol. 16, Selected Executive Session Hearings of the Committee on Foreign Affairs, 1951–1956, U.S. House of Representatives. Washington, D.C.: 1980.

U.S. Congress. "U.S. Assistance to Turkey: Foreign Aid Facts." Congressional Research Service (updated July 16, 1985), Issue Brief IB 85059.

U.S. Congress. House, H.R. 7797, *Report of the Committee on Foreign Affairs*, No. 1802, Part 3 on Foreign Economic Assistance. Supplementary Report of the Committee on Foreign Affairs, March 1950.

U.S. Department of State. *Foreign Relations of the United States*. Vol. 7, 1946; Vol. 5, 1947; Vols. 4 and 6, 1948; Vol. 6, 1949; Vol. 5, 1950; Vol. 5, 1951; Vol. 9, 1952. Washington, D.C.

U.S. Department of State. *Foreign Relations of the United States, 1947,* Vol. 5, 1972; *Foreign Relations of the United States, 1949,* Vol. 6, 1977; *Foreign Relations of the United States, 1950,* Vol. 5, 1978; *Foreign Relations of the United States, 1951,* Vol. 5, 1982.

Utley, Freda. *Will the Middle East Go West?* Chicago: Henry Regnery, 1957.

Váli, Ferenc. *Bridge Across the Bosporus: The Foreign Policy of Turkey*. Baltimore, Md.: Johns Hopkins University Press, 1971.

Váli, Ferenc. *The Quest for a United Germany*. Baltimore, Md.: Johns Hopkins University Press, 1967.

Vere-Hodge, Edward Reginald. *Turkish Foreign Policy, 1918–1948*. Ambilly-Annemasse: Imprimerie Franco-Suisse, 1950.

Walker, Mark. *German National Socialism and the Quest for Nuclear Power, 1939–49*. Cambridge, Mass.: Harvard University Press, 1989.

Walters, Vernon A. *Silent Missions*. New York: Doubleday, 1978.

Weymar, Paul. *Adenauer: His Authorized Biography*. Translated by Peter de Mendelssohn. New York: E. P. Dutton, 1957.

Wighton, Charles. *Adenauer: Democratic Dictator*. London: Frederick Muller, 1963.

Woodrow Wilson International Center for Scholars. *The Federal Republic of Germany and the United States*. Boulder, Colo.: Westview Press, 1984.

Index

Abadan oil refinery, 115–16, 117, 118

Abd al-Aziz, 63

Abdullah Ibn-Hussein, 39, 42, 43–44, 75–77, 94, 129

Abramisov, Peter Andreyevich, 164, 170–71

Abs, Herman, 170

Acheson, Dean, 36, 107–8; on Anglo-Iranian Oil Company, 117; character, 47; on China, 53; and Eden, 119; and Greece, 27, 33, 34; and India, 70; and Middle East, 94–95; and Mossadeq, 117; and NATO, 136; and Pahlavi, 53; *Present at the Creation*, 118; and Turkey, 33, 34; and U.S. policy, 4

Acre, Israel, 39

Adenauer, Konrad, 6, 150, 161, 163, 164, 166, 167, 168, 179, 180

Adoula, Prime Minister, 153, 154, 156

Afghanistan, 13, 15, 56, 72–73, 74, 78, 79

Africa, 50, 60, 79–80

Afrikaner party (South Africa), 58–59

Aga Khan, 134

AIOC. *See* Anglo-Iranian Oil Company

Ala, Hussein, 103, 113

Albania, 8

Algeria, 51

Ali Mohammed Khan, 72–73

Aly Khan, 134

Anderson, Dillon, 133

Anderson and Clayton Company, 124

Anglo-Dutch Shell Oil Company, 118

Anglo-Iranian Oil Company, 99–112, 113, 114, 144

Angola, 15, 78, 80

Apartheid, 58, 59

Arab-American Oil Company, 63, 65, 100, 101, 102

Arab conquest of Palestine, 93

Arab-Israeli War (1948–1949), 93, 94

Arab League, 42, 93

Arab refugee problem, 35–46, 64–65, 75, 76

Arab states, 35–46, 93–98, 105

ARAMCO. *See* Arab-American Oil Company

Arbenz, Jacopo, 143

Argentina, 127

Arms, and Middle East, 94–98

Arnold, Henry "Hap," 83–84, 85

Asia, 60
Aswan Dam, 46, 79, 80
Ataturk, Kemal, 121, 122, 123
Attlee, Clement R., 7, 54
Auriol, Vincent, 68
Austin, Warren R., 36–37
Autobahn incident, 171–72
Azerbaijan, Iran, 49

Ba'ath party (Syria), 79
Baghdad, Iraq, 42
Bahr, Egon, 175
Bahrain, 104
Balaquer, Joaquin, 138, 140, 141
Balieu, Sir Clive, 19
Ball, George, 5, 10, 137–38, 147, 148, 151, 164
Baring, Sir Evelyn, 61
Barkley, Alben, 52
Barnes, Tracy, 145
Baruch, Bernard, 1
Basic Principles of Relations, between the United States and the USSR, 10
Batt, Bill, 19
Bayar, Celâl, 121–22, 125–28, 129–30, 131
Bay of Pigs invasion, 14, 145–47
Bedouin people, 42
Beersheba, Israel, 38
Beitz, Berthold, 173
Belgian Congo Tripartite Agreement, 20
Belgium, 48, 151, 156–57
Ben Gurion, David, 45
Berber people, 67
Berlin, Germany: Brandt on, 174; foreign ministers meeting at (1954), 10; future of, 171; isolation of, 162; and Quadripartite Treaty, 11; and Spandau prison, 164; and Stalin, 4, 8
Berlin blockade, 7, 8
Berlin Wall, 12, 167
Bernadotte, Folke, 35, 38–39
Bevin, Ernest, 7, 33, 96, 105
Biddle, Anthony J. D., 20
Birashug, Gaza Strip, 38
Birgi, Nuri, 31
Bissell, Richard, 145–46

Blessing, Karl, 178
Boeing B-29, 84
Boeing Company, 169
Boer War, 59
Bohlen, Charles, *Witness to History*, 4
Bohr, Niels, 81, 83
Bolshevism, 4
Bomboko, Foreign Minister, 156
Bowie, Robert, 175
Bowles, Chester, 146, 148, 151, 152
Brandt, Willy, 11, 162, 166, 168, 174–75, 179, 181, 183
Brazil, 125, 127
Bretton Woods Conference, 186
Brezhnev, Leonid, 10, 15
British Aircraft Corporation, 169–70
British-American Combined Boards, 19
British Commonwealth, 51
Brown, George, 150
Bryant, E. C., 44
Brzezinski, Zbigniew, 12
Bulganin, Nikolai, 10
Bulgaria, 3, 8
Bullock, Alan, *Hitler and Stalin*, 7
Bunche, Ralph J., 36, 37, 38, 39, 153
Bundy, McGeorge, 147, 148; *Danger and Survival*, 83
Bunker, Ellsworth, 186
Burma, 51, 57–58, 71
Bush, Vannevar, 82
Byrnes, Jimmy, 6
Byrode, Hank, 131

Cadman, Sir John, 100
Capitalism, 49
Carney, Mick, 33
Carter, Jimmy, 10, 15
Casablanca Affair, 67
Casablanca Conference, 2, 68
Castro, Fidel, 14, 145, 146
CDU. *See* Christian Democratic Union
CENTO. *See* Central Treaty Organization
Central Intelligence Agency. *See* United States, agencies and organizations
Central Treaty Organization, 136
Ceylon, 51
Chayes, Abe, 148

Chiang Kai–Shek, 9, 53
Childs, J. Rives, 65
Chile, 127
China: and Burma, 57–58; and Communism, 53; and Four Power Pact, 1; and India, 70–71, 78; and Japan, 2; and Korea, 7; and Nuclear Non-Proliferation Treaty, 180; and South Asia, 50–51; and South Yemen, 78–79; and Tanzania, 80; and the USSR, 49
Christian Democratic Union (Federal Republic of Germany), 179–80
Christian Liberal Progressive party (Eritrea), 62
Churchill, Winston, 1, 10, 17, 83, 119
CIA. See United States, agencies and organizations
Clayton, William L., 18, 25, 30
Cleveland, Harlan, 157
Clifton, Chester, 168
Clive, Robert, 48
Coal and Steel Community, 4
Cockfield, John, 81
Cold War: and CIA, 145–46; and Congo, 152; course of, 1–16; and India-Pakistan conflict, 55; and Middle East, 94; and nuclear weapons, 82, 83; and U.S. aid to United Kingdom, 17
Cold warrior, 9, 13, 48
Colonialism, 48, 50, 71, 105, 152, 156–57
Combined Raw Materials Board, 19
Committee for the Present Danger, 13, 16
Committee of Ten, 146–47
Common Market. See European Economic Community
Communism: American attitude toward, 13; and Burma, 57–58; and China, 53; and CIA, 145; and Dulles, 130; and Eastern Europe, 8; and Ethiopia, 61; and France, 7; and Greece, 26; and Ibn Saud, 66; and Iran, 52, 99, 106, 119; and Italy, 7; and Middle East, 46, 94; and Middle World, 48–51, 77–78, 80; and Morocco, 67, 68; postwar progress of, 49; and Saudi Arabia, 64, 66; Smuts on, 60; and South Africa, 60–61; and South Asia, 50–51; and Turkey, 26; and Union of South Africa, 59; and the United States, 133, 149. See also China; Union of Soviet Socialist Republics
Compton, Arthur Holly, 81
Conant, James B., 83
Conference on Religion and Freedom, 58
Conference on Security and Cooperation in Europe, 11
Congo, 14, 151–59, 186
Cook, Eugene G. (Bud), 89
Copper, 153
Countercoup (Roosevelt), 114, 144
Covert intelligence, 14, 143–50
Cripps, Sir Stafford, 119
CSCE. See Conference on Security and Cooperation in Europe
Cuba, 5, 14, 78, 145–46
Cuban Missile Crisis, 10, 136, 156
Curie, Irene, 81
Czechoslovakia, 8, 10, 14–15, 94, 98

Dallas Council on World Affairs, 58
Danchev, Alex, 111–12
Danger and Survival (Bundy), 83
D'Avignon, Count, 153–54
Davis, Elmer, 118
Dayan, Moshe, 39
De Gasperi, Alcide, 8
De Gaulle, Charles, 5, 78, 161, 163, 164
DeGolyer, Everette L., 63, 101
Democratic Front (Eritrea), 62
Democratic Party (Turkey), 121–22, 123, 124, 125
Denmark, 34
Depletion allowance, 136–37
Détente, 9–13, 15, 16, 78, 161
Developing nation, 71
Diem, Ngo Dinh, 147–48
Dirty trick, 143
Dobrynin, Anatol, 82; In Confidence, 14–15

Dodd, Thomas, 154–55
Dodge, Joseph M., 133
Dominican Republic, 137–41
Domino theory, 9
Draper, Bill, 133, 134
Dulles, Allen Welsh, 145, 146
Dulles, John Foster, 130, 131–32, 144

Eastern Europe, 7–8, 49
East Germany. *See* German Democratic Republic
Eccles, David, 20
Eden, Anthony, 119
EEC. *See* European Economic Community
Egypt: and Arab refugee problem, 41, 42; and colonialism, 50; and Israel, 35, 93; and Tripartite Declaration, 97–98; and United Kingdom, 94, 105, 111; and the USSR, 42, 46, 79, 80
Einstein, Albert, 81
Eisenhower, Dwight D., 10, 14, 129–31, 132, 147
Elkins, Wilson, 174
Elliot, William Yandell, 18–19
El Salvador, 15
Erhard, Ludwig, 149, 161, 163, 166, 168, 173, 174, 175–79, 180
Eritrea, 62
ERP. *See* European Recovery Program
Erzurum, Turkey, 8
Ethiopia, 50, 51, 61–63, 78, 80, 100
Ethridge, Mark, 36, 37, 38, 40, 45
Europe, 167
European-American tariff negotiations, 161, 163, 164
European Economic Community, 4, 162
European Recovery Program, 32
Export-Import Bank, 40, 45, 62, 66

Faisal ibn al Saud, 64–65
Faisal II, 94
Faluga, Gaza Strip, 38
Far East, 60. *See also specific countries*
Farouk, King of Egypt, 48
Fermi, Enrico, 81

Finletter, Thomas K., 18
Fitzgerald, Desmond, 145
509 Composite Group, 87
Ford, Gerald R., 11, 14, 15
Formosa, 70
Forrestal, James, 27
Four Power Pact, 1
France: and Arab refugee problem, 41; and Berlin, 171; and colonialism, 48; and Egypt, 98; and Germany, 4, 162, 163, 171, 177; and Greek–Turkish problem, 34; and Guinea, 78; and Lebanon, 96; and Middle East, 76; and Morocco, 66–70; and Nuclear Non-Proliferation Treaty, 180; and Quadripartite Treaty on Berlin, 11; and Syria, 96; and Tripartite Declaration, 76, 95–96; and Turkey, 129; and the United States, 94; and the USSR, 7; and Vietnam War, 9, 147
Frankfurter, Felix, 52, 83
Franks, Sir Oliver, 19, 104, 107–9, 110–12
Fraser, Sir William, 102, 103, 107
Frederick the Great, 5
Frederika, Queen of Greece, 31
Free Democratic Party (Germany), 162
Free University speech (Kennedy), 167
Front for Liberation of Mozambique, 78

Galbraith, John Kenneth, 147–48
Galilee, Israel, 39, 42
Gass, Neville, 102
Gaza, 38
Gaza Strip, 42, 45
General Electric, 126
German Central Bank, 178
German Democratic Republic, 5, 11, 78, 171–72
German-Russian Pact, 6
Germany, Federal Republic of, 2, 4, 5–6, 8–9, 10–11, 13, 161–84
Germany, Nazi, 81–82
Ghandi, Indira, 52, 56
Ghandi, Mohandas, 54
Goodwin, Richard, 137
Gorbachev, Mikhail, 12

Grady, Henry, 30, 54, 101, 102
Grady, Lucretia, 102
Grand Alliance, 1
Grand Coalition (Federal Republic of Germany), 161, 162, 175, 179
Great Britain. *See* United Kingdom
Greece, 136; and Communism, 49; and NATO, 12–13, 33; and Stalin, 8; and United Kingdom, 3–4; and the United States, 25–34, 56; and the USSR, 77
Greek-Turkish aid program, 4, 28–32
Griswold, Dwight, 30
Gross, Ernest, 113
Gruenther, Alfred M., 133
Guatamala, 143
Guillaume, Augustin, 69
Guinea, 78
Gulek, Kasim, 31
Gullion, Edmund, 152, 153, 156

Habte-Wold, Ate Akililou, 62–63
Hahn, Otto, 81
Haifa, Israel, 39, 42
Hallstein, Walter, 181
Hansell, Heywood, 85
Hare, Raymond, 94–95
Harrar, Duke of, 62
Harriman, W. Averell, 4, 19–20, 114
Hashemite rule, 63, 65
Hastings, Warren, 48
Heath-Ives, W. D., 100
Heisenberg, Werner, 81–82
Hejaz, Saudi Arabia, 75–76
Helsinki Conference, 11
Henderson, Elise, 56
Henderson, Loy W., 27, 51, 56, 57, 70
Hess, Rudolf, 165
Het Volk party (South Africa), 59
Hill, John, 138, 139
Hinton, Dean, 40–41
Hiroshima, Japan, 90–91
Hitler, Adolf, 1–2, 17–18
Hitler and Stalin (Bullock), 7
Hoover, John, 84
Howe, Fisher, 25
Humphrey, Hubert, 52
Hungary, 8, 145

Hussein, Saddam, 79
Hussein, Shariff, 63–64

IAEA. *See* International Atomic Energy Agency
Ibn Saud, 48, 63, 65–66, 75–76, 94
IBRD. *See* World Bank
"Ich bin ein Berliner" speech (Kennedy), 166–67
Ickes, Harold L., 63
In Confidence (Dobrynin), 14–15
India, 51–52; and Afghanistan, 72–73; and China, 78; and Cold War, 55; and Communism, 70–71; independence of, 54–55; and Nuclear Non-Proliferation Treaty, 180; Smuts on, 60; and the USSR, 78
Indochina, 71
Indonesia, 145, 185–86
Inonu, Isiner, 121
Interim Greek-Turkish Assistance Committee, 28
International Atomic Energy Agency, 182
International Bank for Reconstruction and Development. *See* World Bank
Inverchapel, Lord, 26
Iran, 14, 51; and CIA, 144; and Communism, 106, 119; and Mohammed Shah Pahlavi, 52–54; and oil production, 104; and Stalin, 8; and United Kingdom, 99–112, 113–20, 144; and the United States, 14, 49, 106, 108, 109–10, 114, 115, 117, 144; and the USSR, 54, 77, 114
Iraq, 51, 94; and Arab refugee problem, 42, 43; and colonialism, 50; and Israel, 35, 93; and oil, 104, 127; and the USSR, 79
Islam, 67, 68, 93
Israel: and Arab refugee problem, 35–46, 65; and Arab states, 105; creation of, 35, 93; and King Abdullah, 42, 77; and Middle East, 50; and Syria, 79; and Tripartite Declaration, 93–98; and the United States, 32, 94
Israel-Transjordan cease-fire agreement, 38

Istanbul, Turkey, 33
Istanbul Conference, 64
Istiqlal party (Morocco), 69
Italy, 7, 48, 62, 100, 182

Jaffa, Israel, 39, 42
Japan, 2, 13, 84–91
Jerusalem, Israel, 42
Jessup, Philip, 96
Jew, 16, 93. *See also* Israel
Jinnah, Mohammed Ali, 54, 55
Johnson, Lyndon B.: and Bay of Pigs
    invasion, 147; and détente, 164; Do-
    brynin on, 14–15; and Dominican
    Republic, 137; and Erhard, 175–76;
    and McGhee, 150; and Multilateral
    Force, 161; and Vietnam, 149
Jordan, 43–44, 50, 75–77, 93, 94
Juin, Alphonse, 66, 67, 68, 69, 70
Julio, Frederic, 81

Karen tribe, 57
Kars, Turkey, 8
Kashaba, Ahmed, 42
Kashmir, India, 54–55, 56, 73–74, 105
Katanga Province, Congo, 151, 153,
    157, 186
Keeley, James H., 40, 42–43, 45
Kennan, George, 4, 26
Kennedy, John F., 5, 9; and Bay of
    Pigs invasion, 146, 147; and Congo,
    151–53, 154, 156, 157, 186; and
    détente, 164; Dobrynin on, 14; early
    administration, 135–37; Free Univer-
    sity speech, 167; "Ich bin ein Ber-
    liner" speech, 166–67; letter of
    thanks to McGhee, 158; letter to
    Pappas, 140; Paulskirche speech, 166;
    and Vietnam, 147, 149; visit to Ger-
    many, 150, 165–68
Kennedy, Joseph, 137
Kennedy, Robert, 137, 146; *Robert
    Kennedy in his Own Words*, 149
Kennedy Round, of European-American
    tariff negotiations, 161, 163, 164
Khanyumis, Gaza Strip, 38
Khrushchev, Nikita, 5, 10, 14, 145,
    152, 163

Khyber Pass, 55–56
Kiesinger, Kurt-Georg, 161–62, 179–
    80, 181–82, 183
Kim Il-Sung, 9
Kissinger, Henry, 10, 11, 12, 13
Kissner, "Augie," 86
Koprulu, Mehmet Fuad, 122–25, 126,
    129
Koraltan, Refik, 122
Korean War, 7, 9, 10, 14, 32, 70, 71,
    129, 147
Kosygin, Aleksei, 10
Krim, Abd el, 66–67
Krupp, Alfried, 172–74
Krupp, Arndt, 173
Kuter, Harry, 85
Kuwait, 46, 104, 127
Kyushu, Japan, 88

Laos, 135, 136
Lausanne Conference, 45
Lawrence, Ernest, 81
League of Nations, 100
Lebanon, 35, 41, 44, 50, 93, 96
Leggett, Sir Frederick, 112
LeMay, Curtis, 3, 85–89, 92
Lend Lease, 17
Leva, Marx, 133
Liaquat Ali Khan, 55–56, 73–75
Liaquat Ali Khan, Begum, 74
Liberia, 50
Libya, 50
Lidda, Israel, 39, 42
Limited Test Ban Treaty, 181
Linder, Harold, 108
Lippmann, Walter, 52
Lockweed, Admiral, 84
Lodge, Henry Cabot, 149
London Committee, 98
London Daily Mail, 99
Lovett, Robert A., 29, 117
Lübke, 183
Lufthansa, 169–70

Macmillan, Harold, 23
MacVeagh, Lincoln, 30
Madonne, John, 67

Majdal, Gaza Strip, 38
Majlis (Iranian parliament), 52, 101, 102, 120
Makins, Sir Roger, 107, 108
Malan, Daniel F., 58–59, 60–61
Manchuria, 2
Manhattan District Project, 87
Mao Zedong, 9
Mariana Islands, 3
Marshall, George, 26, 27, 30
Marshall Mission, 60
Marshall Plan, 4, 6, 7, 28, 32, 49, 123, 186
Martin, John B., 137–38, 149
Martin, William McChesney, 18
Marx, Karl, 80
Matthews, McFreeman, 19
Maud Committee, 83
McArthur, Douglas, 88
McCloy, John J., 133, 173
McDonald, James G., 41–42
McDonnell-Douglas, 169–70
McGhee, Cecilia, 38, 55, 56, 73, 74, 87, 150
McGhee, George: and Anglo-Iranian Oil negotiations, 99–112; and Autobahn incident, 171–72; as Cold Warrior, 13, 48; and Committee for the Present Danger, 13; in Congo, 5; described by Danchev, 111–12; and East-West African Conference of U.S. Diplomatic and Consular Officers, 58; education, 18, 100; and Eisenhower administration, 130–34; and John F. Kennedy, 149–50; and Johnson, 150; and LeMay, 3, 85–89, 92; letter of thanks from Kennedy, 158; letters to Cecilia, 87–88; letter to Harriman, 20–22; letter to Johnson about Erhard, 176; and NATO, 12–13; and oil, 126–27; resigns as Ambassador to Turkey, 132; and Robert Kennedy, 149; and Rusk, 5, 135; and Tripartite Declaration, 94–95
McGhee, George, appointments of: Ambassador-at-Large, 150; Ambassador to Germany, 149, 150, 157, 161–84; Ambassador to Turkey, 13, 121–32; Assistant Secretary of State for the Near East, South Asia, and Africa, 31–32, 38, 44–46, 47–80, 100; Chairman of Interdepartmental Shipping Priority Committee, 18; Chairman of shadow interdepartmental committee, 135; Consultant to National Security Council, 132–33; Coordinator of Greek-Turkish aid program, 4, 12–13, 26, 30–34, 48, 144, 148; Coordinator of policy for Congo, 151; Coordinator on Palestine Refugee matters, 36; Head of Policy Planning, 144, 147; Member, Combined Raw Materials Board, 19–21, 83; Member, Committee to Study the U.S. Military Assistance Program, 132–33; Member, War Production Board, 2, 83; Naval Liaison Officer to 21st Bomber Command, 3, 83–92; Senior Liaison Officer at Office of Production Management, 18; Special Assistant to the Secretary of State, 36; Under Secretary of State for Political Affairs, 141, 148, 149–50, 151
McGhee, George, meetings: Abdul Hadi Pasha, 42; Abdullah Ibn - Hussein, 43–44, 75–77; Abramisov, 164, 170–71; Adenauer, 183; Adoula, 156; Ahmed Kashaba, 42; Ala, 103, 113; Ali Mohammed Khan, 72–73; ARAMCO, 100–101; Azam Pasha, 42; Bayar, 121–22, 125–28, 129; Biddle, 20; Bomboko, 156; Brandt, 181, 183; British Foreign Office, 100, 101; Bryant, 44; Bunche, 36, 37, 38, 39; Bundy, 147; Sir John Cadman, 100; Carstens, 183; Childs, 65; Clayton, 18; Count D'Avignon, 153–54; Dayan, 39; Dodd, 154–55; Dulles, 131; Eccles, 20; Erhard, 183; Ethridge, 40; Faisal ibn al Saud, 64–65; Finletter, 18; Sir Oliver Franks, 108–9; Sir William Fraser, 107; Frederika, Queen of Greece, 31; Gass, 102; Grady, 102; Hare, 94–95; Harriman, 19–20;

Heath-Ives, 100; Hess, 165; Hill, 139; Hinton, 40–41; I. Ghandi, 56; Ibn Saud, 65–66; Johnson, 150, 175; Juin, 66, 67, 69; Keeley, 40, 42–43; Kennedy, 135–36, 138, 151–52; Kiesinger, 181–82, 183; Krupp, 172–74; Lang, 22; Liaquat Ali Khan, 55–56, 74; Lovett, 29; Lübke, 183; Macmillan, 23; Madonne, 67; Malan, 60–61; Martin, 18; McDonald, 41–42; McNamara, 175; Mehmet Fuad Koprulu, 122–25; Menderes, 122, 129; Mohammed Ayub Khan, 134; Mohammed Reza Shah Pahlavi, 53, 54, 103–4; Mohammed V, 66, 68–69; Mohammed Zahir Shah, 72; Morrison, 34, 104–6; Mossadeq, 113–20; Murphy, 22; Nehru, 52, 56–57, 70–71; Nixon, 154; Nu, 57–58; O'Keefe, 64; Pappas, 140; Patel, 56; Paul, King of Greece, 31; Pinkerton, 41; Plevan, 20; Plitt, 67; Reedman, 38–39; Riley, 41; Baron Rothschild, 153–54; Rusk, 146, 148; Russell, 154; Sardur Mohammed Khan, 74; Schnippenkötter, 182; Schröder, 183; Seddon, 100; Selassie, 61–63; Sharett, 36–37; Sir Francis Shepherd, 102–3; Smuts, 59–60; Spaak, 153–54; Speer, 164–65; Stassen, 131; Stoltenberg, 182; Tawfiq Pasha, 44; Thant, 156, 157; Trevelyan, 43; Trujillo, 138–39, 140–41; Tshombe, 155–56, 157, 159, 183; U.S. African Bureau, 152; U.S. European Bureau, 152; U.S. International Organization Bureau, 152; Von Schirach, 165; West German officials, 183; Westrick, 170; Wheeler, 20; Wright, 101–2

McGhee, George, opinions of: Acheson, 47; Anglo-Iranian Oil Company, 105; Bay of Pigs invasion, 145–47; business and diplomacy, 169, 170; Cold War, 5–6; colonialism, 48; covert intelligence, 143–45; détente, 9–13; diplomacy, 169, 170, 184–86; fall of USSR, 13; Middle East, 105–6, 110–11, 132; postwar Germany, 174; racism, 48; Spaak, 153–54; U. S. in Dominican Republic, 137; United Kingdom, 105, 110–11; USSR, 70; U.S.-U.K. Combined Raw Materials Board, 3; Vietnam War, 9, 147–49

McGhee, George, travels of: Afghanistan, 72–73; Africa, 22–23; Amman, 43–44; Beirut, 37, 40–42; Belgium, 153; Burma, 57–58; Congo, 151, 155–56; Dallas, 91; Damascus, 42–43; Dominican Republic, 138–41; Egypt, 42, 104; Ethiopia, 61–63; Federal Republic of Germany, 164, 165–66, 168–70, 183–84; Greece, 31; Guam, 25, 90; Honolulu, 84; India, 56–57, 70–71; Iran, 99–101, 102–4, 113; Iraq, 104; Jordan, 75–77, 104; and Kennedy's visit to Germany, 165–66; Lebanon, 104; Morocco, 66–70; Pakistan, 55–56, 73–75; Philippines, 88; Rhodes, 38–39; Saipan, 85; Saudi Arabia, 63–66, 94; Turkey, 31, 136; Union of South Africa, 58–61; United Kingdom, 101–2, 104–7; Washington, 94

McNamara, Robert, 175, 177, 179
McNarney, Joseph T., 133
MEDO. See Middle East Defense Organization
Mende, Erich, 179
Menderes, Adnan, 32, 122, 126, 129, 131
Menelik II, 61
Merrill, George R., 61
Middle East, 51; and colonialism, 50; defense of, 33; Dulles on, 132; and Eisenhower administration, 131; and Israel, 50; and refugee problem, 35–46; and Rommel, 6; and Tripartite Declaration, 76, 93–98; and Truman Doctrine, 26; and Turkey, 121, 125, 129; and the United Kingdom, 106; and the United States, 105, 133–34
Middle East Defense Organization, 132
Middle World, 47–80
Midway, Battle of, 3
Millspaugh Mission, 52

MLF. *See* Multilateral Force
Mobil Oil, 127
Mobuto, Joseph, 14
Mohammed, Ghulam, 55
Mohammed Ayub Khan, 134
Mohammed Reza Shah Pahlavi, 48, 52–54, 103–4, 120, 129
Mohammed V, 66, 67–70
Mohammed Zahir Shah, 72
Molotov, Vyacheslav, 7, 8
Mongol people, 6
Montgomery, J. B., 86
Morocco, 51, 66–70
Morrison, Herbert, 33, 34, 104–6, 107
Moscow Council of Foreign Ministers, 7
Moscow Summit Conference, 10
Mossadeq, Mohammed, 14, 54, 103, 113–20
Mozambique, 78
Multilateral Force, 161, 167
Murphy, Robert, 22
Musashino, Japan, 86
Muslim League, 54, 62
Mutual Defense Assistance Act, 32
Mutual Security Agency, 28

Nablus, Jordan, 41
Nagasaki, Japan, 90–91
Nakajima aircraft factory, 86
Napoleon I, 6
Nasser, Gamal Abdel, 79–80
National Front party (Angola), 78
National Front party (Iran), 103, 114
National Iranian Oil Company, 116, 118
Nationalism, 110
Nationalization, in Iran, 99–112
National Liberation Front (South Yemen), 78–79
National party (South Africa), 58–59
Negev desert, 38, 42
Nehru, Jawaharlal, 48, 51–52, 54, 55, 56–57, 70–71, 78, 79, 80
Netherlands, 48, 182, 185–86
Neutralism, 71, 77, 79–80, 162–63
New York *Herald Tribune*, 97
New York Times, 97, 99

Nicaragua, 14, 15
Nimitz, Chester, 84, 86
NIOC. *See* National Iranian Oil Company
Nitze, Paul, 114, 119
Nixon, Richard M., 10, 11, 13, 14, 15, 53, 130, 154–55
Nixon Doctrine, 149
Nolting, Frederick, 148
Nonalignment, 79–80
Normandy invasion, 2
Norstad, Lauris, 85
North Africa, 2, 6, 20
North Atlantic Treaty Organization, 4, 78, 167; creation of, 8–9; and Federal Republic of Germany, 6, 10–11, 162, 163, 164; and Greece, 12–13, 33; and Turkey, 12–13, 31, 33, 121; and the United States, 136
Northern Tier concept, 131–32
North Korea, 9
North Yemen, 79
Norway, 33
Note-taking, 25–26
Nu, U, 57–58
Nuclear Non-Proliferation Treaty, 162, 180–83
Nuclear power, 180–81
Nuclear weapon, 4–5, 12, 15, 81–83, 87–91, 136, 167

O'Donnell, Rosey, 85
Office of Production Management. *See* War Production Board
Office of Strategic Services, 145
Oil, 99–112, 113–20, 126–28, 136–37, 169
O'Keefe, Richard J., 64
Okinawa, Japan, 88
Operation Ajax, 144
OPM. *See* War Production Board
Oppenheimer, Robert, 82
Osaka, Japan, 87
OSS. *See* Office of Strategic Services
Ostpolitik, 11, 174–75, 179
Ottoman Empire, 63, 93

Pakistan, 51, 54–56, 72–73
Palestine, 35–46, 75, 93

Palestine Conciliation Commission, 35, 36, 37–38, 40, 43
Palestine Liberation Organization, 44
Pandit, Madame Vijay Lakshmi, 52
Pappas, Thomas, 139–40
Partial Test Ban Treaty, 10
Pasha, Abdul Hadi, 42
Pasha, Azzam, 42
Pasha, Gubb, 77
Pasha, Tawfiq, 44
Patel, Sardar, 56
Pathan people, 74
Patterson, James, 42
Patterson, Robert, 27
Paul, King of Greece, 31
Paulskirche speech (Kennedy), 166
PCC. *See* Palestine Conciliation Commission
Pearl Harbor, 2
People party (South Africa), 59
People's National Convention, 2
Perkins, George, 33–34
Persian Gulf, 8
Pétain, Henri Philippe, 67
Petroleum. *See* Oil
Philippine Islands, 3
Pinkerton, Lowell, 41
Piraeus, 29
Plevan, M., 20
Plitt, Edwin, 67, 69
PLO. *See* Palestine Liberation Organization
Point Four Program, 50, 58, 60, 62, 66
Poland, 8, 11
Popular Movement (Angola), 78
Population Crisis Committee, 134
Portugal, 48, 78
Present at the Creation (Acheson), 118
Production and Resources Board, 19
Public Law 75. *See* Greek-Turkish aid program
Pushtunistan, 55–56, 72–73, 74–75

Qatar, 104
Quadripartite Treaty on Berlin, 11

Racism, 48, 59
Radford, Arthur W., 133

Radio Free Europe, 145
Ramle, Israel, 39, 42
Ramsbotham, Sir Peter E., 107
Razmara, Ali, 54, 101, 102, 120
Reagan, Ronald, 12, 14, 15, 16
Reed, Ensign, 23
Reed, Phil, 19
Reedman, John, 38
Refugees, and India-Pakistan conflict, 54. *See also* Arab Refugee Problem
Republican Party (Turkey), 129
Rescue, of World War II pilots, 84, 87, 90–91
Reykjavik, Iceland, 12
Rhodes, Cecil, 48, 59
Riff Republic, 66
Riley, William E., 41
Robert Kennedy in his Own Words (Kennedy), 149
Roberts, Sir Frank, 170
Rockefeller, Nelson, 131
Rome, 5, 93
Rommel, Erwin, 6
Roosa Bond, 178
Roosevelt, Eleanor, 56
Roosevelt, Franklin D., 1, 17, 48, 68, 82, 83
Roosevelt, Kermit, *Countercoup*, 114, 144
Rostow, Walt, 147
Rothschild, Baron Robert, 153–54
Rountree, William, 31, 108
Rumania, 8
Rush, Kenneth, 11
Rusk, Dean, 5, 36, 131, 134, 145, 146, 147, 155, 157, 175, 181
Russell, Richard, 154–55
Russia. *See* Union of Soviet Socialist Republics
Russian Social Democratic Party, 4
Rutherford, Ernest, 81

Sadat, Anwar, 79
Saipan, 84–88
SALT. *See* Strategic Arms Limitation Treaty
San Antonio No. 1, 85
Sanchez, General, 138

Sardur Mohammed Khan, 74
Saud, House of, 63
Saudi Arabia, 46, 63–66; and Arab-
    American Oil Company, 100, 101,
    102; and colonialism, 50; and Israel,
    35, 93; and Jordan, 75–76, 94; and
    North Yemen, 79; and oil, 104, 108,
    127
Schnippenkötter, Swidbeer, 182
Schröder, Gerhard, 163, 175, 179
Schuman, Robert, 96
Seddon, Richard, 100
Selassie, Haile, 48, 61–63
Sharett, Moshe, 36–37
Shell Oil, 127
Shepherd, Sir Francis, 102–3
Shipping Board, 19
Silent Missions (Walters), 114
Sinclair Oil Company, 62
Slavery, 61
Smuts, Jan Christiaan, 59–60, 83
Social Democratic Party (Federal Re-
    public of Germany), 11, 175
Socialism, 80
Socony-Vacuum Oil, 100–101
Somalia, 15, 51, 78
Somaliland, 50, 62
South Africa. See Union of South Africa
South Asia, 50–51, 60
Southeast Asia Co-Prosperity Sphere, 2
South Korea, 9
South Yemen, 78–79, 80
Soviet–Iranian Trade Agreement, 54
Spaak, Paul Henri, 152, 153–54, 157
Spandau prison, 164–65
SPD. See Social Democratic Party
Speer, Albert, 82, 164–65
Spirit of Geneva, 10
Squibb (company), 126
Stabler, Wells, 43–44
Stalin, Joseph V., 1, 4, 7–8, 9
Stalingrad, 6
Standard Oil Company of California,
    101
Standard Oil Company of New Jersey,
    100, 140
Star Wars, 12
Stassen, Harold, 131

Stettinius, Edward R., 18
Stevenson, Adlai E., 130, 156
Stoltenberg, Gerhard, 182
Strassman, Fritz, 81
Strategic Arms Limitation Treaty, 10
Strategic Defense Initiative, 12
Struelens, Michael, 154
Sudan, 105
Sukarno, 145, 185, 186
Supplemental Agreement, 100–101
Syria, 35, 42–43, 45, 46, 50, 79, 80,
    93, 96

Taft, Robert, 121
Taiwan, 70
Tanzania, 80
Tariff negotiation, 161, 163, 164
Taylor, Maxwell, 147
Teagle, Walter, 100
Teutonic Knights, 6
Texas Oil Company, 101
Thailand, 135
Thant, U, 152, 156, 157
Thomas, Evan, The Very Best Men, 144,
    145
Thornburg, Max, 52
Tibet, 70
Tinian Island, 87
Tito, Josip Broz, 8
Tokyo, Japan, 85, 87–88
Trade barrier, 163
Transjordan, 35, 41, 42
Treaty of Friendship, Commerce, and
    Navigation (U.S. and Turkey), 124
Treaty of Friendship (Germany and
    France), 4
Treaty of Friendship (Turkey and
    USSR), 49
Treaty of Rome, 4
Treaty of Versailles, 2
Trevelyan, Humphrey, 43
Tripartite Declaration, 76–77, 93–98
Trujillo, Arismendi, 138, 139, 141
Trujillo, Hector, 138, 139, 141
Trujillo, Rafael Leonidas, 137
Trujillo, Ramfis, 137–39, 140–41
Truman, Harry S., 27, 31–32, 121; ex-
    perience of, 7; and Liaquat Ali Khan,

56; mentioned, 65, 115; and Middle
East, 94, 96; and Mossadeq, 117;
and Nehru, 52; and Pahlavi, 53
Truman Doctrine, 3–4, 8, 26, 27–28
Tshombe, Moise, 5, 152, 153, 154,
155–56, 157–58, 186
Tudeh party (Iran), 52, 99, 114
Turkey, 121–32; and Communism, 49;
and Middle East, 129; and NATO,
12–13, 31, 33; and nuclear weapons,
136; and oil, 126–28; and Stalin, 8;
and United Kingdom, 3–4; and the
United States, 25–34, 123–25; and
the USSR, 31, 49, 77
Turkish Straits, 26
Turko–Soviet Treaty of Friendship, 49
20th Air Force, 83–84
21st Bomber Command, 3, 83–92
Tyler, William, 151

Ugba Ibn Nafi, 67
Ukraine, 6
Union Minière, 151, 153, 154, 156,
157, 159
Union of South Africa, 50, 58–61
Union of Soviet Socialist Republics: and
Afghanistan, 72, 73, 78, 79; and
Brandt, 174–75; and China, 49; and
Cold War, 1–16; and Congo, 152;
containment of, 26; Dulles on, 132;
economy, 173; and Egypt, 42, 46,
79, 80, 98; and France, 7; and Germany, 2, 5–6, 11, 162–63, 171, 179;
and Greece, 76, 77; and Hungary,
145; and India, 70; and Iran, 54, 76,
77, 99, 114; and Iraq, 79; and Italy,
7; and Middle East, 26, 76; and
Middle World, 48–51, 77–80; and
North Yemen, 79; and Nuclear Non-
Proliferation Treaty, 180, 182; and
nuclear weapons, 83; and Quadripartite Treaty on Berlin, 11; and Saudi
Arabia, 64; and South Africa, 61; and
South Yemen, 78–79; and Spandau
prison, 165; and Syria, 79; and Turkey, 26, 31, 49, 76, 77; and the
United States, 76, 82, 161, 162, 170–
72, 181; and U Thant Plan, 153;

and World War II, 18. *See also* Communism
United Kingdom: and Arab refugee
problem, 41, 43; and colonialism, 48;
and Egypt, 94, 98, 105, 111; and
European Economic Community,
162; and Four Power Pact, 1; and
Germany, 8, 169–70, 171; and
Greece, 3–4; and Greek-Turkish
problem, 33, 34; and Hashemite
rule, 65; and India, 54; and Iran, 99–
112, 113–20, 144; and Middle East,
26–27, 76, 93–94, 106; Ministry of
Fuel and Power, 107; and Mossadeq,
114–15; and Nuclear Non-
Proliferation Treaty, 180; and Pales-
tine, 35; and Quadripartite Treaty on
Berlin, 11; and Saudi Arabia, 63–64,
65–66; and Transjordan, 42; and Tri-
partite Declaration, 76, 95–96; and
Turkey, 3–4, 129, 132; and the
United States, 17–23, 83, 94; and
World War II, 17–18
United Nations: and Arab refugee
problem, 35, 76; and Congo, 151–
52, 156, 157; and Ethiopia, 62; and
India, 71; and Indonesia, 186; and
Iran, 8; and Italy, 62; and Mossadeq,
113, 115, 116; Relief and Works
Agency, 28
United party (South Africa), 58–59
United States: and Angola, 78; and
Arab refugee problem, 76; and Arab
States, 94; and Cold War, 1–16; and
colonialism, 152, 156; and Communism, 13, 133, 149; and Congo, 14;
and Ethiopia, 62; and Europe, 167;
and France, 94; and Germany, 8–9,
13, 162, 168–70, 171, 177–78, 180;
and Greece, 25–34, 56, 136, 148;
and Greek-Turkish aid program, 4,
28–34; and India, 70–71; and Iran,
14, 49, 106, 108, 109–10, 114, 115,
117, 144; and Israel, 94; and Italy,
182; and Japan, 2, 13; and Laos,
135, 136; and Middle East, 76–77,
93–98, 105, 133–34; and Middle
World, 77–80; and Morocco, 67, 68,

69; Mutual Security Program, 123; and NATO, 136; and Netherlands, 182; and North Yemen, 79; and Nuclear Non-Proliferation Treaty, 180; Point Four Program, 50; public opinion, 14; and Quadripartite Treaty on Berlin, 11; and Saudi Arabia, 64, 65–66; Smuts on, 60; and South Africa, 61; and Thailand, 135; and Tripartite Declaration, 76; and Turkey, 25–34, 123–25, 127–28, 129–30, 132; and Union of South Africa, 59; and United Kingdom, 17–23, 83, 94; and USSR, 76, 82, 161, 162, 170–72, 181; and Vietnam War, 135–36, 147–49, 178, 179; and World War II, 6

United States, agencies and organizations: African Bureau, 151; Air Force, 30; Army, 30; Army Corps of Engineers, 29; Bureau for Near Eastern, South Asian, and African Affairs, 47; Bureau of the Budget, 30; Central Intelligence Agency, 137, 143, 144, 145–46; Committee of Ten, 146–47; Congress, 28, 29, 40; Defense Department, 30; Department of Agriculture, 30; Department of Commerce, 30, 170; Department of Labor, 30; Department of the Treasury, 30; European Bureau, 151; Federal Security Agency, 30; International Organization Bureau, 152; Joint Chiefs of Staff, 95; National Security Council, 95; Navy, 30; Policy Planning, Kennedy Administration, 147; Public Health Service, 30; Public Roads Administration, 30; State Department, 28, 29

University of Maryland, 174

UNRWA. See United Nations, Relief and Works Agency

USSR. See Union of Soviet Socialist Republics

U.S.-U.K. Combined Raw Materials Board, 3

U Thant Plan, 152–53, 155, 186

U-2 spy plane, 145

Vandenberg, Arthur, 27

Van Fleet, James, 31

Venezuela, 100, 108, 127

Very Best Men, The (Thomas), 144, 145

Viet Cong, 135, 147

Vietnam War, 7, 9, 14–15, 135–36, 147–49, 178, 179

Volk party (South Africa), 59

Von Brentano, Heinrich, 163

Von Hassel, Kai-Uwe, 177

Von Schirach, Baldur, 165

Wadsworth, George, 121

Wallace, George, 85

Walters, Vernon A., 113, 116, 117; Silent Missions, 114

Ward, "Bud," 84

War Production Board, 2, 18

Warren, Avra, 73, 74, 131

Webb, James E., 133

West Bank, 75

West Irian, 185–86

Westrick, Ludger, 170

Wheeler, C. R., 20

Wilds, Walter, 31

Williams, Mennen, 151, 152

Wilson, Edwin, 30

Winship, North, 58

Wisner, Frank, 145

Witness to History (Bohlen), 4

World Bank, 40, 116

World War I, 6

World War II, 1–3, 6, 17, 129, 143

WPB. See War Production Board

Wright, Michael, 101–2

Yama gas pipeline, 12

Yemen, 50

Yugoslavia, 3, 8, 31, 49, 136

Zaim, Husni, 45

Zambia, 80

About the Author

George C. McGhee, a native of Texas, received his D.Phil. from Oxford as a Rhodes Scholar. He worked as a geologist for various petroleum companies before establishing his own oil producing firm in 1940. Mr. McGhee joined the War Production Board in 1941 and also served as Deputy Executive Secretary of the U.S.-U.K. Combined Raw Materials Board. He was later a Lieutenant in the U.S. Navy and was awarded the Legion of Merit and three battle stars for his service in Guam. He joined the Department of State in 1946 as Special Assistant to Under Secretary William Clayton, was Coordinator for the Greek-Turkish Aid Program, and in 1949 was appointed Assistant Secretary of State for Near Eastern, South Asian, and African Affairs. Mr. McGhee was Ambassador to Turkey from 1951 to 1953. In 1961, under President Kennedy, he was Counselor of the Department of State and Chairman of the Policy Planning Council and later Under Secretary for Political Affairs. In 1963, President Kennedy named Mr. McGhee Ambassador to West Germany in 1963. He returned as Ambassador-at-Large in 1968 and retired from government in 1969. In addition to Mr. McGhee's years of public service, he has been a director of twelve corporations and has served as trustee to numerous civic, charitable, and educational organizations, including five universities.